Making Movies, Music & DVDs on Your Mac

Using Apple's Digital Hub

Jesse Feiler

McGraw-Hill Osborne

New York   Chicago   San Francisco   Lisbon
London   Madrid   Mexico City   Milan   New Delhi
San Juan   Seoul   Singapore   Sydney   Toronto

The **McGraw·Hill** Companies

McGraw-Hill/Osborne
2600 Tenth Street
Berkeley, California 94710
U.S.A.

To arrange bulk purchase discounts for sales promotions, premiums, or fund-raisers, please contact **McGraw-Hill**/Osborne at the above address. For information on translations or book distributors outside the U.S.A., please see the International Contact Information page immediately following the index of this book.

Making Movies, Photos, Music & DVDs on Your Mac: Using Apple's Digital Hub

1234567890 FGR FGR 0198765432

ISBN 0-07-222554-8

Publisher:	Brandon A. Nordin
Vice President &	
Associate Publisher:	Scott Rogers
Acquisitions Editor:	Megg Morin
Project Editor:	Mark Karmendy
Acquisitions Coordinator:	Tana Allen
Technical Editor:	Amy Hoy
Copy Editor:	Marcia Baker
Proofreader:	John Gildersleeve
Indexer:	Claire Splan
Computer Designers:	Tara A. Davis, Lucie Ericksen
Illustrators:	Michael Mueller, Lyssa Wald
Cover Series Design:	Dodie Shoemaker
Cover Illustration:	Eliot Bergman

This book was composed with Corel VENTURA™ Publisher.

Dedication

This book is dedicated to your grandchildren and your grandparents,
to your colleagues and customers,
to your neighbors and friends—close by and on the Internet.

I hope it helps you share the memories,
express the ideas, and
tell the stories
they're waiting for.

About the Author

Jesse Feiler is the author of a number of Mac OS X books including *Mac OS X: The Complete Reference* and *Mac OS X Developer's Guide*. He is also the author of *Building WebObjects 5 Applications*, as well as many books on the Web-based enterprise (such as *Database-Driven Web Sites* and *Managing the Web-Based Enterprise*), the Y2K problem, home offices, databases, and FileMaker. His books on OpenDoc, Cyberdog, Apple Guide, and Rhapsody are now collector's items.

He has worked as a developer and manager for companies such as the Federal Reserve Bank of New York (monetary policy and bank supervision), Prodigy (early Web browser), Apple (information systems), New York State Department of Health (rabies and lead poisoning), The Johnson Company (office management), and Young & Rubicam (media planning and new product development). He founded Philmont Software Mill in 1989 and now serves as Software Director.

His interests in new forms of technical training have led him to MediaSchool (**http://www.mediaschool.com**), for which he has authored several Mac OS X courses available over the Internet in conjunction with Apple Developer Connection, as well as to Geek Cruises' Mac Mania cruise to Alaska (and Mac Mania II to Hawaii in 2003). He is also the first author of a technical book to be published both on paper and on an ebook. He appears regularly on WAMC, Northeast Public Radio, on their Roundtable and Vox Pop shows.

Active in the community, he served for three years as President of the Mid-Hudson Library System, was Chair of the Philmont Comprehensive Plan Board, founder of the Philmont Main Street Committee, and Treasurer of the HB Playwrights Foundation.

He lives 100 miles north of New York City in the Village of Philmont with a rescued greyhound and a cat. His research into iMovie, iPhoto, iTunes, and iDVD has earned him the sobriquet "The Digital Scourge of Philmont." More information is available on his Web site, **http://www.philmontmill.com**.

Contents

Acknowledgments

No book like this is possible without the hard work of many people. Working on tight schedules with very complex material (including many, many figures and illustrations), these people have assisted the author far beyond the call of duty.

Megg Morin, Acquisitions Editor, started the ball rolling; her assistant, Tana Allen, provided great support and coordination as the book took shape. On the editorial side, Mark Karmendy was unflappable as changes to the text (as well as to Apple's software) required changes up to the very last minute. Copy Editor Marcia Baker and Proofreader John Gildersleeve helped decipher and clarify the occasional obscurity and tracked down the mysteries of spelling and orthography that seem to be endemic to the world of computer software. Technical Editor Amy Hoy did the same on the technical side. To complete the production process, Claire Splan provided the index, and Illustrator Michael Mueller helped make the book look as good as it does. Carie Abrew and Kathleen Edwards set the pages. Yes, where a page ends matters and how a sentence flows across pages helps make the book more readable. Fortunately, you don't notice their work—that's the point of it.

Bettina Faltermeier, Publicity Manager at McGraw-Hill/Osborne and Susannah Greenberg of Susannah Greenberg Public Relations were an enormous help in getting the word out about *Mac OS X: The Complete Reference* last year, and I'm very pleased to be working with them again on this book.

Friends and colleagues who have been kind enough to share their digital hub experiences with me have made the writing of the book a pleasure; they are acknowledged throughout the pages of the book. And, of course, the brilliant designers and engineers at Apple have—once again—defined the future of personal computing. They deserve enormous thanks for putting these ideas into motion.

Lastly, Carole McClendon of Waterside Productions, who has represented me for many years has helped move this project—as many others—along.

Notwithstanding the help of so many people, any errors are the sole handiwork of the author.

Introduction

One aspect of the digital hub that I've noticed in my travels is how social the whole thing is. I'm sure there are scores of people locked in their rooms alone with these tools, but it's amazing what happens when you put a PowerBook, a digital camera or camcorder, and iPhoto or iMovie into a public space. The first amazing thing is that most people aren't amazed (this is part of the Apple's "just works" technology). The second is that, having immediately accepted what I think are technological miracles, everyone has an opinion on sequences, cropping, titles, organization, and so forth. The digital hub turns out to be a social hub and the digital hub tools are all communication tools.

This book shows you what's behind the digital hub and its tools, as well as how to use them. It then goes on to help you *understand* how to use them—not just where to click and what to plug in, but how to work with communication tools that rely on images and sound in addition to text.

Since the invention of photography in the early nineteenth century, ours has become a world where communication, memories, and information have become increasingly visual. Rather than supplanting text, images have become integrated with it. The ease with which you can use digital hub tools to create composite media—text with pictures, DVDs with movies and documents, and the like—means that the barriers between the different media forms are coming down. As you'll see in this book, most of the principles involved in storytelling, persuasion, and recording history and memories are the same regardless of medium—or composite medium. This book is designed to help you get past the basic principles and the mechanics of how to use these tools quickly; you can then move on to using them effectively and integrating them effortlessly.

How this Book Is Organized

There are four parts to this book.

Part 1: Getting Started

First you will see what it's all about. You'll learn about the digital hub as well as the basics of photography and video. This part of the book gives you the grounding in technology and vocabulary that you'll need for the rest.

Part 2: Making Movies, Photos, Music, and DVDs

Here's where the fun starts. The chapters in this section show you how to use the digital hub tools. By the end of this part of the book, you should be ready to start using them all productively.

Part 3: Making Better Movies, Photos, Music, and DVDs

Here you'll learn how to move on. These chapters present more advanced topics ranging from how to work in front of (or behind) a camera to how to manage projects. It ends with a chapter that introduces Apple's professional digital hub tools, and it also describes how you might set up your own digital studio.

Part 4: Case Studies

Finally, here are five chapters that explore specific uses of the digital hub. You'll see how to make scrapbooks for and with kids and find out how to prepare instructional materials; there's a chapter on creating portfolios, one on advertising, and one that examines archives and exhibitions. Rather than focusing on the tools and technology, these chapters focus on real-life projects. Throughout this part of the book you'll see how to integrate the various tools and their media. Unless you're producing one of Apple's commercials, your own story or message is what you want to tell—not the story of the camera or technology.

A Note About Versions

One aspect of Apple's digital hub technology (and of its new operating system, Mac OS X) is that more frequent but smaller updates are made than in the past. As a result, the software that you have may look slightly different from that shown in this book. It may be earlier or later, but its functionality is basically what is described here.

Ongoing changes (such as the conversion of iTools to .Mac, the addition of DVD-ROM to iDVD, which allows you to store documents and applications as well as movies on your DVDs) will continue. Apple's architecture of Mac OS X and of the digital hub tools makes this particularly easy.

If you want to check the version of your software, you can do so by choosing the first About command for any application. For example, if you are running iPhoto, the first menu to the right of the Apple menu is labeled iPhoto, and the first command is About iPhoto. That will show you the version number. To check the version number of your operating system, choose About This Mac from the Apple menu at the left of the toolbar. You can compare those versions to the ones used in the preparation of this book:

- Mac OS X 10.2 (screen shots are from Mac OS X 10.1.5, but the text reflects the newer version)

- iMovie 2.1.2

- iPhoto 1.1.1

- iTunes 3.0

- iDVD 2.1

Getting Help and Support

Support is available from Apple in several areas. On the main Apple Web site (**http://www.apple.com**), there are specific areas for each of these tools. Just add the product name to the Apple URL—for example, iPhoto is located at **http://www.apple.com/iPhoto**. On these pages, you'll find detailed product information as well as marketing materials.

Discussion boards and the Apple Knowledge Base are accessible through **http://www.apple.com/support**. Here you'll be able to search for technical information and to join in discussions about the products. The discussions are particularly useful for problems that occur outside the realm of Apple software and hardware—for example, issues with specific cameras and camcorders made by other vendors.

Yet another area of support from Apple is available to .Mac subscribers. Once you log in to .Mac (click the .Mac button on Apple's home page), you can click the Support button to go to moderated discussions. Questions here are monitored by Apple employees, and answers are provided by other users and by them.

For more intense support from Apple, consider their fee-based services located on the Support page cited previously. And for even more support, consider joining the Apple Developer Connection (ADC) located on the Web at **http://developer.apple.com**. A variety of membership levels are provided (including student and online memberships). ADC provides documentation for developers; many power users, network administrators, and advanced Webmasters also find it useful.

Additional support is provided to readers of this book through the author's Web site, **http://www.philmontmill.com**. Here you'll find questions and answers as well as tips and updates related to this book. You can post your own questions and answers as well as tips that you discover.

Part 1

Getting Started

Chapter 1

Introducing the Digital Hub

In This Chapter...

■ Think Digital. What exactly does "digital" mean? How is it different from analog? And why does this matter? Here are the answers.

■ Components and Standards-Based Communication. The reason you can simply plug everything in and have it work is because industry-wide standards have rapidly replaced proprietary formats, and the consumer wins. Here's a summary of the standards you'll use and talk about.

■ The Role of Mac OS X. Mac OS X plays a big role in the digital hub. This section highlights the key under-the-hood features that make your digital hub life easier.

■ Consumer? Prosumer? Professional? Where do you stand regarding the digital hub? Technology is targeted to these different groups, with different price tags to match.

■ Tips for Surviving and Thriving with the Digital Hub. Finally, here are some tips to help you learn—and continue to learn—to work in this new world.

The digital hub—with the Macintosh at its center—makes your digital lifestyle possible. Here's how Apple describes it: "Apple is the only company that makes the hardware, the operating system, and the software—all completely integrated with Apple's ease of use. With the help of some select electronics, Mac OS X and applications like iTunes, iMovie 2, iDVD 2, and iPhoto, Apple helps make your digital lifestyle possible." This book is about it all—the electronics (in the Macintosh and in cameras, camcorders, and other devices), iTunes, iMovie 2, iDVD 2, and iPhoto.

It's not only about being able to move the photos from your digital camera onto your computer and, from there, onto the Web or your ink jet printer. It's also not just about being able to capture the video from your digital camcorder with iMovie and edit it, adding sophisticated transitions such as cross fades. True, those topics are covered, but the digital hub—and this book—are about shooting a digital photo that you import with iPhoto and then export to iDVD to use as a background for your movie title. It's also about using iMovie to add some iTunes music as a soundtrack for the video you shot and edited yourself. And it's even about converting a PowerPoint presentation to a QuickTime movie, which can then wind up on your DVD along with your movies, photos, music, and other graphics.

In short, it's about moving almost effortlessly among the digital media and the digital hub authoring tools from Apple.

This chapter provides an introduction to the digital hub and the digital lifestyle. The terms might be used in advertising, but they are real and important concepts that make your life easier (and different). The first three sections of this chapter focus on the technology and concepts: digital technology, components, and standards-based communication, and the role of Mac OS X. The last three sections focus on you: the expanded ideas of who can make movies, photos, DVDs, and music, as well as how you can adapt to this changing world.

Think Digital

Digital matters. A lot. Today's computers are digital, and much of our media is now digital. Digital media includes everything from CDs to DVDs, ebooks, scanned images, and digital tape formats for both audio and visual.

Two digital milestones have occurred. Many people believe that in the two decades between the mid-1930s and the mid-1950s when modern computers were being developed, the shift in thinking from analog computing to digital computing made today's computers possible. The second milestone was the emergence of digital media. This began with CDs in the late 1970s, and it gained momentum

Think Digital

QuickTime Beginnings

I'll never forget seeing QuickTime demonstrated for the first time at Apple's Worldwide Developers Conference. (I don't think anyone who was there will forget.) The technological feat of playing video on a desktop computer was impressive, but the possibilities it suggested were truly mind-boggling. You could write an instruction manual that contained a video illustrating how to replace a photocopier's toner cartridge, for example. What could be simpler? But the mind-boggling part was understanding that such a document would not only be much clearer and more understandable than several pages of description (even with many illustrations), but that the document couldn't be printed. This was the first time I saw a document—something that anyone could create sitting at a desktop computer with a keyboard and mouse— exceed the capabilities of paper. (Until then, we were struggling to make computer-produced documents as good as paper with desktop publishing and laser printers.)

with digital text and graphics in the desktop publishing revolution of the late 1980s (led by the Apple Macintosh computer and LaserWriter printer). This continued with the development of digital time-dependent media (audio and video, as in Apple's QuickTime technology) in the early 1990s.

Digital refers to the use of numeric representations of information or phenomena (sound or images) that often consist of continuous variations of wavelength frequencies. Its opposite—the continuous variations of wavelength frequencies or other phenomena—is analog.

The word "digital" can also apply to numeric and structured representations of data. You can have a digital scanned image of a book's page, just as you can have a digital representation of that page using PostScript, PDF, or the proprietary format of a program such as AppleWorks, Microsoft Word, or FrameMaker.

Analog Beginnings

Analog registration of real-world entities often is accomplished by converting physical movements in one medium to another. For example, in Thomas Edison's original phonograph, a diaphragm vibrates in response to sound waves. Its vibration is transferred to a needle that records the diaphragm's movement on a surface, such as tin, wax, or vinyl. That tracing is the analog of the diaphragm's motion. The sound is played back by reversing the process: the needle's movement is transferred to a diaphragm, which vibrates. Those vibrations are amplified mechanically or electronically into the sound you hear. The most important characteristic of analog computation or recording is that the devices can represent an infinite range of values. If you're nimble enough, you can move a slide rule (an analog device) one micron to the left or right. A sophisticated audio recorder can record tones, half-tones, and micro-tones known to no musical scale.

Digital Advances

Digital technology isn't continuous with regard either to values or time. Values are assigned with a certain degree of precision, and no values can fall between them. In the case of digital recording, instead of a diaphragm's movement being transferred, a value (usually of the sound wave) is recorded with a certain degree of precision. That value is rerecorded ("sampled") at constant intervals.

A system based on numeric values, rather than a physical basis, has many advantages over the analog system. One major advantage is that perfect copies are possible: you simply repeat the numeric (digital) values. A copy of an analog recording loses some of the fidelity of the original. Each time you copy it, the recording (or transmission) process might subtly change the physical characteristics of the stored sound or other data.

Furthermore, the numeric data can be manipulated in the same ways all numeric data can be manipulated. This allows arithmetic calculations to be done to verify the digital data and to transform it in specific ways.

As a final benefit, digital representations of analog signals often take fewer resources than their counterparts. In the move to high-definition television (which is digital), a single station's frequency can be used to transmit as many as four separate programs at the same time, using the same bandwidth as an older, analog station's transmission.

Digitization

The world contains a wide variety of data and phenomena, which are basically analog in the sense that they have infinitely varying values of sound and light waves, as well as other such characteristics. Measuring and sampling these values in discrete units and at a given rate is the process of digitization. *Digitization* requires a significant amount of computer processing power and a reasonably fast processor in the case of time-dependent media, such as sound and video. Special digital signal processing (DSP) chips are often used to do the work of digitization.

As recently as five years ago, digitization was done in computers: you plugged analog devices, such as VCRs or camcorders, into your computer and digitized the analog signal. Today, digitization has moved outside the computer into digital cameras, digital camcorders, digital televisions, and digital phones. Converting sound and images to digits as early as possible in the process of recording and transmitting them allows the benefits of digital media to be exploited as much as possible.

Components and Standards-Based Communications

Components and Standards-Based Communications

There's no better way to understand what has happened with the digital hub than by comparing a Macintosh today with one from five years ago. If you looked at the back of a Macintosh 8600 in 1997, you would have seen the following connectors, in addition to those for power, headphone/speakers, and microphone:

- A pair of RCA jacks for 16-bit stereo input

- Another pair of RCA jacks for 16-bit stereo output

- An RCA jack for 24-bit composite video input

- Another RCA jack for 24-bit composite video output

- A multipin connector for 24-bit s-video input

- Still another multipin connector for 24-bit s-video output

- A GeoPort (serial) connector for the modem

- A GeoPort (serial) connector for local area networking or a printer

- An SCSI connector to connect disk drives and scanners

- 10-Base-T Ethernet connector

- AAUI-15 Ethernet connector

- An Apple Desktop Bus (ADB) connector to connect a keyboard or mouse

That is a grand total of 14 connectors of 8 different types (still others exist for power, microphones, display, and headphones/speakers). Some of these connectors, such as the RCA jacks or the multipin S-video connector, also appeared on VCRs and camcorders of the era.

In February 2002, the G4 QuickSilver model was released. Looking at its back, you would find the following connectors:

- Two FireWire connectors for digital video, disk drives, and other high-speed devices

- Two USB connectors for digital cameras, microphones, and the keyboard

- 10/100/1000-Base-T Ethernet connector

That makes a total of five connectors of three different types. (An optional SCSI connector was also there, as well as the power, microphone, and headphone/speaker connectors.) Today's digital camcorders and digital cameras also sport connectors like these.

Many of the older connectors are specific to the types of devices they connect—ADB connectors, for example, were used almost exclusively for keyboards and mouse devices. The RCA jacks were for audio and video; the multipin connectors were for S-video.

Two standards for wired digital connections—USB and FireWire along with n-Base-T Ethernet connections—have replaced all other technologies for connecting and communicating over wire. And the digitization process has moved out from the computer to digital cameras and camcorders, as described in the previous section. Once information is digitized, the different types and formats are indistinguishable.

Video, word-processing documents, and images are all only sequences of digits. Communicating and storing these sequences of digits is, therefore, the same, regardless of what they represent.

Wireless connections have been made possible in large part by the move to digital communications and media. Wireless networking using AirPort (IEEE 802.11) and wireless connectivity of devices, such as telephones and organizers using Bluetooth (part of which forms the core of the IEEE 802.15.1 standard), are becoming commonplace. Arguably the capability to include error-correcting code in digital communications contributes to the feasibility of wireless communications, which otherwise could be less reliable than wired connections.

NOTE   *If you haven't heard of Bluetooth, you will. A wireless technology designed to connect small devices such as telephones, personal digital assistants, keyboards, and cameras with one another and with personal computers, its focus is short range (a few meters or yards). In the spring of 2002, Apple adopted Bluetooth as its wireless technology for peripherals, providing a significant boost to the technology.*

These standards are true industry-wide standards. As a result, it's no longer necessary to buy connectors that specifically work with Macintosh computers. This has brought down the price of cables and connectors. This has also produced savings for consumers because the USB cable that was used to connect a now-defunct printer can now be reused to connect a brand new scanner.

Also worth noting is that all these connections are fast and they're getting faster all the time. Digital images and particularly digital video involve enormous amounts of data. Storing and moving this data require high-volume data stores and transfer mechanisms.

You'll find much more on communications and connections in Chapter 4.

The Role of Mac OS X

People at Apple talked about what had become known as the digital hub long before Mac OS X arrived. At the end of the 1980s, there were short- and long-term predictions of where computer technology would go, and those predictions were right. In addition to the standard faster-cheaper-more powerful prediction, the short-term prediction was that computers would become more complex as new technologies (such as sound and video) were added to them. The long-term prediction was that computers would then become less complex as those technologies moved outside the computer itself to special-purpose devices and computers: this is the *digital hub*.

The Role of Mac OS X

Many of the components of the digital hub work on Mac OS 9 and earlier operating systems (OSs), but applications such as iPhoto run only on Mac OS X. In addition, many of the features of Mac OS X make the digital hub hardware and software particularly effective. This section provides a brief overview of some of those features and why they matter when you're making movies, photos, music, and DVDs. The theme is simple: Mac OS X implements much of what is necessary to use digital cameras, digital camcorders, MP3 players, and other such devices. Individual applications don't need to reinvent the wheel. They build on Apple's infrastructure and implement only the features that aren't part of the OS.

NOTE   *Jesse Feiler's* Mac OS X: The Complete Reference, *(Osborne/McGraw-Hill, 2001) provides much more extensive information about the design and implementation of Mac OS X.*

Kernel-Based Hardware Access

Mac OS X is built in layers of increasing specialization and complexity. At the top are applications and the Aqua interface. Supporting them are internal tools that provide programming support for common application and interface functionality. (Not only does this assist developers by providing ready-written tools, but it also helps to assure uniformity in the interface.)

Beneath these layers are imaging tools for two- and three-dimensional graphics, as well as for QuickTime. Still lower is the *kernel,* a rather small core of the OS that runs swiftly and supports everything else above it.

The kernel interacts with hardware—both the computer itself and peripherals, such as disks and cameras. When an application program wants to access an external device, it invokes code in the kernel, which does the actual work.

This means application programs interact with the kernel and its representation of devices. As new devices come along, the kernel needs to recognize them (this is Apple's job), and, in many cases, applications can continue to run without modification by making the same calls to the kernel.

QuickTime

QuickTime is Apple's technology that supports time-dependent media, such as audio and video, as well as numerous other media technologies, such as virtual reality. QuickTime runs on both Macintosh and Windows computers and is an integral part of the OS.

For developers, QuickTime is an important tool. They can add movies or audio to their applications with a minimum of fuss. This is why so many Macintosh applications incorporate video: QuickTime makes it easy for the developers to do so.

Memory Protection and Symmetric Multiprocessing

Two features of Mac OS X are widely featured in Apple's promotional materials, yet they appear quite esoteric to many people. *Memory protection* is a set of technologies that prevent one application program from accidentally causing another program's memory to become corrupted. Under Mac OS X, each program has its own memory partition outside which it can't move.

Symmetric multiprocessing is the architecture that allows the OS and its applications to take advantage of the multiple processors built into the high-end Macintosh computers. (Other implementations of multiprocessing require the programs to be specially written for multiple processors.)

Both these features help to support the digital hub concept. Many of the tasks you do with digital media (particularly video) are time-related and time-intensive. Burning a DVD, for example, takes quite a bit of processing power because it isn't only a matter of transferring files, but also of preparing them for the formatting expected by a DVD player. Making the OS more stable (with memory protection) and more responsive (with symmetric multiprocessing) makes these lengthy tasks run faster and helps to ensure that you don't have your machine crash after an hour of (incomplete) DVD processing.

Consumer? Prosumer? Professional?

For Apple, there are two categories of computer user: consumers and professionals. The iMac and iBook are marketed to consumers. The desktop models and PowerBook computers are marketed to professionals.

In the world of electronics—particularly cameras and video—three categories exist. Products aimed at the consumer (or amateur or home) market are the simplest to use. The highest-quality (and most expensive) products are marketed to professionals. In between is a third category. In the world of digital cameras, for example, the consumer market is dominated by point-and-shoot cameras with minimal focus controls, which sell for about $200–$300 dollars. The professional cameras exceed $1,000, sometimes going up to $5,000. These provide automatic focusing as well as manual overrides for all their settings. They accommodate all sorts of lenses and filters, and are ruggedly built.

Between those two markets, the prosumer cameras sell in the range of $600–$1,000. They provide much of the functionality of the professional cameras but with somewhat less detail and quality.

Knowing about these markets is important when you shop for cameras and other electronic devices. But it's also important to think about prosumers because of what that third category says about how people use these digital devices.

Access to High-Power Tools for All

Prosumers are not only advanced amateurs. They often are people who are using professional (or near-professional) tools in their work and other activities. The realtor who makes a DVD showing properties for sale is working. The teacher who creates a movie illustrating how different types of bushes should be pruned is also working. In the past, these people wouldn't have dreamed of producing DVDs or movies, but with tools such as iDVD 2 and iMovie, they can now do so.

A common sense of wonderment is expressed by many people who have been in fields such as moviemaking or advertising for a decade or more. They shake their heads in amazement at finding tools more powerful than the ones they used not long ago available to a vast range of people.

New Ways of Authoring Media

The availability of these tools changes the way in which many projects are done. Rather than a complex production process standing between an idea and its creation on film, a limited number of people—sometimes even one person—can do everything. In the past, rare geniuses of the cinema such as Orson Welles, Jacques Tati, and Charlie Chaplin did everything from writing scripts to directing to scoring their films' music. But they did everything with the help of hundreds of people ranging from actors to designers and cinematographers.

Being able literally to do it all yourself if you want to makes it possible to create very personal movies, photos, and other digital creations. Working alone isn't for everyone, but the possibilities of this personal form of content creation have barely been explored.

NOTE
The word "authoring" is commonly used when describing the process of creating new media or mixed media projects. Words such as "writing" or "painting" suggest one specific medium, and so authoring is a good choice for cases in which more than one medium is involved. To some ears, this is a strange and new usage. This is an old use, though—more than four centuries old. Using authoring in this way rescues it from the endangered words list. In fact, the Oxford English Dictionary declares the word "authoring" obsolete everywhere except in the United States!

Tips for Surviving and Thriving with the Digital Hub

This book provides you with an overview of technology to help you make movies, photos, music, and DVDs on your Macintosh. It also provides you with tips, ideas, and suggestions to make your life easier and your projects better. But you have to do your part. Here are three points to consider.

Criticize Constructively

Constantly criticize your authoring projects and those of others. Learning the art of constructive criticism is difficult for some, but it's essential to improve your work. Destructive or merely flattering criticism isn't helpful, but asking questions such as "How was that done?" "How could it have been done differently?" and "Why was that done?" will help you develop your own style and way of working.

Learn to look at things you normally don't look at, things you're not supposed to look at. When you're watching a movie, a TV news broadcast, or a commercial, watch what happens when one scene ends and another begins. Search out shows that break new ground and succeed, as well as those that get terrible reviews—in both cases, you can learn a lot.

Look at photographs in magazines, museums, and on the Web. Look beyond the substance of the photo to see how it's framed—is the subject in the center? Where is your eye drawn first? You can also learn a great deal about organizing images by wandering through art galleries and looking at books about art. After all, painters have been composing images for centuries.

Even if all you want to do is take a few snapshots at a silly party, why not make them the best snapshots you can take? If your standard today is making sure you don't cut off the top of your subjects' heads, try to surpass it tomorrow with still more sophisticated techniques.

When it comes to creating DVDs, look carefully at the various DVDs you come across. For many people DVDs are videotapes on discs: they simply press Play and sit back. But DVDs allow a highly structured format of mixed and interactive media. Examine how they're put together. Watch yourself as you explore a DVD you like—or one that's particularly frustrating.

The Basic Rule: Be There and Be Ready

Whether you're taking photos in real time of spontaneous events or filming a Hollywood epic that's been carefully rehearsed, your concern is capturing a fleeting image on film or pixel. There are no identical repetitions. If your toddler does something wonderfully cute and appealing, but your camera is in the closet, chances are by the time you've found and set it up (and replaced the dead batteries), the little tyke will be fast asleep—or bawling with rage.

The equipment for most digital authoring is small and portable. If you want to explore digital photography and digital video, get in the habit of taking your cameras with you. Check the batteries regularly and make sure the lenses are clean, but be sure to observe the cautions on privacy and digital etiquette discussed in Chapter 18.

The Corollary: Digital Images Are Cheap

Many amateur photographers try for the perfect shot. Not surprisingly, they often miss. Professional photographers (both still and movie) almost always shoot far more than they'll ever use. In movies, the ratio of film (or tape) shot to film or tape used in the final movie is called the *shooting ratio*. Ratios of 5:1 are common, but rates of 20:1 and even 50:1 are far from unheard-of.

When using digital media, there's no cost to develop or print film. There is a cost to store images (until you decide to delete the ones you don't use). There also is a cost involved in sorting through all those images, but as you learn to evaluate your own work effectively, you can discard outtakes and unusable shots immediately.

If you're shooting still photos, similar ratios apply. Actors traditionally hire photographers to shoot head shots—rolls of film with slightly different shots in each frame. From a roll of film with 36 images, finding one worth reproducing isn't always possible. Finding two or three is lucky.

You might have heard that photographs are made in the darkroom (or in the digital darkroom of iPhoto or Photoshop). Movies are made in the editing room (or in iMovie). A lot of truth is in those sayings, but if you haven't taken enough images or video, you have nothing to work with later on. This is why taking as many photos and as much video as possible is so important.

Particularly as you're learning, take as many shots as you can, critique them, and then go out and take more.

Summary

This chapter provided an introduction to the digital hub and the digital devices it includes. In this chapter you've seen the importance of digital technology. The main advance digital technology provides is that digits are digits, and the same hardware and software that store and communicate digital images can store and communicate digital video as well as spreadsheets and word-processing documents. The big change in the last decade is that digitization has become cheaper and has moved out of the personal computer into digital devices such as cameras and camcorders.

The digital hub is also made possible by the use of components and standards-based communications. Fewer types of connectors, jacks, and cables do the same work of many only a few years ago.

Those issues—digitization and standards-based communications—apply to all vendors in today's digital marketplace. However, Apple has some unique advantages in this area. Apple has always been a leader in graphics (and graphics are a big part of the digital hub), but Apple's architecture of Mac OS X with its kernel-based hardware access, Quartz imaging, and QuickTime technology also provide significant benefits to users of the digital hub tools. Similarly, the increased stability provided by the OS's memory protection and the higher throughput achieved with multiple processors and symmetric multiprocessing make the processor-intensive multimedia tasks manageable.

In this world three groups of players exist: consumers, professionals, and prosumers. The prosumer market consists not only of advanced amateurs but also of professionals in other fields who are becoming as comfortable with creating movies and DVDs as they are with writing or using a spreadsheet. A significant effect of this technology also exists in one-person projects. The benefits of single-person projects have long been known when it comes to productivity. Now that media authoring can be done by an individual, those benefits can be obtained by more people.

Finally, you need to learn some new rules. In a nutshell, learn from everything (including your successes and mistakes), be ready to use your cameras, and shoot enough images and footage to be able to edit them later.

With that introduction, you can put digital issues aside for the moment: the next chapter deals with camera basics, with scarcely a mention of digitization or pixels. Those concepts return in the following chapter.

Summary

Chapter 2

Camera Basics

In This Chapter...

- ■ It's All About Light. The basis of all photography (still and video) is light. Here's an introduction to the concepts you'll need to know.

- ■ Types of Cameras. This section provides an introduction to the types of still and video cameras you'll find, along with the terminology you'll find in advertisements.

- ■ Focusing Light with Lenses. These are the basics of shutter speed, lens aperture, and other standard photographic terms.

- ■ Filtering Light. You can add filters to most cameras and camcorders to produce special effects, protect your expensive lens, and improve your images.

- ■ How to Use Viewfinders Properly. Digital cameras and camcorders provide traditional viewfinders, as well as LCD previews. Here's information about how and when to use each.

- ■ Capturing Sound. Your digital video has a stereo sound track. Making the most of it requires some planning.

- ■ Batteries. Many batteries are available for digital cameras and camcorders: this section explains the differences among them, which ones are interchangeable, and how to get the most out of your batteries.

- ■ Camera Maintenance. Some routine tasks can help you take better pictures and prolong the useful life of your camera.

This chapter takes a break from digital issues and looks at the basics of cameras—both still and video cameras. Whether your goal is taking candid snapshots at your birthday party, video of your vacation, art shots of flowers, or assembling a digital album of still and moving images that document your child's growth, you need to know a little about how cameras work and how to use them best.

The images you take with digital cameras and camcorders are temporarily recorded on chips, rather than on film or video tape. From the chip, the data is then stored on removable memory or MiniDV tape. This process is discussed in the next chapter.

NOTE   *Many of the concepts described in this chapter are illustrated on the author's Web site, **http://www.philmontmill.com** and at **www.osborne .com** in the content area under this book's title. On the philmontmill.com site, click the Mac OS X button, and then visit the area for this book. You'll find a number of images to view online. You can also download them to view on your computer or to print. The reason the images are placed online is that many of the concepts they demonstrate can't be shown using the printing technology available for this book (color, for example).*

It's All About Light

Light is the basis of everything you do with a camera. Light itself is a form of electromagnetic radiation, that part of the spectrum perceivable by the human eye. The branch of physics called *optics* studies light, as well as the nearby spectra of ultraviolet and infrared radiation. (*Infrared* is just above the visible spectrum, while *ultraviolet* is just below the visible spectrum.)

This section provides a brief overview of the science of light and how people perceive it. This is designed not only for background information, but also to give you an understanding of how and why some things happen—and how you can improve your movies and photos. Be aware that this section deals with the common cases in which you want your photos and videos to look as much like real life as possible. Art photography and cases in which you want to distort reality in one way or another are a different matter. The suggestions in this section might not apply—or you might want to apply them in reverse.

Having Enough Light

Perhaps the most general issue to consider is having enough light for your photo- and filmmaking. Today's digital cameras and camcorders are sensitive. They function in extremely low-light levels. In fact, you can use a digital camera or a digital camcorder to photograph someone lit only by a single candle in an otherwise darkened room!

Having enough light makes it possible for the camera to record the image properly. In low-light conditions, color might be distorted and the image could be unclear. A properly lit image can be darkened using an application such as

Entirely New Creative Directions

Steve Benson, a friend who describes himself as an educator, scholar, and serious amateur of photography, just got a Canon PowerShot G2 digital camera. I asked Steve what he thought:

"Spoiled by almost 40 years of using nothing but Nikon SLRs [single lens reflex 35mm cameras], I was a reluctant convert to digital. The rewards, however, have far exceeded my expectations. What I have enjoyed most is a new-found sense of freedom—freedom from buying and handling film, freedom to fire away with no concerns about "wasting" film, freedom to play and experiment, freedom to enjoy absolute control over all stages of the picture-making process. The intuitive ease and flexibility of both camera and computer software have opened unlimited possibilities, and taken me in entirely new creative directions."

Photoshop or iPhoto. iMovie enables you to darken video. A large difference can exist between an image taken in low light and one taken in normal light that's manually darkened. In the second case, the image could be significantly sharper.

If you're trying for special effects, remember, creating the appearance of low lighting can be done in many ways and having low lighting is only one of them. The great actress Gwen Verdon told the story of her father, an MGM electrician (lighting designer) who worked on many movies, who was once told by a director to light a nighttime scene with extremely low lighting. Verdon's father replied that, in this case, the audience wouldn't be able to see anything. His solution was to light part of the set brightly (as with a streetlight) so, by contrast, the rest of the set appeared almost pitch black (even though it was lit well). That, together with the behavior of the actors, convincingly made the well-lit set appear dark.

Almost all cameras today come with an electronic flash. This is effective for adding light to close-up subjects. The range of a flash is about 3–4 meters/9–12 feet. This means it's useless for anything beyond that distance, and you might as well turn off the flash. (In fact, in some cases, turning off the flash might force the camera to change its settings and produce a better image than if you have the ineffective flash turned on.) You can buy a rechargeable floodlight that attaches to your camera and provides significantly more light. You can also buy studio lighting for relatively little money (that is, if you'll be using it frequently). Once you've taken a photograph in poor light, there's little you can do to rescue it. The details that haven't been captured because of the low-light level simply aren't there. You'll read more on lighting options in Chapter 20.

Visual Perception

You should know about two important issues in this area to take better pictures and movies.

Seeing and Recognizing Things

The process of seeing is a complex interaction of physics, anatomy (largely in the eye), and mental processes. Without the brain's involvement, you can't see anything. This matters in two ways when you're taking photographs or movies:

- Some of the information your mind uses to identify objects might be distorted or missing in photographs. For example, your two eyes provide dual inputs that make it possible for your brain to construct three-dimensional images. The camera's single lens flattens the image.

- When you look at objects in the real world, you can focus your attention on them without even thinking about it. You might recognize a loved one standing on a street corner a block away. When you look at a photograph of the same scene, you might not recognize anyone at all.

As you become more experienced, you'll learn how to account for these issues. In short, remember that your eyes are smarter than the camera's lens. What you see is a highly edited and refined version of what the lens "sees."

Reflected and Refracted Light

Although all the light entering your eye is the same, it can be generated in two ways. *Reflected* light is reflected off a surface (such as that of a printed page). *Refracted* light passes through a medium (such as a computer display, a television screen, or a 35mm slide). After you make every possible adjustment in the images themselves, a noticeable difference still exists in an image printed on a high-quality printer and one viewed on your display.

Measuring Light

Light, like all other electromagnetic radiation, consists of waves. All electromagnetic waves behave in the same way. This is why sound, light, infrared, X-rays, and gamma rays all exhibit similar behavior.

It's All About Light

This is demonstrated in some higher-end prosumer cameras that can work not only with visible light but also with infrared light. Their infrared sensors record images in the same way the sensors record visible light. In this way, you can take a photo in a totally dark room. No visible light is there, but there is infrared radiation. Some cameras not only let you take photos using the infrared spectrum, they also let you use the infrared spectrum in the viewfinder to frame a shot. You then use the flash to take a photo with visible light.

Working with Color

You should be aware of several issues related to color. The first is this: in low-light conditions, cameras (like your eyes) don't register colors as vividly as they do in full light. This effect isn't nearly as noticeable indoors as it is outdoors on a moonlit night—everything seems in shades of gray to most people. Having enough light will eliminate many color-related problems.

The second aspect of color you should know about is this: despite scientists' ability to measure light waves and physical aspects of light, the perception of color is highly individual, and largely dependent on the context of the color. In extreme, but not particularly unusual circumstances, a swatch of color can change dramatically. It can appear in one context as blue and in another as green or even red.

NOTE   *The classic work on this subject is* Interaction of Color, *by Josef Albers (Yale University Press), available in paperback and CD-ROM editions (also available in a number of translations).*

Different types of film have different sensitivities to color, which is why some types are preferred for indoor work and others for outdoor photography. Digital cameras have no film, and the differences in sensitivity are built into the camera itself. Some cameras have a bias toward (or from) certain types of colors. Color correction is something that can be done with Photoshop (and to a limited degree, with iPhoto) for still images and in iMovie for video.

Types of Light

Not all light is the same. Daylight is different from artificial light in an office, and that, in turn, is different from the light in a home. Many of the more advanced cameras have settings for different types of light. They automatically adjust their color balance.

In addition, in many cameras you can set the *white balance*: using the lighting for the image you're going to shoot, you focus on something that's white and flat, such as a piece of paper. You then use the camera's white balance control (usually a button or menu choice) to, in effect, say to the camera, "This is what white looks like under the lighting conditions I'll be using." Once the white balance is set, all other colors fall into line.

Most of the time, the automatic white balance in the camera or camcorder is fine. In special cases (including low light), though, you might want to adjust it manually. When you return to normal lighting, you can return to automatic white balance.

Some cameras have preset white balances for known conditions: the greenish tinge of fluorescent lighting can be accommodated and the reddish distortion from incandescent lighting can also be accounted for. Check your camera's instructions to see what, if any, white balance settings are available.

Where Light Comes From

In making certain that you have enough light to shoot, pay attention to where the light is coming from. If the light is coming from behind you, it will light the person or object you're photographing well. If the light is coming from behind you and shines directly into a person's face, though, you'll wind up photographing an unpleasant squint.

Bright sunlight is good, but it also tends to cause harsh shadows. Somewhat diffused light can be most helpful for photographing people. If your camera has a setting that forces the flash to be used, you can use that for fill lighting in taking close-up photos of people.

Types of Cameras

Today's digital world has two types of cameras: still and video. Many of the cameras that are above the basic models have some type of crossover features: you can shoot limited video on still cameras and you can shoot stills with video cameras. Except in the most general sense, however, there's still no single digital camera/camcorder. If almost all your work is still with the rare video, you might be able to get by with the video features of a higher-end still camera, but that's unlikely for most people. (The limit of video on a still camera is likely to be measured in seconds, rather than in minutes or even hours.) More conceivable is that you can manage with only a video camera because to one degree or another, you can create stills with any camcorder. (You certainly can always use iMovie to create a still from any video.) You should know, though, that the quality of stills from digital camcorders isn't comparable to even entry-level digital cameras. The choice is yours, and it probably will come down to money.

Types of Cameras

In describing these cameras, reference is made to their resolution, which is measured in megapixels. Zooming is also mentioned. These issues are covered in Chapter 3. For now, just know that more is better (to a certain extent) when it comes to resolution and megapixels. Optical zooming is more useful than digital zooming. Note, too, that resolution and megapixels change most over time: the quality found in professional cameras becomes standard in prosumer models in a year or two. That quality filters down the next year to consumer models. The point-and-shoot (consumer) models seem to have reached a plateau currently.

Still Cameras

Digital still cameras fall into three groups, which roughly correspond to the three basic market segments (consumer, prosumer, and professional). In all groups, you should expect to find these features:

- Automatic exposure with little, if any, manual override
- Built-in flash
- Red-eye reduction
- Delayed-release shutter (timer)
- Tripod connector
- USB connector
- Internal removable memory

Point-and-Shoot Cameras

These are the basic cameras for most consumers. They are comparable in many ways to the old Kodak Brownies and to the disposable cameras you can buy in the supermarket today. They have limited controls for you to worry about, hence the term "Point-and-Shoot."

Priced from under $100 to about $300, these cameras typically include the following features:

- Image resolution of 1280 × 960 to 1800 × 1200
- Pixels in the range of 1.3 to 2.3 megapixels
- Optical zoom either nonexistent or 2–3×

The lens is a good all-purpose lens. It handles close-ups of about a meter/yard, as well as distant shots. It isn't designed for attachments, such as filters, without an adapter.

If you want a general-purpose camera, this is probably fine for you. The greatest limitation for most people is that the images can't be enlarged much beyond the size of a snapshot. They're fine for display on computers that have relatively low resolution, but if you plan to print your photos or to enlarge them (or both), the results probably won't be satisfactory. If you plan to put them in an album (either in a book or on your computer), you'll probably be happy.

If you want to spend a little more money, you're probably better off buying more removable memory (and larger memory) than comes with the camera. Most rolls of film are 24 or 36 exposures. Whether through habit or not, people seem to be comfortable changing film after that number of shots. Try to get enough memory so at least 24 or 36 shots of the highest quality fit on it. You'll normally download your images from the camera's memory to your computer, but you need enough memory to store the images until you can do that. If you'll be photographing an important event, such as a wedding, you might need several removable memory cards, so you won't have to excuse yourself at critical moments to download images (if a computer is even available).

Midrange

You can split the midrange cameras into two sets (or you can look at the range as fairly large). All are geared either to demanding consumers or to prosumers.

The first set of midrange cameras is priced from about $400 to $800. You should find the following features:

- Image resolution of 1600 × 1200 to 2272 × 1704

- Pixels in the range of 2–4 megapixels

- 3–6× optical zoom

- Autofocus (as in point-and-shoot)

- Manual focus in a variety of modes (shutter only, aperture only, both, and so forth)

- Excellent autofocus technology to accommodate a variety of special cases

The lens will be a better lens than in point-and-shoot cameras. In addition, it will probably be designed to take filters. The removable memory supplied with these cameras is much larger than in the point-and-shoot cameras. Given the larger size of these images, though, the provided memory still only holds about 8–12 images at high resolution.

These cameras can be used as point-and-shoot cameras, but if you want to use manual controls, you can do so without finding them too daunting. Images can be enlarged to about 8.5 × 11 without serious degradation.

The second set of midrange cameras is priced at around $1,000–$1,200.

- Image resolution of 2560 × 1920

- Pixels in the range of 5–6 megapixels

- 3–7× optical zoom

- Autofocus

- Manual focus in a variety of modes

- Advanced autofocus technology to improve images further

- Additional features, such as infrared photography (features vary by camera and manufacturer)

- You might find a remote control for the camera as an optional accessory. Use this with a tripod to take photos without worrying about the camera moving as you press the shutter. Some remote controls also let you zoom the lens.

- Adjustable ISO settings let you change the sensitivity of the camera's imaging system

What you're paying for in this second set of midrange cameras is the highest resolution. Experience has shown this resolution filters down into the lower part of the midrange category in about a year. Whether that will continue is unclear. Images at this resolution can successfully be blown up to poster size without serious degradation.

Professional Cameras

Professional cameras start at a little over $1,000 and go up—and up—from there. Many are camera bodies only: photographers use lenses they purchase separately (or already have). The features include even more powerful focusing tools and, in the cameras that have them, even better lenses. Resolution and pixels are in the same range as cameras in the midrange. In fact, you will find resolutions akin to those in the lower end of the midrange in some professional cameras. This is because resolution and pixels aren't everything (see Chapter 3).

Video Cameras

Video cameras are much easier to categorize. The professional models cost several thousand dollars ($4,000 and more). Below that, you'll find a number of models ranging from about $600 to $1,400.

The big difference between the low end of this range and the high end is size. All models have image stabilization technology to hold the image steady as you move the camera. All models provide the capability to shoot video, still images, and progressive photos (quick sequences of still shots). All record sound, and all provide a FireWire port for connecting to your Macintosh. All the digital video camcorders now use the MiniDV tape format, which allows for just over an hour of high-quality video on a single cassette.

Resolution of video cameras is lower than comparably priced still cameras. This is why video still images generally don't look as good as those from digital cameras. (You'll find resolution of under 1 megapixel on many camcorders. This reflects the different requirements of video display devices from those that print still images.)

Focusing Light with Lenses

Your camera's lens is one of the critical components of every camera and camcorder. The quality of the lens has a major impact on the quality of your images. At the low end of the price range for cameras (digital as well as film), basic lenses that are often made of optical quality plastic are common. At higher prices, fine glass optical lenses are found. Many film cameras enable you to substitute lenses, but only a few digital cameras let you do so.

Lenses have two important roles to play in a camera. The first is they must transmit light and all its components to the film or the chip that will receive it. For this purpose, lenses must be clear, clean, and unscratched. The second purpose of the lens is to focus the light it receives onto the film or chip. For this purpose, the lens is curved, so a relatively large area in front of the camera is focused down on to the much smaller film or chip.

The simplest lenses are single-element lenses that allow for no-focus adjustment. Higher-quality lenses combine several elements, each of which has its own characteristics for focusing the incoming light. In zoom lenses, lens elements move in relation to one another. Other parts of a zoom lens and parts of other lenses are stationary. The number of elements in a lens is determined by the design of the lens. The most important distinction is between single-element lenses with fixed focus and all others.

Point-and-shoot cameras have either fixed focus or autofocus capabilities. Higher-end cameras have autofocus features, and all except the most basic let you override these. This section describes some of the important concepts related to lenses that you can adjust when you override autofocusing. It suggests what you should look for in your images as you change those settings.

Focal Length and Angle of View

Focal length and *angle of view* are the issues that determine how wide your image is. With replaceable lenses, a photographer might have a normal lens, a wide-angle lens for landscapes, and a telephoto lens for capturing relatively close-up images from afar. Most digital cameras don't have replaceable lenses, but they do have adapters you can screw on to the front of the lens that refocus the incoming light into a broader or narrower area.

Almost all digital cameras and camcorders have zoom lenses. Rather than worry about replaceable lenses or adapters, you can simply use the zoom. These cameras have two types of zoom lenses: optical zoom and digital zoom. An *optical zoom* works the way a zoom lens on any camera works, that is, it physically changes the position of parts of the lens. A *digital zoom* has no physical movement. How it works is described in Chapter 3.

NOTE   *Most people feel a digital zoom is something that was easy for digital camera manufacturers to implement, and it adds no price to a camera. This is probably how a feature that delivers no apparent benefits is included on all digital cameras.*

The *angle of view* (also known as *picture area* or *field of view*) refers to the size of the area visible through the lens, horizontally and vertically. Because the size of the image itself is constant, when the size of the visible area decreases, its detail increases. This is what happens with a telephoto lens. When the size of the visible area increases, its detail decreases, and this is what happens with a wide angle lens.

The angle of view is determined by the *focal length,* which is the distance from the sensor (film or chip) to the lens. On 35mm cameras, certain focal lengths are common for lenses:

- 50mm is normal (the same as the human eye's angle of view)

- 24–35mm is a wide angle lens

- 80–300mm is a telephoto lens

Other values exist for super telephoto, extreme wide angle, and other lenses.
Because most adjustments to the field of view on a digital camera or camcorder
are with the zoom rather than with a replaceable lens or adapter, you generally
don't need to worry about these numbers. And, because everything on a digital
camera is smaller (smaller lens, smaller chip compared to film), the focal length
values on digital cameras are different. Manufacturers often supply comparable
35mm values for their focal lengths, so you can compare when you're shopping.
If you're used to 35mm cameras and are partial to particular fields of view (that
is, specific focal lengths), check to see that the ranges of the digital camera's
zoom will be satisfactory.

These ranges vary significantly. One camera might have a range of 36–110,
while another could have a range of 38–190. In this comparison, the first camera
(which happens to be less than half the price of the second) would be able to focus
much less tightly on distant objects.

NOTE   *Some people fidget with the optical zoom as they hold the camera at
rest. On some models, it's easy to let your thumb slide the zoom back
and forth for no good reason. This is the most effective way to drain
your camera's battery.*

The advent of high-resolution cameras has introduced some changes to the way
people think about both zoom and telephoto lenses. With a high-quality image,
you can use iPhoto and other tools to enlarge areas of it, zooming in digitally long
after you've taken the photo. Because you can do this, even an image taken with a
normal field of view can be manipulated to show the detail you'd otherwise need a
telephoto lens to see. In the same vein, you can consider the digital zooming with
iPhoto as an example of multiplying the optical zoom built into the camera. You
can use the optical zoom to zoom in on something as much as possible, and then
zoom in further digitally with iPhoto.

As noted, this is possible with the advent of high-resolution cameras—those
above 3 megapixels in resolution. When you zoom in digitally, you're cropping
the image to that area and viewing it at a higher resolution. As long as the resolution
of the picture is sufficient, you won't get a blurry image. As you continue zooming
in with iPhoto, you can see the image degrade.

Focusing Light with Lenses

Note, this applies to zooming in (telephoto). You can't zoom out because if something is beyond the boundaries of the photo, there's nothing to manipulate in iPhoto.

Depth of Field

When you focus the camera, the image is as crisp as possible for the area on which you're focused. In the case of a snapshot of a person, this is normally the person's face. The background might be somewhat blurred. The *depth of field* refers to the distance in front of and behind the focus that's clear. When you're shooting a fairly long shot where the focus is more than a few yards or meters away, almost everything except for nearby objects is in focus. When you're shooting a fairly close-up object (such as a portrait), the depth of field could be quite limited and you might have to worry about it.

You can handle depth of field issues in two ways. First, be aware of the issue and simply avoid having objects that should be in focus located significantly in front of or behind the subject of your shot. Second, increase the depth of field. You can do this by manually decreasing the aperture of the lens, which requires a corresponding increase in the speed. Those two issues are discussed in the next sections.

Aperture

In all but the most basic lenses, you can vary the *aperture*—the size of the opening through which light passes. This changes the amount of light that can pass on to the chip (or film). Note, changing the aperture changes only the amount of light that can pass through. It doesn't change the angle of view, which is changed by adjusted the focal length.

The aperture of a lens is measured in *f-stops*. (The *f* is commonly believed to be an abbreviation for *finestra,* Italian for window.) F-stops are inverse to the size of the aperture, so a low f-stop indicates a wide opening for the lens. Adjustable lenses in all but the most basic cameras provide a variety of f-stops.

When the aperture is smaller (the f-stop is higher), the depth of field is greater, and more of the image (from front to back) is in focus. This is often what you want, but sometimes you want to focus on one flower in a long flower border. In this case, you would make the aperture as wide as possible to make only that one flower in full focus. You can achieve similar effects with advanced editing tools, such as Photoshop. In those, you can manually blur the parts of the image you want to be slightly out of focus. The end results are similar, but not the same.

Speed

You can control the amount of light entering the lens with the aperture or with the speed at which the shutter operates. The shorter the time the shutter is open, the less light can enter.

To keep the amount of light entering constant, you must increase shutter speed as you increase aperture openings (which means decreasing f-stops). If you've followed the strategy in the previous section for manipulating the depth of field by changing the aperture, you need to compensate by adjusting the speed accordingly. Most mid-range to high-end digital cameras provide manual overrides for aperture, speed, or both. Thus, if you're adjusting the aperture to change the depth of field, the camera can automatically set the correct speed.

Sometimes, you need to work in reverse by starting from the speed setting. If you're photographing something that moves or changes rapidly (such as a sporting event), you need a high speed, so the image isn't blurred. In these cases, the aperture will need to be enlarged so enough light can enter. Thus, high-speed photography is going to mean your aperture settings will be relatively high (low f-stops) and your depth of field will be on the low side.

In practice, you can use the autofocus features on your camera most of the time and not give these issues any thought. If you have special conditions, you can use the manual overrides. On most mid-range cameras and better, you can use automated settings for some controls and manually override others. Many cameras now come with a variety of controls for setting the autofocus features for different conditions. Experiment to see how the settings affect the images.

NOTE *In experimenting with settings, a good idea is to start with a controlled environment. If possible, use a tripod and place it in front of simple objects, such as tables or chairs. Include strong horizontal and vertical lines (the edge of a table, for example, or a coat rack). The results of changing lens settings are less noticeable if you're looking at faces instead of man-made objects.*

Filtering Light

The light that enters your camera's lens consists of many wavelengths (colors). You can place filters in front of the lens to manipulate that light, so it's transformed. Most medium- to high-end digital cameras let you add filters to them. The camera's documentation will indicate the size of the filters it uses— each camera might be different.

Filters as Protection

Many photographers always have a filter on their camera to protect the lens. Remember, the lens is one of the most critical components of the camera, and it's vulnerable to dirt and scratches if it isn't protected. A lens cap comes with all cameras except the most basic, and it provides protection when the camera isn't in use. When you're using the camera, however, it isn't difficult to touch the lens accidentally and leave a fingerprint or even to scratch it.

If you place a filter on the lens and something like that happens, you either clean the filter or replace it. A basic filter (such as the UV filter described next) can cost under $20. If you have a digital camera that costs $500, a repair to a scratched lens will cost far more than the filter.

UV Filters

Ultraviolet (UV) filters prevent ultraviolet wavelengths from passing through. In this way they appear to cut through light haze and make pictures somewhat sharper. UV filters are commonly used for that purpose and, because they minimally modify the image, they're used as permanent filters for lens protection.

Special Purpose Filters

A variety of other filters can be used to change colors and provide a host of interesting effects. However, programs such as Photoshop let you do many of these tasks on the computer. iMovie and iPhoto both provide basic image-manipulation features that can substitute for the use of filters.

Viewfinders

On both digital cameras and camcorders, the *viewfinder* lets you see the image you're shooting. The viewfinder has its own opening next to the lens, and you might need to compensate for the fact that it's a short distance above or next to the lens.

In addition to a traditional viewfinder, many cameras have a small LCD display you can use as a viewfinder. This displays the exact image the chip is receiving. It typically swivels and rotates: you can turn it around so the subject of the photo can see it. This is particularly helpful if you're photographing yourself (for example, if you're preparing a video presentation). This is also useful because, instead of squinting into a small viewfinder, you can hold the camera at arm's length and see what you'll be photographing.

LCDs take more power than the small viewfinders, so if you are accustomed to using the LCD, make certain you have enough battery backup. If you're accustomed to using traditional viewfinders, experiment with the LCD viewfinder. It can change the way you use cameras.

Capturing Sound

Many higher-priced digital cameras have small microphones you can use to record spoken comments about the pictures you take, but sound is primarily a feature of digital camcorders. All digital camcorders come with a built-in microphone, which usually records sound in two-channel stereo.

Using Microphones

The built-in microphones are good for general purpose work, but they're essentially the sound world's equivalent of point-and-shoot cameras. Using a better microphone is often a good idea if you care about the quality of your video. Your digital camcorder has a receptacle where you can plug a standard microphone. (In some cases, the receptacle is on a separate dock to which you must attach the camcorder.)

You can use two types of microphones. The first type either attaches to the camera or can be placed wherever you choose. The second type clips onto a person's clothing and is called a *lavaliere*. Each kind normally comes with a windscreen, which is typically a small piece of foam that protects the microphone from the whooshing sound of wind.

The first type of microphone simply replaces the built-in microphone with one that's more powerful or can be positioned better. A typical use for such a microphone would be taping a panel discussion from the back of the room using the camcorder's zoom to get a close-up view of the panel. If you place a microphone on the table where the panel is speaking, you'll pick up their voices but not the stray sounds from other people in the room. Using the camcorder's built-in microphone, you might find that when you listen to the tape, the sounds closest to the camcorder (the audience sounds) are louder than the voices of the speakers.

Lavaliere microphones originally were used by television broadcasters. They hung from cords that looped around the neck, much as emeralds and diamonds hang from lavaliere necklaces. (The term "lavaliere" has also been used to describe the flamboyant and flowing neckwear affected by men in the aesthetic movement in the late nineteenth century. The word dates back to the Duchesse de Lavalliere, famous first as a mistress of King Louis XIV and, later, for her piety in a Carmelite priory.) Today, lavaliere microphones typically come with a clip to attach to a shirt or tie. They can consist of a single small microphone or a pair of microphones that provide stereo sound. Using the pair of stereo microphones provides better quality, as well as a degree of protection in case one channel is unusable. (If you have a stereo lavaliere that terminates in two connectors, you can buy an adapter into which you can plug them. The adapter's single stereo connector can then be plugged into your camcorder.)

Lavaliere microphones can be purchased in audio and hi-fi stores for under $25. A two-to-one stereo adapter should cost under $5.

A lavaliere microphone is an excellent solution if you need to capture an individual's voice, but it's a poor choice if you want to capture the sound of a group of people.

For $200 and up you can purchase a wireless lavaliere microphone. This is an excellent investment if you'll be taping individuals who are speaking. (If you confine your taping to scenery or to parties, it won't be helpful.) A wireless lavaliere has two components. The first is the microphone that's connected by wire to a small transmitter, which can be clipped to the back of a person's belt or clothing, or placed in a pocket. A companion receiver is placed near the camcorder and plugged into the sound input receptacle. This allows someone to speak into the camera even if intervening people and objects generate sound or cause a microphone cable to snag.

Adding Sound

You can add sound to your videos with iMovie. As you see in Chapter 10, you can use a microphone connected to your Mac to record a sound track to add to your video. You can use this to add narration or to substitute for sound you were unable to capture properly.

Batteries

All cameras today use batteries. In fact, few film cameras can function at all without a battery. Power consumption and battery capacity are significant variables in digital cameras. Some can go through a battery charge in a few shots, while others can last for days. If you're comparison shopping, make certain you look at the battery specifications of the models you're considering because they're likely to vary greatly.

Types of Batteries

Some digital cameras (often the lower-priced ones) use common batteries—often AA batteries. You can buy these in many places, and they aren't expensive. You can find rechargeable AA batteries and, over time, these provide a bargain, even though you need to buy a charger. Nickel Cadmium (NiCD) and Nickel Metal Hydride (NiMH) rechargeable batteries are made in AA sizes.

NiCD batteries suffer from *memory effect*: If they're recharged before they're fully exhausted, they "remember" that battery level and subsequently can't be charged fully. You can recondition them with many chargers, but the memory effect can be frustrating. Nevertheless, they're relatively cheap and still widely used.

NiMH batteries don't suffer from memory effect, but they're more expensive and they lose some of their charge over time, even if they're not used.

If your camera takes AA batteries, you can alternate between traditional batteries, NiCD batteries, and NiMH batteries. Note that you should never mix and match batteries at any time. In other words, if your camera takes four batteries, use four NiCD batteries or four standard batteries.

Lithium ion (Li-ion) batteries are used in higher-end devices such as laptop computers, digital camcorders, and higher-priced digital cameras. These batteries are usually designed specifically for a given camera, and they aren't interchangeable. Li-ion batteries have no memory effect, and they hold a charge longer than other rechargeable batteries. If your camera comes with Li-ion batteries, it also will come with its own charger. If you use your camera a lot, you might want to buy a spare battery, even though it could well cost over $50. On the other hand, you might choose a camera with a long-lived battery so no matter how many shots you take, you won't exhaust it until the end of the day.

Battery Management

Batteries last longer if they aren't stored in cameras (or any other devices). NiMH batteries in particular lose power as they're stored. Other batteries lose power when they're stored, but not nearly so fast.

Many cameras draw on batteries even when they're turned off. A digital camcorder that's turned off can exhaust its battery in a day or two. If your camera does this, store it with the battery removed. Your instruction manual will indicate if your camcorder should be stored with the battery removed. Or you can perform a simple test. Leave the battery in and the camera turned off. Turn it on the next day and see what the battery level is. Recharge it, and then perform the same test for a day with the battery removed. If there's no difference or only a minor difference, don't worry. If the turned-off camera is draining the battery, the result will be quite significant, even over the span of a single day.

Traditional batteries last longer if they're stored in a refrigerator when not in use. They, too, should be removed from devices when they aren't needed. (Don't take this to extremes, though. There's no need to remove batteries between shots. Just remove them when you finish shooting for the day.)

Battery Disposal and Replacement

All batteries eventually need to be disposed of (even rechargeables). They all contain substances that can pollute the environment, but they can be recycled. Make it a point not to toss used batteries in the trash. You can put them in a bag in a bottom drawer and periodically take them to a recycling center. Some places that sell batteries will take old batteries for recycling at no cost.

Maintenance

Digital cameras and camcorders are expensive. A mid-priced digital camcorder can easily cost the same as your computer. Perhaps because they're smaller than computers and because they're designed to be carried around, some people don't pay enough attention to caring for them. Remember these few points:

- First, make sure to follow the manufacturer's suggestions for care. In particular, know whether batteries should be removed when not in use. Consider the use of a filter to protect the lens.

- For cleaning of the lens (and of filters), use photographic lens cleaners. These are available in photo stores as well as where eyeglasses are sold. Don't use window cleaners on lenses (or, for that matter, on eyeglasses).

- Digital camcorders need to have their tape mechanisms cleaned periodically. You can buy a cleaning cassette for this purpose. Follow the instructions for its use and avoid over-using it—but do make certain to use it regularly. If the recording head in your camcorder gets dirty, it will need to be repaired, and that could well cost several hundred dollars.

- If you travel with your camera or camcorder, make certain you have written down the model number and the serial number. If it's lost or stolen, this can help you to file an insurance claim. And, before traveling, check to see what coverage you have while you're away. Some general policies provide insurance. Others require you to get a temporary rider.

Summary

This chapter provided an overview of camera basics in the digital world. The most important point to take away is this: photography is all about light. Make sure you have enough light, that it comes from the right direction, and it's the right kind of light.

The basics of photography—lenses and filters—are covered here. If you're new to photography or videography, many books are available, so you can learn more about how to use the equipment. Just because you're using digital media doesn't change the basic techniques.

This chapter also touched on augmenting your camcorder's built-in microphone, caring for batteries, and maintaining your equipment.

The next chapter goes to the heart of digital photography (both in cameras and camcorders). It examines resolution and the chip that's at the heart of your camera or camcorder.

Summary

Chapter 3

Image Quality: Pixels and Resolution

In This Chapter...

- **What Is a Pixel?** Pixels (and megapixels) are prominent in all advertising for digital cameras and camcorders. What exactly are you paying for?

- **What Are You Doing with Your Photos?** Your camera might have different settings for different resolutions. Knowing what you'll do with your photos, you can use those settings wisely.

- **Zooming and Enlarging Images.** What is zooming? How does zooming differ from enlarging? Here are the answers.

- **Storing Images on the Camera.** You probably have removable media in your camera or camcorder: here's a guide to different types.

- **File Formats on the Camera.** Many cameras enable you to choose from several standard file formats. You'll find out what they are and when to use each one.

- **Other Data in Your Pictures.** Cameras and camcorders can store information in addition to the photo image (such as the date and time of the shot). Here's a rundown on that subject—metadata.

The previous chapter examined camera issues that apply broadly both to digital and film cameras. This chapter, however, looks at issues specific to digital cameras and camcorders although some of them, such as the issue of resolution, also apply, but in different ways, to film.

What Is a Pixel?

Pixel is a constructed word (*pix* + *element*), which refers to the smallest element that makes up a picture on a digital display. A pixel on a display can show any of a wide range of colors. A pixel on a digital camera or camcorder's sensor can receive any of a wide range of colors. On displays, colors are commonly represented by three numbers representing the value of red, green, and blue (a color system called *RGB*) that are to be combined to produce the needed color. The number of digits in these numbers determines the range of colors. On the Macintosh, if you choose Millions of colors, you use 24-bit color, which consists of three 8-bit values for the three basic colors. The result is a range of over 16,000,000 colors (the human eye can perceive about 10,000,000 colors). If you choose Thousands of colors, you use 16 bits to represent 65,000 colors.

The reason you can choose between these settings is because using more bits requires more memory. Today, video display memory is usually separate from the computer's main memory, and it's usually adequate to display millions of colors without a problem.

On a digital camera, the chip on which the light through the lens is focused consists of pixels, each of which can sense a single color. A common system for digital cameras, *GRBG,* has four sets of pixels: two sets sense the intensity of green light, and one each senses the intensity of red and blue. Once the image has been registered, it's quickly processed, and each pixel's neighboring pixels are evaluated and combined into a full 24-bit color value for each pixel. This is the value that's stored and ultimately transferred to your computer.

You often have a choice of image size. On a fairly high-end camera today, you may have 5 megapixels on the sensor. The largest image size available might be 2,560 × 1,920. If you multiply those numbers together, you get a value of 4,915,200—the effective output of your chip. You can usually choose smaller values that use only some of the camera's pixels. The reason for this is that the more pixels you use for each image, the more memory is taken up both in the camera and on your computer. Image size is generally referred to as *resolution* on digital cameras.

Five Megapixels = No More Film

I've had digital cameras for years (my first was Apple's QuickTake camera in 1994). With each new generation, the quality has improved. I've gone from one-third of a megapixel in resolution (the QuickTake) to 1, then 2, and then 5 megapixels. The industry has also produced cameras with 3 and now 6 megapixels, but I haven't owned them. I never gave up my film camera because I needed its superior imaging for travel photos. You couldn't get the quality of a landscape image with the digital cameras. And, if you're traveling, you might be unable to get back for a retake.

Finally, I put my old Pentax 35 mm SLR camera away for good when I got the 5-megapixel camera. This was the one with sufficient resolution that I trusted it not only for casual snapshots but also for wildflowers among the Greek ruins in Sicily, sequoias in California, and panoramas in the Adirondacks.

I have friends who take snapshots at parties and rarely take travel photos. For them, the 2- and 3-megapixel point-and-shoot cameras are fine. Each person finds a level of resolution that's sufficient to finally put the film camera away for good.

The size of the optical image (that is, what you see through the lens) is unaffected by resolution. The number of pixels used to create the digital image determines its quality: a smaller number can result in distortion or lack of clarity.

A digital camera normally comes with a minimal amount of removable memory. It almost always makes sense to buy a larger memory card when you buy the camera. Otherwise, you'll constantly have to replace your memory or unload the card. Or, you'll reduce image size or quality to squeeze more lower-resolution images into memory.

NOTE   *For both digital cameras and camcorders, you can effectively increase the quality of your images in still another way. If you're using ambient light (the light that happens to be available), you can augment it with flash or flood light. The brighter the image is, the clearer it will be as long as you do not overexpose the image (if you do, you will be unable to recover the data that is flooded out with light). Photos and videos taken indoors at a nighttime event—even one that appears to the naked eye to be well-lit— will be improved substantially.*

Choose Resolution Based on Photo Use

If you want the highest quality images, use the highest resolution setting on your camera. It uses more memory, but you'll have better images and more options when it comes time to work with them in iPhoto.

But you don't always want the highest quality images. What you want are the highest quality images for what you'll do with the photos. In an ideal world, you would use the highest resolution possible for each photo, and you wouldn't have to worry about running out of memory, but this isn't an ideal world.

If you have a new camera, spend some time experimenting. Take several snapshots using different resolution settings, then print them on the printer you'll be using (and on the quality of paper you'll be using). Use the highest resolution setting that makes a difference to your eye. If you plan to print photos of your green beans on the labels of the packets of the special hybrid seeds you breed, a small image and low resolution might be fine.

Note that each camera has slightly different image sizes. The examples shown here might differ slightly from those on your camera. These suggestions are from the manual for the Sony DSC-F707 camera, a 5-megapixel prosumer model.

If you want to build in a margin of safety, use a higher resolution and then use iPhoto to scale it down. But that margin of safety will cost you in being able to store fewer shots in your camera's memory.

- **Email Snapshots**   If you plan to send photos inside email messages to your friends for them to view on their computer display, low resolution and small size, such as 640 × 480, is fine. In fact, sending a 5-megapixel image that's larger than the display and has to be scrolled is a nuisance (and it can take a lot of time on a dial-up connection).

- **Printing as Snapshots or Post Cards**   An image size of 1,280 × 960 is perfect here. Anything larger will have to be reduced to this size.

- **Posting on a Web Site**   If you're using a small photo on a Web site, the smallest image is usually fine. However, you might want to allow users to click the small image and see a larger version—or even download a high-quality version. If this is a possibility, use the high-quality settings and use iPhoto to create the small version.

- **High Quality**   Use the largest image size and focus closely on the part of that image in which you're interested. The next section demonstrates this.

Zooming and Enlarging Images

Image resolution depends on two primary factors: the quality and characteristics of your lens (particularly its capability to zoom) and the number of pixels that make up the image. Your primary objective is to produce an image that will be clear when it's displayed at the size you want, using the medium you want.

You can use the camera's zoom to photograph only that part of a scene in which you're interested. By zooming into the area of interest, you can devote as many of the camera's pixels as possible to your subject. This produces the best image. You can subsequently crop the image (cut out extraneous parts). You can also enlarge the image, so all or part of it is increased in size. To enlarge an image, you need enough resolution so the image doesn't break up. By zooming in on an object of interest, you maximize its resolution, so you can subsequently enlarge it. (You also often reduce image sizes but, in general, difficulties arise with enlargement, not reduction.)

Zooming and Enlarging Images

NOTE   *In this book, zooming is used to refer to operations on a camera; enlarging or reducing is used to refer to operations on the computer (iPhoto, for example). Elsewhere, the terms are used interchangeably, but this distinction is enforced in the book for the sake of clarity and to avoid having repeatedly to describe which size manipulation tool is being used.*

Zooming the Lens

As you've read several times, the best way to get a sense of how cameras work is to use them in controlled settings. Here, two cameras are used to photograph the same scene. The low-resolution camera is an Olympus D600-L with 1.3 megapixels and a zoom from 36–110mm. The high-resolution camera is a Sony DSC-F707 with 5.24 megapixels and a zoom from 38–190mm. The cameras are comparable in that each in its time occupied the same product category—prosumer—and each sold for approximately the same price. Today even the simplest cameras have higher resolutions than the Olympus D600-L. However, comparing those point-and-shoot cameras to a prosumer model such as the Sony DSC-F707 isn't particularly productive.

The four photographs in this section were all taken from the same location. For each camera, a pair of photos was taken with the widest and narrowest zoom settings. Figures 3-1 and 3-2 start with the widest zoom.

Taken with the camera's zoom at its widest, the image shown in this iPhoto window is 50 percent of the actual image size. (iPhoto automatically resizes images to fit in its window, which is a constant size.)

In Figure 3-2, the high-resolution camera has taken the same photo—widest zoom. Note two important points here. One, the image is about the same, which is because the two zoom lenses have similar wide angle settings (36 and 38). The second point is the image size is different: iPhoto has resized it to fit in the window, but what is shown is only 25 percent of the actual image. (The full dimensions of each image are displayed in the lower-left of the iPhoto window.) Note, while the actual images in both cases are larger than what is shown, they've been scaled: the image shown in the iPhoto window contains the entire image. You can see the difference between the two lenses in Figures 3–3 and 3–4.

The tightest zoom for the low-resolution lens is 110. You can see in Figure 3-3 how closely you can focus on the sugar bowl on the table in the photo. The narrowest zoom for the high-resolution lens is 190mm. In Figure 3-4, you can see how much closer you can get to the sugar bowl just by zooming the lens.

Because the high-resolution camera has a much more powerful zoom lens, you can get "closer" to objects in the image. This is important if you're subsequently enlarging them, as you see in the next section.

Enlarging Images

The four figures in this section demonstrate enlargement of the four photos from the previous section. In Figure 3-5 you can see the low-resolution image at widest zoom enlarged.

Comparing it to the original image (Figure 3-1), note that it's only slightly enlarged. (You can also see the size control slider in the lower-right of the iPhoto window is moved only slightly.) Enlarging the image beyond this size causes it to degrade because of its low resolution.

In Figure 3-6, by comparison, the high-resolution image at widest zoom is enlarged until it, too, starts to break down.

The two zoom lenses are similar at wide zoom, as shown previously in Figures 3-1 and 3-2, where the images were almost the same. Thus, the difference in the quality of the enlarged images is almost entirely because of the higher resolution of the camera (5 megapixels rather than 1.3). The fact that you can use iPhoto to enlarge the sugar bowl from Figure 3-2 to the image shown in Figure 3-6 is quite impressive, and it requires high resolution.

If you combine the zoom lens with enlargement, the results are more impressive. Figure 3-7 is an enlargement of the narrowest zoom low-resolution image, shown previously as Figure 3-3.

Enlarging the zoomed image provides a significant increase in size and detail until the image starts to break down. However, the results in Figure 3-8 are, by comparison, spectacular.

This is the enlarged version of Figure 3-4. Unlike the others, it isn't enlarged until the image starts to break down. By enlarging it to that degree, the resulting image (a small piece of the decoration on the sugar bowl) is unrecognizable—not because of blurring, but because it's so large.

Overenlarging Digital Images

With both digital and film images, you frequently enlarge or reduce the image for display. Enlarging an image eventually causes it to break down. In digital images this is referred to as *pixelization*. Figure 3-9 shows pixelization appearing in an image that's been enlarged too much.

FIGURE 3-1   Low-resolution image at widest zoom

FIGURE 3-2   High-resolution image at widest zoom

FIGURE 3-3   Low-resolution image at narrowest zoom

FIGURE 3-4   High-resolution image at narrowest zoom

Zooming and Enlarging Images

FIGURE 3-5 Enlarged low-resolution image at widest zoom

FIGURE 3-6 Enlarged high-resolution image at widest zoom

FIGURE 3-7 Enlarged low-resolution image at narrowest zoom

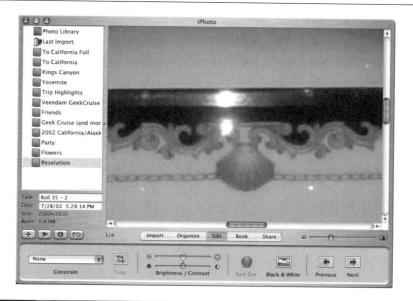

FIGURE 3-8 Enlarged high-resolution image at narrowest zoom

Zooming and Enlarging Images

FIGURE 3-9   Pixelization occurs when you overenlarge an image.

You can prevent pixelization from happening by not overenlarging an image. Make certain the image you shoot is zoomed in, so you use your camera's pixels for the image you want, not for extraneous material. The more pixels you have in your image, the more possibilities you have for enlargement. And the closer in you've zoomed, the less need you'll have for it.

Storing Images on the Camera

Once you take the photo and it's been processed, the photo is stored on removable media on the camera. You then need to transfer the image to your computer.

Types of Removable Memory

Five basic types of removable media exist for cameras. Unfortunately, each is a different size and shape. When you buy a second digital camera, your old removable memory quite possibly won't fit if you switch brands. The good news, though, is the cards are compatible: if your camera uses a SmartMedia card and your friend's camera does, too, you can share. Each of these cards is available in a variety of sizes.

- **Sony MemoryStick**   Used primarily on Sony cameras; you can buy MemoryStick media from Sony and from third parties.

- **SmartMedia**   Cameras from manufacturers such as Olympus, Minolta, and Fuji frequently use these cards.

- **Compact Flash**   Canon, HP, and Kodak cameras often use Compact Flash cards. ("Flash" refers to *flash memory,* a type of memory that retains its values when power is removed. "Flash" doesn't refer to a flash attachment that adds light to your photo.)

- **MultiMediaCard**   Canon uses this format—the tiniest—to store the still images on its digital camcorders. Not all models support this feature.

- **PCMCIA**   Some high-end cameras use PCMCIA cards. These are the same cards you can insert in slots in laptop computers. (Personal Computer Memory Card International Association is an international trade organization that issues standards for PC cards. PCMCIA is the association; it is also correct to speak of the PCMCIA interface, which is what they promulgate, and PCMCIA cards, which are PC cards adhering to the PCMCIA interface.)

Your camera's instruction manual will give you a guide to the number of images—at different sizes and qualities—that you can store on a given size of memory card. Many people are used to the standard film sizes of 24 and 36 exposures. If you're among them, make certain you can get the number of images of the size and resolution that you want onto the memory card. As noted previously, this generally means purchasing a larger memory card at the time you buy your camera. (Many people wish the camera manufacturers would supply no memory card with the camera. They pay for a card that's too small, and they'd rather take the money and put it toward the purchase of a usable one.)

NOTE   *Chapter 4 discusses the tools and techniques you need to move images from your camera's memory card to your computer.*

File Formats on the Camera

Once the image data is received by the sensor, it's stored in the camera. One of the most significant advances of recent years has been the development of standard formats for image storage.

File Formats on the Camera

Video Formats: DV

DV (which stands for digital video) is now the standard format for digital video. MiniDV cassettes used in many of today's digital camcorders can typically record 80 minutes of digital video. At a lower quality, they can record two hours' worth of video. When imported to your computer, DV takes up a lot of space: you need 3.6MB of disk space per second of video.

Because digital video takes up so much disk space, you need a large disk to work with it. Generally, you also need some way to move the data temporarily off your disk. Chapter 9 addresses these issues.

NOTE   *In its professional video editing application, Final Cut Pro, Apple supports the OfflineRT format. This downloads digital video for editing, but it's highly compressed. When you finish editing, the needed video—and only what is needed—is downloaded at full resolution.*

Still Formats

Your camera might provide you with a choice of formats to use in storing images in memory. Three formats are common.

JPEG

The *JPEG* format is widely used on computers and on the Internet. It converts the original image (usually in RGB color values) to a different system based on brightness and color, and it compresses that data. This is referred to as a *lossy* file format because it destroys some of the original image's data (the RGB values), which is lost forever and can't be restored. For most purposes, this loss—at least the first time—doesn't degrade the image substantially (or even noticeably to the human eye). And this compression can reduce the image's file size by a factor of 8–10.

A problem does arise with JPEG images that are repeatedly saved: gradually; they lose more and more data. If you're taking digital images and move them to the computer, you might want to change their format to another one before embarking on changes. *Graphic Converter,* a shareware utility, lets you make such conversions. (You can download Graphic Converter from **http://www .lemkesoft.com**.)

You needn't worry if you're importing a JPEG image into iPhoto, because iPhoto saves the original image, even as you modify it. (What you think you're doing with modifications is actually storing instructions to be applied to the original image each time iPhoto displays it.)

The conversion of the image from RGB to a system based on brightness and color exploits the characteristics of the human eye. JPEG isn't a good format to use for images that will be used in optical scanning or other nonhuman purposes.

TIFF

JPEG was designed to store images with as much fidelity as possible in as little space as possible. In fact, you can adjust the degree of image quality.

The *TIFF* format isn't a lossy one. The TIFF format stores the maximum amount of data about the image in a standardized way. Printers frequently prefer TIFF files to JPEG files because of their higher quality. Your camera might be able to store images as TIFF files rather than JPEG ones. If so, they'll take up more space. If you need TIFF files and don't have a problem with the slight loss that occurs in JPEG files, consider downloading the JPEG images to your computer and using Graphic Converter to convert them to TIFF for further processing.

RAW

Proprietary formats also exist for each manufacturer. Because these are idiosyncratic, it's generally a bad idea to use them. The only reason to consider doing so is there's less processing to the image than in the JPEG and TIFF formats (it isn't finished yet). Thus, you can import the file and manipulate it. That process is beyond the scope of this book.

Other Data in Your Pictures

Finally, you should know that digital images today have space in their files for comments. Your camera can automatically timestamp images (digital camcorders automatically do this). The time stamp might not be displayed, but it's usually there. For this reason, make certain your camera or camcorder's date and time are correct.

Some cameras have built-in microphones that let you record a brief period of sound as a comment. All of this is referred to as *metadata*.

Other Data in Your Pictures

Summary

This chapter has covered the purely digital aspects of photography. You've seen how the sensors work and how pixels, resolution, zooming, enlarging, and picture quality are all related. The digital storage formats and types of memory cards were described here. All this is background you should know. What's important to remember from this chapter is the following:

- Use zooming and your camera's resolution and quality settings to get the highest quality image you can.

- Consider your purpose, though, and don't get higher quality (and use more memory) than you need.

There's one more important aspect of your digital camera or camcorder: getting the pictures onto the computer. This is the topic of the next chapter.

Chapter 4

Connecting the Digital Hub

In This Chapter...

■ Plug and Play. From sensing a digital camera or camcorder to sensing an iPod automatically launching iTunes, plug and play makes it possible. Here's how it happens.

■ Power. Somehow, each of your digital hub components needs power. Sometimes that's a direct corded connection to a power source. Other times, it's a battery. In still other cases, the data connection doubles as a power connection. This section looks at those possibilities.

■ Network and Internet Connections. Your computer connects to other computers and network printers (not to mention the Internet) through a network connection. This can be wired or wireless.

■ Using Plug and Play to Get All Your Devices Communicating. Your camera, camcorder, or iPod (or other music player) is a peripheral. These use different connections than do computers and network printers. Like network and Internet connections, these can be wired or wireless.

One of the most significant changes to computers in the last five years has been the introduction of sophisticated connection technologies. Unlike the proprietary designs of a decade ago, industry standards now exist and are widely used. These connection technologies are more sophisticated, too, often incorporating power and communication in the same cable. And, as you would expect, they're more powerful and faster.

This chapter provides an overview of the types of cables you encounter, along with the types of wireless technologies you need to know about. Fortunately, because of the rise of the industry standards, two categories (wired and wireless) exist for each of three types of connections (power, network, and local), making a total of six.

In this chapter, you see the wired and wireless choices you have for power, networks (including the Internet), and peripherals. The rise of wireless connectivity reflects its maturity as a technology and its affordable pricing. The price of wireless is still higher than that of wired connections. However, when you consider you don't have to keep purchasing cables with each new peripheral you buy, you don't have to worry about stringing them behind furniture or through walls, and the limitations on where you can work are significantly reduced, you might well think wireless technology is cheaper than wired.

The Impact of Wireless Technology

David G. DeLong is professor of architecture at the University of Pennsylvania and a long-time friend. His books include *Frank Lloyd Wright and the Living City, Louis I. Kahn: In the Realm of Architecture,* and *Frank Lloyd Wright: Designs for an American Landscape.* I asked David to put on his architect's hat to think about the impact of wireless technology. Here's his response:

"Architects have only begun to envision new spatial configurations that wireless technology will make possible. Freedom from cords is an advance in a class with indoor plumbing."

Plug and Play Connections

The rules for connecting something to your computer used to be simple: power everything off, make the connection, and then power on—toward the computer (that is, printers and disk drives first). Violating these rules could lead to serious problems, sometimes even the demise of one or more components.

Plug and play has two critical features:

- ■ You can connect and disconnect computers and devices without powering them off.

- ■ Devices can identify themselves in a standard way: they can be sensed by identity and location in the computer's environment.

Sensing a Connection

The plug and play protocols specify how devices should identify themselves. As a result, the computer can tell if a camera—and which camera—is connected to it. Periodically, devices communicate to identify themselves.

Power-Up Connections

When a USB device is powered up, it sends a message out to the computer to which it's attached, identifying itself. In most cases, a digital camera that's plugged into a computer will, eventually, identify itself to the computer. The easier way is to turn the camera off, and then back on again.

Optional Power Supply

The wired connections for peripherals (USB and FireWire) allow a small amount of power to be passed over the cable. This means you don't need a separate power supply for the peripheral. If you're using wireless technology, you'll need a separate supply for the peripheral.

Peripherals on the Macintosh Desktop

When you connect your digital camcorder or camera to your computer and turn it on, the plug and play sensing enables Mac OS X to open the appropriate application, such as iPhoto, shown in Figure 4-1. (If your digital camera is old, it might not work directly with iPhoto. In that case, you need to transfer the images with a reader for the memory card in your camera. See Chapter 11 for more on this.)

FIGURE 4-1   iPhoto opens automatically when you connect a camera.

As you can see in the lower-left portion of the window, not only has iPhoto discovered a camera, but it has used standard USB protocols to identify the manufacturer.

When you finish unloading photos from your camera, don't turn it off or disconnect it. It has been mounted on your desktop as a removable disk. Click the Finder icon in the Dock (at the left or top if it's displayed vertically), and then click Computer in the Finder toolbar. You'll see the disks mounted on your computer. The camera is shown as a removable disk (not as a camera), possibly with a name such as Unlabeled, as shown in Figure 4-2.

Before turning the camera off, drag it to the Trash to eject it. Or use a contextual menu to eject it. For still another option, select it, and then choose Eject from the File menu. If you turn the camera off without doing this, a message like the one shown here appears:

In most cases with cameras, no damage will be done, but it's best to get in the habit of disconnecting devices properly (dragging them to the Trash, and then turning them off).

Powering Your Computer and Components

Your computer, digital camcorder, digital camera, disk drives, and the like all need power to run. Improvements in battery technology now allow heavy power-consuming devices (such as the computer itself or a digital camcorder) to run for three, four, or more hours without being recharged.

Thus, your laptop, digital camcorder, or any other device can run in wired or wireless mode. As you will see, your desktop computer can also run in cordless mode for limited periods of time.

Powering Your Computer and Components

FIGURE 4-2   Cameras appear as removable disks.

Replaceable Batteries

If you're using replaceable batteries (such as AA) for a digital camera, a good idea is always to have a spare set available. Batteries aren't expensive, and if you purchase a recharger at an electronics store (or even a supermarket!), you can get many uses out of a set. (See Chapter 2 for more on the types of rechargeable batteries available.)

Lithion-Ion Batteries

If you're using Lithion-Ion rechargeable batteries, these are much more powerful than the AA or AAA batteries. They also are generally custom-made for each device, so you can't swap them between your digital camera and digital camcorder (or, often, even between two digital cameras from the same manufacturer). Thus, your laptop or digital camcorder batteries might well cost over $50 each—

sometimes much more. For most people, this means not having a backup battery. Instead, you monitor the battery charge and make certain you charge it overnight or when it's not in use.

Mixing Batteries and Wired Power

You can mix wired and battery power. If you're doing something mechanically intensive (such as using a digital camcorder and frequently rewinding or fast-forwarding the tape), if at all possible, it's best to have the camcorder plugged in. Likewise, if you're using your laptop for file maintenance and you're copying many files back and forth, this is a good time to make certain you have direct power. (Or if you're running on the battery, postpone those file maintenance chores until later.)

Universal Power Supplies

Another source of power is a *Universal Power Supply* (UPS). Formerly the bailiwick of major data centers and mainframe computers, these products are now widely available for the home and small office. They combine a constantly recharging battery with surge suppression for incoming power, network, and telephone lines.

For under $100, for example, you can purchase a UPS system with six outlets. The constantly recharging battery holds a charge sufficient to power a computer for some time. An iMac, for example, can run for 16 minutes after the power fails. A desktop Macintosh G4 can run from 5 to 12 minutes, depending on the size of the display (larger displays need more power).

Furthermore, a USB connector on the UPS can plug into your computer. If you install the software provided with the unit, it checks to make certain the UPS is functioning properly. If it senses the UPS is running on battery power, the software automatically shuts down your computer, so files aren't damaged when the power fails.

Network and Internet Connections

A *local area network* (LAN) contacts computers, routers, cable/DSL modems, and networkable printers. If you have any two or more of these connected together, it almost certainly uses the Ethernet protocol. If all you have is a cable or DSL modem and a computer, you've got a LAN.

Network and Internet Connections

A LAN normally covers a relatively small area, such as an office or building. The same technology can cover a wide area and it's then called a WAN (wide area network). WANs can span the Internet. LANs might typically connect to the Internet, but they focus on the computers and network printers attached to them.

LANs frequently have dedicated computers on them. A *file server,* for example, is a computer on a network with a large disk (or an array of disks). This is used for primary or backup storage for the computers on the LAN.

You can use a LAN to connect to the Internet. You can also use it to connect various computers together. You don't normally use a LAN to connect digital devices, such as cameras or camcorders, to one another or to a computer. In part, this is because a LAN connection requires an Ethernet card or controller, and those aren't built into devices, such as cameras and camcorders. These devices are typically "slaves" to an individual computer, not shared among several computers on a network. Network devices are normally computers, networkable printers, routers, and other computers.

Subject to security constrains, all the devices on a LAN can communicate with one another. LANs are a way of sharing these devices (particularly network printers, file servers, and Internet connections).

Wired Ethernet

Ethernet is a standard used for LANs. Developed originally by Xerox, and then Intel and DEC, Ethernet is now codified in standard IEEE 802.3. It originally used coaxial cable, but now can use high-grade, twisted-pair cables (specified as Category 5 or 6—Cat 5 or Cat 6). Ethernet is a packet-switching network (just as the Internet is). Messages are split into packets and sent separately to their destination. The only serious competitor to Ethernet today for LANs is the token ring standard.

Today, most Ethernet connectors use the flat RJ45 connector (somewhat wider than the standard RJ11 telephone connector). In addition to connecting these devices to one another, you can connect several of them to a hub or router, and then connect it to other devices or other hubs. (Hubs have ports—4, 16, 32, or more—into which you plug other devices. A single port then connects to the rest of the LAN. Instead of the single port that connects to the rest of the LAN, routers have a single port that connects to a cable, DSL, or other modem. They also have 4, 16, 32, or more ports for network devices.)

AirPort Wireless Ethernet

If you have a wireless network connection, you have no cables to worry about. Instead, you have an AirPort card in your computer that communicates wirelessly with a router—the AirPort base station. Except for the fact that the physical connection is wireless, the same technology is used. This technology includes an Ethernet card or controller in each device connected to the network. All Macintosh computers ship with Ethernet controllers (other computers have separate cards added in for Ethernet). Many high-end printers also contain Ethernet cards, and this is a build-to-order option on others.

The *AirPort base station* is functionally the same as the router you buy in the office supply store (for well under $100 these days). Like the router, it's connected via a wire with another router or DSL/cable modem or to a dial-up connection. Unlike the router, the AirPort base station is connected wirelessly to the computers with AirPort cards.

NOTE   *AirPort is Apple's proprietary name for the 802.11 standard. Other manufacturers make wireless equipment that interoperates with AirPort.*

AirPort Issues

AirPort uses radio frequencies to communicate between the base station and AirPort cards in computers and other devices. These radio frequencies have a range of 100 meters/300 yards in an unobstructed area. Certain materials (such as masonry and concrete) decrease the range of the signals. If you have an AirPort base station, you can experiment with its placement to see where the signal is strongest. (All AirPort devices have a display for the signal strength.) Many people report significantly improved results by placing the base station high up in a room rather than on the floor amid a welter of cables.

AirPort base stations have connectors for a cable/DSL modem or wired LAN, as well as for a dial-up modem. You need one of those connections to connect to the Internet. Wireless communications, such as AirPort, are generally slower than the fastest wired connections. However, it's worth remembering that if you're surfing the Web, the speed of your Internet connection determines responsiveness. If your network (wired or wireless) is faster than the Internet connection, it won't do you any good.

Network and Internet
Connections

Peripherals

Peripherals are relatively small devices that normally are attached to a single computer rather than to the network as a whole. They include disk drives, scanners, individual (as opposed to networked) printers, and digital cameras, digital camcorders, iPod and other music players, personal digital assistants (PDAs), and, now, some cell phones.

Two wired technologies, FireWire and USB, exist, along with a single wireless technology, Bluetooth. FireWire is the faster of the two wired technologies. Both are now on their second generations, so if you see comparisons that suggest USB 2.0 is comparable in speed to FireWire 1.0, this is the reason. Macintosh computers today ship with both USB and FireWire ports, so you can connect either type of device. Because you can connect devices to one another as described in the following section, connecting five FireWire and six USB devices to a computer is easy with only two USB connections and two FireWire connections.

You can find out more about FireWire at **http://www.apple.com/firewire**.

FireWire

FireWire is the highest-speed connection available on the Macintosh, except for the connections within the computer itself. It's used for devices that need to transmit large amounts of data quickly. These include disk drives, high-end printers and scanners, and digital camcorders.

FireWire also enables you to connect peer-to-peer devices. You can connect two computers together using FireWire, and you can connect some FireWire devices directly to other ones in the right circumstances. Normally, though, you connect your FireWire peripherals to your computer.

Developed originally by Apple, FireWire is now an international standard (IEEE1394). Sony uses this standard and markets it as *i.Link*.

Types of Connectors

Standard FireWire connectors connect to your computer and to FireWire devices. A second type of connector that's smaller is used to connect certain small peripherals (such as digital camcorders).

Connecting Multiple Devices

You can connect FireWire devices in a chain, one to the other. Each device identifies itself, and data destined for one device is sent over the chain and bypasses all except the intended destination. (An older technology, Small Computer System

Interface (SCSI), required you to assign unique numbers to each device on the chain. Also, you needed to power everything off to add or remove devices.)

Because FireWire is a standard, you can buy replacement or extension cables at ordinary stores. Unless a nonstandard connector is used to connect the FireWire cable to your camera or camcorder, you don't need a special (expensive) cable.

> **NOTE**   *The first thing you should do when unpacking a new FireWire device is to check if a nonstandard connector is used. If it is, hoard that cable like gold because its replacement could be expensive.*

USB

The Universal Serial Bus (USB) standard is used for lower-speed peripherals, such as keyboards, digital still cameras, and for some printers and scanners.

USB Implementors Forum at **http://www.usb.org** has more information and detailed specifications of USB.

Types of Connectors

Two types of standard USB connectors exist.

- A connectors are flat connectors that connect USB cables to computers.

- B connectors are smaller connectors that connect USB cables to peripherals.

In addition, some companies use proprietary small connectors, rather than the standard B connectors.

> **NOTE**   *As with FireWire, check to see if your peripheral uses an idiosyncratic connector.*

Connecting Multiple Devices and/or Hubs

Unlike FireWire, where devices are usually connected in a chain, you can have USB hubs. Similarly to a LAN, the hub is connected to a USB port on the computer (or other device) and several USB devices are plugged into the hub. If you have a recent desktop Macintosh, you probably have at least two hubs: the display and the keyboard. The display is connected to the computer and, in the back, has two open USB connectors into which you can plug other devices: it is a hub. Likewise, the keyboard has two USB connectors: one is to connect to the computer and the other is for whatever you want.

Peripherals

Hubs can be powered or unpowered. Because power can flow over the USB cable both to power devices and to improve the signal, a powered hub (priced at about $50) can be a good investment if you have several devices to attach.

Bluetooth

Finally, *Bluetooth* provides wireless connectivity on the Macintosh. You need a special adapter, which plugs into a USB connector on your computer. The price is about $50. You also need to download and install software for your OS if that hasn't been done for you.

When you want to connect a Bluetooth device, it, too, needs a Bluetooth adapter. Some are built into new devices. In other cases, you need to buy an add-on card, as is the case for older PDAs from Palm. Such cards cost about $150.

Bluetooth is designed for short-range communications—about 10 meters/ 30 feet. It's wonderful for minimizing cable clutter, and avoiding plugging and unplugging components. Anyone who has gone wireless swears never to come back. It completely changes the way you use your computer and its peripherals.

Summary

Certainly one of the advances that has made Apple's digital hub concept so popular and easy to use is the standardization of communication technologies. Wired technologies for power, networking (Ethernet), and peripherals (USB and FireWire) are standards across the industry. Apple has adopted leading-edge, but standard, wireless technologies for networking (AirPort) and peripherals (Bluetooth).

The heart of the peripheral technologies is plug and play. You don't have to turn devices on and off: they just work. In fact, if you're experienced with connecting devices to your Macintosh, most of what you have to do today is to unlearn the old rules.

Here's one more combination to consider: you can have a remote disk attached to your computer over the Internet. Apple's .Mac provides disk and applications for you to use, and these are mostly free. The applications of the digital hub are highly integrated with .Mac, and the next chapter tells you more.

Chapter 5

.Mac: Apple's Suite of Internet Tools for You

In This Chapter...

■ What is .Mac? Apple has a suite of Internet tools providing you with email disk space, backup, anti-virus software, greeting cards, support, and more. They're closely integrated into the digital hub applications. This chapter shows you what they are and how to use them.

■ Accessing Your iDisk. Having an additional 100GB of disk space at your disposal—particularly when it's located offsite and maintained by someone else—can be a blessing. That's what your iDisk is.

■ HomePage: Creating Your Web Site. You have a Web site waiting for you on .Mac. You can create pages easily online—or with the click of a mouse from inside iPhoto.

■ iCards. Send greeting cards with your own photos to friends (or colleagues or business acquaintances). Here's how.

Apple provides a suite of Internet-based tools called *.Mac,* which you can use with your Mac and Mac OS X. This chapter provides an overview of .Mac, focusing particularly on how it can be used to share your files, and how you can create Web pages and greeting cards from the photos you've made on your Mac.

NOTE *In addition to iDisk, HomePage, and iCards, Apple offers email on .Mac. Periodically, other services are offered. Email isn't covered in this book. To learn how to use your .Mac email account, see* Mac OS X: The Complete Reference, *by Jesse Feiler (Osborne/McGraw-Hill, 2001).*

What Is .Mac?

The tools and resources on .Mac are added value features for users of the Macintosh and, particularly, of Mac OS X. You can create an .Mac account during the installation and registration process of Mac OS X. Also, at that time, you can automatically set your computer to use an already existing .Mac account. (If you aren't ready for .Mac, you can bypass it entirely. You can go back to it and register by logging on to Apple's Web site, **http://www.apple.com**, and clicking the .Mac button at the top.)

Some of the resources on .Mac, such as email at **mac.com** or a home page at **homepage.mac.com**, have obvious benefits. Others are more for fun—such as *iCards,* the tool that lets you create and send greeting cards to your friends.

And another one, *iDisk,* has significant benefits that might not be immediately obvious (iCards and iDisk are discussed later in this chapter. Email at **mac.com** is discussed in *Mac OS X: The Complete Reference*).

You get to .Mac from the tab buttons at the top of the Apple Web site, as shown in Figure 5-1.

If you indicated that you want to use a .Mac account during installation and registration, you might never need to see this page. iPhoto automatically stores

FIGURE 5-1   .Mac Home Page

What Is .Mac?

photos to the proper place in your .Mac account, and it can also automatically create a Web page for your Web site at **homepage.mac.com**. This is part of an emerging trend in the world of personal computers, with Apple leading the way. The desktop metaphor that has stood in good stead for a quarter of a century is becoming less and less relevant. At the start, this metaphor was necessary because people neither knew what personal computers could do nor how to make them do those things. The idea of files, folders, and the trash helped suggest solutions to these questions. Today, we all know those answers, and advanced application programs, such as iPhoto, can perform tasks with less and less user involvement. In other words, you don't need to know where your pictures are located on the Internet because, if you use .Mac, they'll be in a specific location. iPhoto will remember where that location is as well as your .Mac user name and password.

Accessing Your iDisk

Each .Mac account comes with an allocation of disk space on Apple's servers called your *iDisk*. You can get to it once you log in to .Mac. Click the tab in the second row at the top, as shown previously in Figure 5-1. You can also click iDisk icons on various other screens.

If you created or entered your .Mac information in your computer installation or registration, your iDisk is also available directly from the Finder. Choose iDisk from the Go menu and your iDisk will be mounted automatically for you.

Use iDisk Utility to manage your iDisk. iDisk Utility is found in the Utilities folder inside the Applications folder. If it's not there, you can download it from the .Mac Web site by clicking the iDisk button. It lets you manage your iDisk in many ways. The buttons across the toolbar at the top of the window provide access to the various features, as shown in Figure 5-2.

You can log on to an iDisk from here—you need the user name and password. This is useful if you are using someone else's computer and want to get to your own iDisk.

Even more useful is the iDisk Public folder. You can log on to any user's Public folder from here—provided you are given access. Use the Public Folder Access button, shown in Figure 5-2, to determine if everyone can see your Public folder files or if they need a password. You can also let people view the files (Read-Only) or update them as well (Read-Write).

Finally, note that you can add disk space to your iDisk. If you want more than the minimum allocation, you must pay for it. Click the Upgrade Now button to see

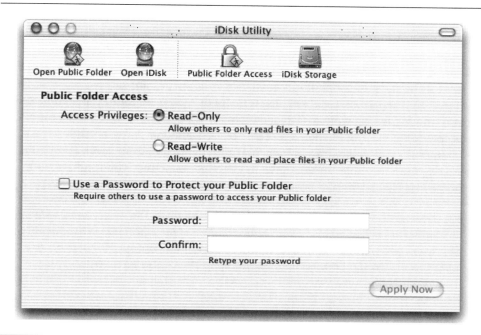

FIGURE 5-2   iDisk Utility

the current prices (you won't actually purchase the additional disk space until later in the process, so there's no harm in clicking Upgrade Now).

You can use this disk space for your Web page on **homepage.mac.com**. You can also use it to put files, such as movies and photos, into your Public folder for your friends to download.

Perhaps one of the most important uses of your iDisk is to back up critical files. As you see in Chapter 9, having your computer backed up in case of problems is critically important. While you should be using removable storage such as tapes, CD-ROMs, or data DVDs to do so, storing important files in a secure location away from your computer is also a good idea (in case of fire, for example). You can store these files on your iDisk (most emphatically *not* in your Public folder).

Apple maintains your iDisk in a secure data center that's backed up on a regular basis. You needn't worry about the files once they're placed on your iDisk. Except for the most unusual of circumstances, these files are safe.

If you're using iDisk to store files, remember, you need an Internet connection to get to those files, as well as to place them on your iDisk. If you have a high-speed Internet connection, such as a cable or DSL modem, moving files across the Internet isn't a big deal. However, if you're using a dial-up connection and, especially if it's unstable, so you have to keep reconnecting, you might want to minimize your use of iDisk.

NOTE   *Originally, files in your Public folder were accessible only to people using Macintosh computers. Now, your Public folder can be accessed from any Internet-capable computer, no matter what operating system (OS) it's running. Your .Mac home page and email account have always been accessible from all OSs.*

iDisk Folders

When you open your iDisk—from the .Mac Web site, the Go menu, or from an iTools button in your Finder toolbar—you can see the disk mounted on your desktop. If your Finder display uses the icon view, your iDisk appears as shown here:

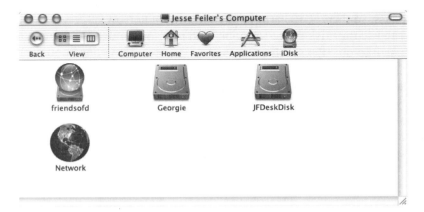

The iDisk icon is a disk drive with a globe on top of it. It's the left-hand icon in the first row of icons in this figure.

If you open your iDisk, you can see a standard set of folders inside it:

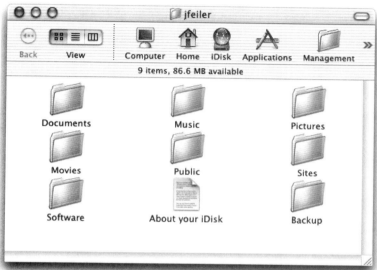

You can't create new folders at this level, but you can create new folders within each of these folders. Note, the list that follows is the current configuration of folders. This list might change over time. The iDisk folders are described in the following table.

Folder	Description
Documents	Just like the Documents folder in your Home directory, use this to store any documents you choose. (If you're using your iDisk for backups, you probably will create subfolders here, such as Monday032902Backup, and place your backup files in this location.)
Music	Use this for music, just like the Music folder in your Home directory.
Pictures	This is for pictures and photos. You can use it like the Pictures folder in your Home directory, but iPhoto also is aware of this. When you click a button to move your photos automatically to your iDisk when you're using iPhoto, this is where they'll go. The HomePage software, as well as iCards software, will look here to let you add photos to your Web site or to iCards.
Movies	As on your desktop in your Home directory, this is for movies. Your **homepage.mac.com** Web site will look here for movies to add to your Web site.
Public	As noted previously, any files you place in this directory are visible by anyone who knows your .Mac name (your **mac.com** email address). iPhoto can also automatically place files here.
Sites	This is where your **homepage.mac.com** Web page is located. The files here are created and maintained by the HomePage software you use to create your Web site. Under almost all conceivable circumstances, *never* move or rename these files.

Folder	Description
Software	This is a list of software you can download to experiment with or use. It includes Apple software as well as software from third parties. This list also includes some additional digital files, such as royalty free music, which you can use as a soundtrack or background music in your iMovie.

Moving Files to and from Your iDisk

Because your iDisk is integrated into the Finder, you can see it and its folders in the Finder windows, as shown previously. To move files to or from your iDisk, simply drag them as you normally would in the Finder. Only a few differences exist.

- Copying files to or from your iDisk takes longer than copying them on your hard disk. As a result, you should watch to see if the spinning cursor has stopped before continuing. If the cursor spins for a few seconds, don't panic: you're communicating over a long distance.

- In some circumstances, deleting files on your iDisk can cause them to be deleted immediately (they won't be placed in the Trash). If this is going to happen, you'll be warned and you'll have a chance to cancel the operation.

HomePage: Creating Your Web Site

You can use as much of your iDisk space as you want for a Web site. You build it with the HomePage software built into .Mac. This space is available only when you're online. There's no offline version.

HomePage builds on the files you placed in your Pictures and Movies folders on your Web site. For this reason, if you want to include photos or movies on your site, first move them to the appropriate folders on your iDisk.

NOTE *When HomePage includes photos or movies on your Web site, it references them from their locations in the Pictures or Movies folders. This way, you needn't duplicate storage for the files, but they must be in the appropriate folders.*

When you start out to create your Web page, click HomePage from the tabs in the second row under the .Mac tab. You see the window shown in Figure 5-3.

FIGURE 5-3   Beginning a HomePage Web site

Once you choose a look for your Web site or if you're modifying an existing Web site, you see the screen shown in Figure 5-4.

You can use the buttons at the top-right of the screen to put a password on your site. You can also create *subsites*—sites within sites. Each of these subsites can have its own look (or *theme* in HomePage parlance), and each can have its own password.

NOTE   *.Mac refers to your basic page as a HomePage, and you have sites within it. Some people refer to the inner sites as subsites of a main site.*

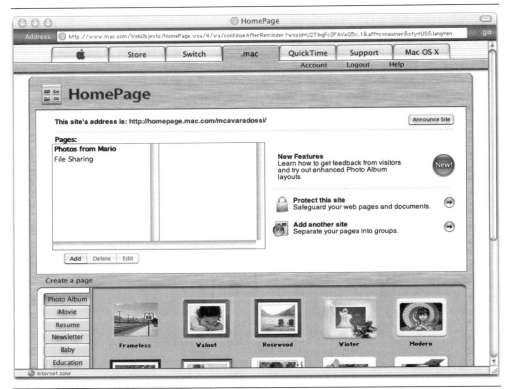

FIGURE 5-4 Updating a HomePage Web site

If you choose to password all or part of your site, you can enter the password, as shown here:

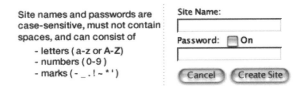

iCards

The iCards part of .Mac is available to everyone—you click the iCards tab underneath the .Mac button, as shown in Figure 5-5.

FIGURE 5-5   Creating an iCard

If you're an .Mac member, however, in addition to the standard images you can choose for an iCard, you can click the button in the lower-right. The images in your Pictures folder are displayed, and you can create a card using any one of them.

Summary

Many companies offer Web storage for your photos. Other companies offer email accounts. What's different about .Mac is the degree to which it's integrated with Mac OS X and with the applications that make up the digital hub. You can use your iDisk as just another disk connected to your computer, moving files to and from it, as you see fit. Or, because its directory structure is known, you can manipulate your photos stored on your iDisk by clicking buttons in iPhoto or by using HomePage.

As you've seen, the essence of the digital hub is digital files that can be moved around on your computer, your local area network, and across the Internet—to your iDisk, for example. However, some nondigital aspects still exist to the digital hub and to the media files, which you're going to use. The next chapter focuses on the critical issue of printing—on paper! Music, DVDs, and movies can't be printed, so that chapter deals solely with photos.

Chapter 6

Printing Your Photos

In This Chapter...

- Mechanics of Printing Images. If you only print text or if you only print photos, you can buy a laser printer or a special photo printer and be done with it. But, if you print a variety of things (as most people do), you need to know a little bit about printing, so you can make each of your documents look its best.

- Connecting Printers. It's not just a matter of plugging in cables: some computers can be shared over a network, while others are only for a single computer. Here's how to tell the difference.

- Using Print Center. Most of the time, Mac OS X takes care of printing for you. But sometimes you need to monitor the progress of printing and check problems with printers. Print Center helps you do that.

Digital data—images, sound, video, or even traditional numerical data—is at the heart of the digital hub and makes it possible. However, sometimes you need to produce nondigital output or to get data from a nondigital source. This chapter deals with printing photos, the only nondigital data you need to worry about in the context of the digital hub. (You can't print video or sound: their playback is often digital. Even when it isn't digital, though, the conversion from digital to analog is handled for you by the playback equipment.)

Mechanics of Printing Images

This section provides you with information about printing that can help you improve the quality of your printed output, as well as guide you to buying the most appropriate paper and printer for the job. The most expensive printer or paper isn't always the best. Here's what matters.

The Components of Print Quality

To understand the printing of images, go to a library armed with a magnifying glass and examine several books closely. First, look at an illustrated weekly newsmagazine. Then, look at a newspaper with color photos. Finally, look at an art book with reproductions of fine art. (Look for a publisher such as Abrams, Rizzoli, or a museum.) With few exceptions, almost all printed materials of this nature today use an offset process. The offset process is suitable for large print runs, and it differs from the processes used by printers connecting to computers. Many of its characteristics apply to computer printers, however. (Other printing processes, such as silk-screen printing and printing from special plates and blocks, are used for smaller print runs and for special purposes, including artwork.)

Two points should be apparent. First, with the magnifying glass, you can see the color image is made up of many small dots of ink. The higher-quality images have smaller dots and more of them. This is resolution, again.

But you'll notice a second important point. A tremendous difference exists in the paper used in weekly newsmagazines, newspapers, and art books. The paper contributes to the quality of the image. Uncoated stock, like the paper in a newspaper or the common copier or office paper, absorbs ink. The ink is not only absorbed, it is also somewhat diffused as it spreads into the fibers of the paper. Coated stock—glossy paper—has one or more thin layers of material that overlay the paper itself. Each of the layers absorbs ink in a different way.

Another aspect of print quality might not be visible when you look at printed illustrations. The colors aren't mixed in advance as an artist would do on a palette. Instead, the colors of the printed image are created by combining three, four, or six colors in the printer. Separate plates for each of the colors can be prepared. With a typical home or office printer, cartridges containing the basic colors are controlled by the printer, so the single image is divided into tiny dots covered by each of the colors. The human eye takes care of the rest. (You can see how color printing works when you find an image that's been printed incorrectly. *Registration marks* help printers align the separate color images directly on top of one another. If they aren't aligned properly, you'll see, for example, an offset yellow image above or next to a red image, and so forth.)

Home and office printers typically use three to six colors, as well as black, for printing. The three colors can be in a single, three-part cartridge or they can be separate. Commercial printing presses can be configured to use up to six colors. In both cases, the specific types of ink involved are usually determined by the press.

How Printers Work

As you've seen, printing consists of laying down ink on top of (and sometimes drawn into) paper. Two major technologies are used today in computer printers: laser printers and ink-jet printers.

Laser Printers

Laser printers ushered in the desktop-publishing revolution. Providing high speed and high-quality output, laser printers make it possible to publish newsletters, brochures, and crisp documents with a word-processing or desktop-publishing program.

Laser printers use the same technology as photocopying: fine particles of toner are magnetically charged on a drum and transferred to paper, where they're sealed in place with high heat. The clarity of laser printing is due, in large part, to the fact that no ink is involved. The toner particles land on top of the paper. No absorption and no diffusion occur, so the image is crisp.

Color-laser printing works the same way, but instead of having a single color (black) of toner, four colors are used. The tiny dots of toner in each of the four colors make up an image that appears to be in color as the dots blend together. The four colors normally used are the same four used in offset printing: cyan, magenta, yellow, and black (CMYK). The combinations of these color provide the widest range of color.

Laser printers are fast, and they're the workhorses of many offices. The entry-level laser printers are personal printers, which are connected to a single computer. More advanced printers can be networked and shared among computers on a local area network (LAN) or even across the Internet (see the upcoming section "Connecting Printers to Your Computer").

Except for the most basic laser printers, almost all use the PostScript imaging language. The print job sent to the printer uses this standard to describe the image to be printed. Any PostScript printer can print the same PostScript file with almost the same results.

Mac OS X directly supports PostScript and an even more sophisticated document description language, Portable Document Format (PDF). You can create a PDF file from any print dialog on Mac OS X. As shown next, choose Output Options from the pop-up menu, and then click Save to File and select the format you want. (Note, PDF is a Mac OS X-supported format and it should be available in all cases. The choice of PostScript depends on each individual application.)

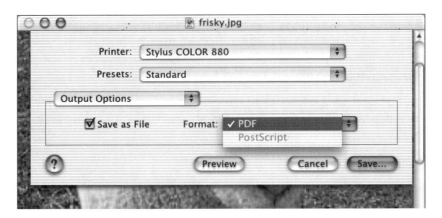

Ink-Jet Printers

Ink-jet printers are less expensive than laser printers and their quality was long considered inferior. They can't provide the crisp text and fine black lines of a laser printer. Ink-jet printers use real ink, not toner powder, and that ink can be absorbed into paper, making the images less distinct.

As people began to use digital cameras, the ink-jet printer industry changed dramatically. Today, ink-jet printers are optimized for printing photos. Some, in fact, enable you to connect a digital camera directly and to print images from it without using a computer. Because people are using photo-quality ink-jet printers to replace film processing for their keepsake photos, a wide variety of specialty paper has been brought to market that enables you to create ink-jet photo images that rival those of a photo-processing shop (see the upcoming section, "Output Media").

Ink-jet printers are slower than lasers and they're usually connected to an individual computer. In most cases, ink-jet printers aren't networkable; however, they can often be shared indirectly if the computer to which they are connected is networked.

Most ink-jet printers don't use PostScript to describe their images. For that reason and because they don't have the capability to print fine lines the way laser printers do, ink-jet printers normally aren't frequently used for text documents.

> NOTE
>
> *If you're creating documents, templates, or stationery to be used with an ink-jet printer, you can take its advantages and limitations into account when you create the document. Knowing that fine lines won't print properly, you can exploit other features—such as good color imaging— in your documents and logos.*

Special Purpose Printers

A variety of special purpose printers are available. They might use other types of ink or dyes in their imaging, and they might accommodate paper sizes larger than those used in standard office papers. A typical large-size printer enables you to print a four-fold newsletter. (The paper size accommodates two pages next to one another. When printed on both sides, you have a newsletter or tabloid format on a single page that has four sides.)

The prices of printers are coming down rapidly. If you thought that certain capabilities were beyond your means, check again.

Mechanics of Printing Images

Output Media

The printer is only one part of the equation that determines how your photos will look when you print them. The paper is equally important.

Printing on Paper

If you're printing color images and photos, it's almost certain that standard office photocopy paper won't yield satisfactory results. You need higher-quality paper designed for photo reproduction.

When using an ink-jet printer, select from the specialty papers you can find in an office supply store. They'll be heavier than standard photocopy paper and have some degree of glossy coating on them. Many ink-jet printers have settings for a variety of papers. If so, those settings will appear in the Print dialog, as shown in Figure 6-1.

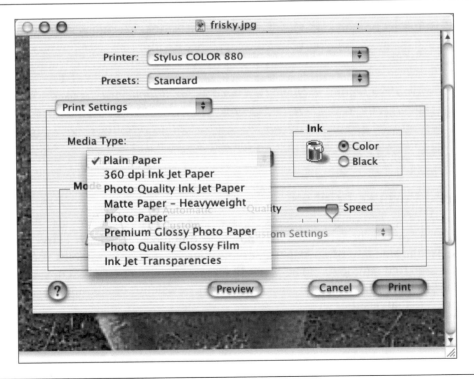

FIGURE 6-1   Paper settings for a color ink-jet printer

NOTE   *These special settings are automatically added to the Print dialog by the selected printer's driver code. This is installed automatically as part of Mac OS X or when you install your printer. If you need to install a printer driver manually (or to check which ones are installed), look in your computer's /Library/Printers directory. (That is, the Library directory at the root level of your computer, not in your Home directory.)*

These papers are even more sensitive to humidity than ordinary paper. To prevent printer jams, keep them in a cool, dry place. Furthermore, note that most of these papers come in plastic (not paper) wrappers that can be resealed with tape. Keep them in the plastic wrapper.

NOTE   *Your ink-jet printer might come with a sample pack of specialty papers. Don't simply toss these into the paper tray and run off a few memos. Save them and test them on photos. Each printer maker has its own line of papers. While they're all comparable, they might have different brand names.*

Keeping good-quality paper safe before printing is only half the battle. Color images fade over time, and some colors are more prone to fading than others. (Some newer ink-jet printers use dyes rather than inks to minimize fading.) Keep your printed photos under similar conditions to the unprinted paper: cool, dry, and dark. Photos placed behind glass (framed, for example), are less subject to fading than those left lying around or pinned to a wall. Nevertheless, for the most precious of your photos, make sure to keep the original digital image, so you can reprint the photo if it fades.

Printing on Transfers and Transparencies

In addition to printing on paper, ink-jet printers can easily print on overhead transparencies and on transfers you can iron on to T-shirts and other items. If you're printing to a transfer, you might need to reverse the image. If your printer supports this feature, it will be available in the Print dialog, as shown in Figure 6-2. This might have a different name and it might be in a differently named item in the pop-up menu, but it should be available. (If reverse printing isn't available, consult your printer's manual to see if it supports the feature.)

Mechanics of Printing Images

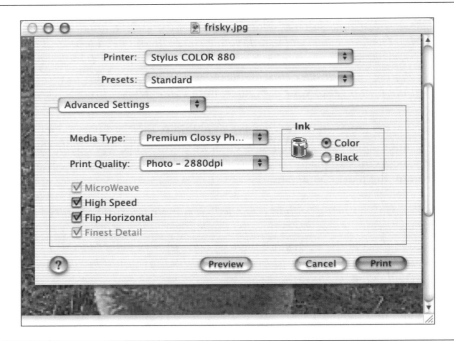

FIGURE 6-2   Reversing an image for printing on a transfer

When to Call the Print Shop

You can do much of what a print shop would do in your home or office with an
ink-jet printer (or a laser printer for text-oriented and large jobs). If you compare
costs, however, you'll notice that for large print runs—in the hundreds, for
example—the print shop (or copy shop) will probably be cheaper.

Today, many print shops are capable of printing directly from PDF files. You
can use the Output Options section of the Print dialog to produce a PDF file,
which you can email to a printer.

If the files are big, you and the printer might decide not to use email but,
instead, a more appropriate file transfer mechanism such as File Transfer Protocol
(FTP), as described in Chapter 7.

NOTE   *If you haven't done this before, try it with a two-page document of no
great importance. Sometimes it can take a little work to coordinate with
a printer, but once the two of you have set up your communications, you
should be able to ship large documents to the printer without any fuss.
Make sure to do your testing far in advance of approaching deadlines.*

The View from the Print Shop

Ryan Scott is the production manager at Pro Printers, a small commercial printer in Hudson, New York, which has been serving customers since 1989. I asked Ryan how the Internet and digital printing has changed his business. Here's Ryan's reply:

"My customers never have to leave their homes or offices. Customers can send their PDF files to me electronically, day or night. I, then, produce their jobs and ship the work right to their door. The Internet has truly altered the way I do business."

Connecting Printers to Your Computer

If you have printers installed on your network or connected to your computer, Mac OS X will normally recognize them when you install the software or when you turn on your computer. If not, here are the few steps you need to take.

USB Printers

USB connections for printers are common for ink-jet printers and personal (nonnetworked) laser printers. (These are the same USB connections described in Chapter 1.) You simply plug the printer into an available USB port on the computer, the display, or the keyboard. If you're all out of ports, you'll need to purchase a small USB hub. These typically have four ports you can use and a single additional port to connect the hub to your computer, display, or keyboard.

Some USB hubs are powered and, chances are, if you need a hub because you've run out of USB ports, you should get a powered one. They draw little power, and they work better.

Your USB printer should be recognized as soon as you connect it and turn it on. Because USB is a plug-and-play technology, you don't need to turn equipment off to connect and disconnect it. You might need to power the printer on (or off, and then on), however, to force it to be recognized promptly by the computer. (Or you could simply wait.)

Networked Printers

Laser printers with Ethernet cards require the same installation as any other Ethernet device. Connect a cable from the printer's network interface to an Ethernet hub or to an Ethernet receptacle in the wall if you have a wired office. The printer should be recognized as soon as you turn it on.

Using Print Center

Print Center is the application that manages printing for you on Mac OS X. Print Center is described fully in *Mac OS X: The Complete Reference* by Jesse Feiler (Osborne/McGraw-Hill, 2001). Each print job you create (by selecting the Print command) is sent to the printer you selected for it. A queue of jobs is created.

If you're having trouble printing—for example, if nothing happens—check to see that the appropriate printer queue hasn't been stopped. Open Print Center (from the Utilities folder in the Applications folder), and double-click the printer you want to know about. Its printer queue window is shown, as you can see here:

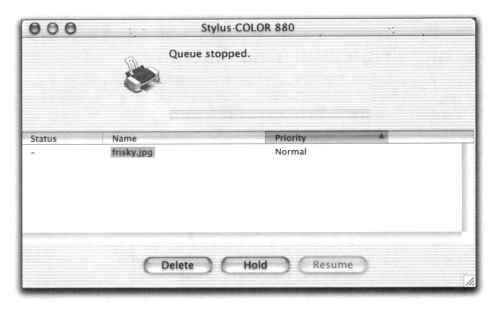

You can click an individual job to select it, and then hold it or delete it. If you're trouble-shooting a printer that doesn't print, check to see if the print queue is stopped (as it is in this example). To restart the printer queue, choose Start Queue from the Queue menu in Print Center:

You might wonder how this could happen. If your printer encounters an error, Print Center might stop its queue. That will enable you to "print" to the queue and, when the queue is restarted, those print jobs will go to the printer. Problems that can trigger this usually aren't the basics, such as out-of-paper conditions. If this happens repeatedly, you might want to troubleshoot it (or just restart the queue, as needed).

Summary

This chapter has provided an overview of printing photos. The technology and tools you use are quite different from printing text-based documents. For most people, the best results when printing photos come from using ink-jet printers (especially those marketed specifically for photo printing) and from using the papers designed for photos.

These printers aren't particularly expensive: The home printing market is large and the manufacturers are providing excellent printers at little more than $100 (sometimes less). By comparison with standard photocopy paper, photo-quality paper might seem expensive, but all photographic papers are expensive.

Remember to store your photo paper in cool, dark places both before and after printing. If you do so (and if you remember to keep an archival copy of the original digital image), you should be pleased with the printed results for a long time. You can share the photos with your friends and relatives, just as you do with film-based photos.

One of the great advantages of digital imaging, though, is you can share photos (and movies and music) over the Web. The next chapter shows you how to do this.

Chapter 7

Using Web Sites and Email for Sharing

In This Chapter...

■ Using Web Albums. Share your photos online with Web albums.

■ Filename Extensions. When you send files to other people—particularly those using other operating systems—you need to pay attention to those extensions that follow a filename. Otherwise, the files might be unreadable.

■ Compression Strategies. You can save transmission time and disk space by compressing your files. This section shows you how.

■ Using FTP. One of the oldest Internet protocols—File Transfer Protocol (FTP)—lets you send files without using email.

■ Using Email to Send Attachments. You can also send files as attachments to email messages. Here's what you need to know.

■ Using iDisk to Share Files. Finally, you can use your iDisk (part of .Mac) to share files easily with others. You can access your iDisk from the Finder without worrying about FTP, email, or extensions.

Much of the fun of making movies, photos, and music on your Mac is sharing with friends and colleagues. If you're using the technology at work or at school, sharing is an essential part of the process.

This chapter introduces you to a number of ways to share your digital files over the Internet. You can send them via email or using a file transfer mechanism. You can also post them to the Web where your friends, colleagues, and others can see them at their leisure. (Note the distinction: with email and file transfer, the files are sent and received at your convenience. When you post them to the Web, you send them at your convenience, and they're received at the other party's convenience. This includes the possibility that they'll sit on your Web site until someone decides to look at them, which may never happen.)

Overall, remember this one important point: iPhoto and .Mac make moving and sending files easy for you because you simply click a button. Just as you can manipulate files directly in the Finder, you also can manipulate them with email, file transfer, and the Web. The trend, though, is to hide the actual file manipulation from users, while providing them with simpler and more powerful interfaces that let the computer do the work.

Using Web Albums

Apple's .Mac site is a great way to share your files. As noted in Chapter 5, you can have your own public iDisk and you can post photos automatically to your Web site using iPhoto. HomePage, the iDisk online Web site creation tool, also lets you easily share photos, movies, and music.

.Mac is perhaps the easiest Web-based file-sharing system to use, but many others exist. A number of companies offer free Web albums for your photos: you upload your photos to public or private areas where your friends and relatives can see them. Features similar to iCards and HomePage let you create greeting cards from your photos, and create your own Web pages. Most Web albums let you have both public and private areas for your photos.

In general, these services are free—free in the sense that you needn't pay for them. Costs are involved, however, that might or might not concern you. The first "cost" is you might see advertisements on these Web album sites. Furthermore, your friends and relatives might see advertisements as they look at your photos. The sponsors of these Web album sites frequently promote their own products, and a look at the sponsors makes it clear what they're promoting.

Sony provides **http://www.imagestation.com**. This Web site includes advertisements for Sony products (particularly digital cameras and accessories). Special offers are also available on the site. Epson, a major printer manufacturer, provides Epson PhotoCenter at **http://photo.epson.com**. This site also provides advertisements and special offers, and it provides printing options for your photos. If you purchased a printer or digital camera, you might have information about the vendor's Web album site. .Mac is a terrific site to use because it's integrated into the Apple products and is available to users of Macintosh computers, as well as those running Linux and Windows. You might want to augment your .Mac site with one or more other albums, however, for special purposes or to take advantage of special offers.

In signing up for any Web album site (including .Mac), you'll be asked to agree to terms of use. This is a long document that spells out your rights and responsibilities, as well as those of the vendor. An option might be available where you can choose to receive email from the vendor and/or from its partners. You might want to reduce your incoming email but, in doing so, you could lose out on notifications of special offers. This is your choice (and you should be able to change it at any time).

Filename Extensions

One of the most complicated issues on all personal computers is linking data files to the applications that should open them. This is a simple matter with proprietary

Watch Your Rights

If you intend to use your photos for commercial purposes, be sure to read the terms of service carefully. In most cases, you retain the ownership of your photos if you post them to a Web album. By posting them to a Web album, however, you could relinquish all rights to further use and reproduction to the proprietor of the Web site. In other cases, you might relinquish those rights only if you post them to a public area of the Web site (not your private album). In still other cases, you relinquish rights only while the photo is posted: if you remove the photo, you regain the rights.

formats—Application A knows all its files are identified in a certain way and might even be stored in one location. With standards-based formats, however, the problem is more complicated.

Your digital camera images could be JPEG or TIFF files. You might want to open them in Preview to view them or in iPhoto to manipulate them. What's the correct action for the operating system to take when you double-click an image file?

Mac OS X has a number of rules it applies to open the correct application with a double-click. Prominent among these rules is the use of a file extension that identifies the type of the file. (This strategy is used on many operating systems.) You might have an image file called MyHouse but, in fact, this likely is called MyHouse.jpeg (or MyHouse.tiff). If you select a file in the Finder and choose Show Info from the File menu, you can choose whether the extension is shown, as you can see here:

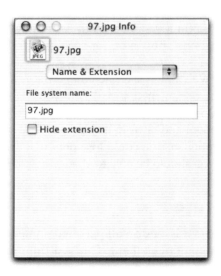

On Mac OS X, extensions aren't limited in length (for all practical purposes). On older versions of Windows and some other operating systems, they might be limited to three characters. Mac OS X makes the appropriate conversions: .jpeg is treated as .jpg, for instance. If you're sending files to another operating system, however, you might have to ensure the extension on the file is what that operating system expects. A common cause of unreadable files you send to someone on another operating system is an incorrect or missing extension. The other person can often change the extension and "recover" the file.

To change a file's extension, simply rename it as you normally would by clicking the name in the Finder, and then typing a new name. Type the extension you want after a period. You'll be asked to confirm you want to change the extension and when you confirm the dialog, the file will have been renamed.

Using the same Show Info window, you can also specify whether that file, or all files with the same extension, should be opened with a certain application. Use the Open With Application settings, as shown next. The small downward-pointing triangle in the icon of the application indicates this is a pop-up menu. You can select from any application on your computer.

On the Macintosh, these extensions aren't required and, as you saw, aren't always visible (although they frequently exist). Other strategies are used by the operating system to select an application to open a file. On other operating systems, the extensions are the primary means of determining an application to open the file.

Compression Strategies

If you're sending files to someone else, you might want to compress them. This saves transmission time and also enables you to compress a number of files into a single compressed file (often called an *archive*). Three common compression techniques are discussed in this section.

Compression takes advantage of the fact that many files contain a lot of information that can be mathematically reduced in size without losing any information. The page you're reading, for example, could be scanned to produce a graphic image. In that image, the background—the white paper—would be part of the image and it would be the largest part of the image. The background would be a prime target for compression.

The compression algorithms used don't destroy any information, so you can use them without fear. Note, some files are more amenable to compression than others. JPEG or GIF files, for instance, are already compressed as part of the JPEG and GIF formats, so compressing them further has little effect.

The compression strategies discussed in this section (Stuffit, ZIP, and TAR), are supported on most major platforms. You certainly shouldn't have trouble sending them to friends using Windows, Unix, or Linux. (Friends can decompress files if they know how, but they needn't know any special tips for decompressing files from a Macintosh.)

NOTE   *One easy way of reducing file size is to send a lower-resolution version of a file. If you're sending a digital image for someone to view online (a snapshot of your new baby or pet, for example), low resolution is fine because monitors don't display the high resolution needed for printing. This is the easiest approach and the one iPhoto does for you automatically.*

Using Stuffit to Compress Your Files

Stuffit, from Aladdin Systems, Inc., is the classic Macintosh compression utility. You'll find a version of Stuffit Expander installed with Mac OS X. *Stuffit Expander* enables you to unstuff files you receive. If you want, you can purchase *Stuffit Deluxe,* which provides tools for creating archives. (Aladdin Systems, Inc. is at **http://www.aladdinsys.com**.) Stuffit archive files have an extension of .sit. Your email and browser programs can automatically be configured to unstuff files you receive with those extensions.

Archives can be passworded. You can create an archive on your system and password it, so other people can't see the files inside it.

> NOTE
>
> *Stuffit archives can be used on Windows computers, but they aren't so widely used there as on Macintosh computers. If you're sending an archive to a Windows or Linux user, you might want to use one of the two following techniques.*

Using ZIP to Compress Your Files

ZIP files compress data. You can create an archive of one file or, as with Stuffit Deluxe, you can create an archive containing a number of files. As with Stuffit files, you can password a ZIP file. ZIP files are commonly used on all platforms. (If you purchase Stuffit Deluxe, you receive an application called *DropZip* that creates ZIP files. DropZip is in addition to *DropStuff,* which creates Stuffit files.)

A variety of programs, including Stuffit Expander, which ships with Mac OS X, can decompress ZIP files. ZIP files are a good choice for sharing compressed files across platforms.

Using TAR to Compress Your Files

Finally, *UNIX TAR* files are provided with Mac OS X. *Tar* files are uncompressed archives (*tar = tape archive*). You can ZIP a TAR file to create a compressed archive. You compress and decompress TAR and ZIPped TAR files from the command line using Terminal. The advantage of using TAR files is you don't need extra software. The disadvantage is you need to use the command line. If you're used to creating TAR files from a command line (perhaps on other operating systems), the commands are the same on Mac OS X. If you're not used to doing so, chances are you'll be better off with ZIP or Stuffit files.

Using FTP to Transfer Files

FTP, one of the earliest Internet standards, was devised to allow people to send files back and forth. In fact, email evolved from the FTP protocol when people realized the files they sent could consist of messages to one another.

FTP is a convenient and polite way to transfer files. You post a file to an FTP server, notify the recipient (often via email), and the recipient downloads the file from the FTP server. This prevents an email message with a large attachment from preventing other email messages from getting through.

Often, an FTP server is a file server on a LAN. If you're on the LAN, you move files to the file server, just as you normally would. Subject to security, people from outside the LAN access the file server with FTP. URLs for FTP servers start with the FTP schema. One such URL could be ftp://commonserver.yourcompany.com.

Two types of FTP software exist: FTP clients and Internet browsers with FTP capabilities.

Using FTP Client Software with an FTP Site

Programs such as Anarchie and Fetch are classic FTP programs available on the Macintosh. *Anarchie* and *Fetch* connect you to the FTP server you specify, and then you can browse, upload, or download files, much as you would with the Finder.

Programs like these are typically the fastest for transferring files.

Browsers for FTP

Many Internet browsers today handle FTP. You can type in an FTP URL, just as you would an HTTP URL, and you'll be connected to the appropriate server. Browsers typically are slower than dedicated FTP clients. If you only occasionally use FTP, the great virtue browsers have over FTP clients is this: you probably have a browser while you might not have an FTP client.

Using Email to Send Attachments

Most email programs enable you to send attachments. If you're sending a small photo, this isn't a big deal. If you're sending large images (or many of them), though, you should create a Stuffit or ZIP archive, and then attach the archive to the message.

Note, many ISPs limit the size of attachments. Some limits are quite small (this is particularly true on free email servers). In addition, a certain number of ISPs prohibit any attachments. Likewise, some receiving email servers refuse attachments (usually for security reasons). Also, users have an option in most email programs not to download attachments, so you can't be sure your email attachments will get through.

Because a large attachment might not get through or it might prevent subsequent messages from being delivered until it's been transmitted, consider using FTP instead to transfer large files.

NOTE   *Many email applications will attempt to expand image files into the message. Thus, attaching a TIFF file could display the actual image in your email message. Your recipient might not be using the same software and, thus, could see the attachment displayed as a link to a file that's been downloaded to disk.*

Using iDisk to Share Files

If you have an .Mac account, your iDisk is your very own FTP server. You can use it to share files with other people (on Macintosh and other platforms) without worrying about the problems of transferring files using email. The only point to consider is you can't exceed your iDisk disk allocation. If you need more space, you can purchase it.

Summary

Sharing files over the Internet is easy, and it's one of the most enjoyable aspects of using the digital hub. Sharing files can also be a vital part of your business or professional life. You can use free Web albums to post your photos. You can also transfer files to others using FTP (or your .Mac). And, you can use email to send files as attachments.

When transferring files, always consider your recipient. The photos you think are cute might not be cute to someone else—or they could be cute, but not at this exact moment. That is why Web albums and FTP transfers can be so valuable.

Remember, too, to create archives of compressed files when you send them (either via email or FTP). This reduces transmission time and, in the case of multifile archives, helps prevent them from getting lost.

Summary

Chapter 8

Using AppleScript Automation with the Digital Hub

In This Chapter...

■ What Is AppleScript? More than a macro or keystroke-automation tool, AppleScript has true computer programming capabilities. Here's an overview.

■ Automating Your Work with AppleScript. For tasks that are simple and repetitive as well as for those that are complex—and for everything in between—AppleScript can make your life easier. It can also keep your computer chugging away while you're asleep, out playing, or doing anything else you want to do with your life.

■ Creating and Using Droplets. A new feature of AppleScript, these special scripts let you manipulate the contents of files without opening them in another application first.

■ Toolbar Scripts. The Mac OS X Finder windows have a toolbar at the top into which you can drag-and-drop scripts for easy reference.

■ Using the Script Menu. The script menu (new in Mac OS X 10.1) lets you quickly access all your scripts from the menu bar. *All*—as in AppleScript, Perl, and shell scripts. Here's how.

■ Downloadable Scripts. Apple provides you with lots of scripts to help you use its applications and to tie them together into sophisticated workflows. This section shows you some of the digital hub scripts you can use.

AppleScript has long reigned as one of the most important of Apple's productivity tools. In Mac OS X, it takes on renewed importance. This chapter explains what AppleScript is and how to use it with the tools of the digital hub.

You can write scripts yourself, or you can use scripts provided by Apple (or others). Either way, your work will be easier.

NOTE   *Many references in this chapter are made to the AppleScript site, from which you can download the scripts described here. The AppleScript site is located at **http://www.apple.com/applescript**. Go to the Mac OS X section from the first page of the Web site to find these scripts. Over time, this step will become unnecessary as existing AppleScript users migrate to Mac OS X. For now, though, you might have to explicitly go to the Mac OS X section.*

What Is AppleScript?

AppleScript is a suite of tools and features that helps you automate your work. It consists of the AppleScript language with which you write scripts, as well as tools for editing those scripts, such as Script Editor (included with Mac OS X). AppleScript, which is based on the Apple Events technology programmers use, also includes dictionaries that applications incorporate showing the AppleScript syntax they support.

Why Script?

The graphical user interface provided tremendous power to users: instead of having to haul cartons of punched cards to a central site where an anonymous computer operator fed them into the computer, users could sit at their own computers and point, click, and type their way through exactly what they wanted to do.

Terrific!

And also a tremendous waste of time in some cases. If you know what you want to do, and you want to do it over and over and over, all that pointing, clicking, and typing wastes your time. AppleScript provides a way to automate your work so you can do other things. For example, a sample AppleScript script that's distributed in the AppleScript folder (inside the Applications folder) will replace a given string in file or folder names with another string. The script is named *Replace Text in Item Names*. Thus, you can replace *test* with *production* (or even with a blank string—"") for all the files within a given folder. This is a common and tedious task you must do often, and AppleScript can do it for you. Thus, the first use of AppleScript is for automation of repetitive simple tasks.

The second use of AppleScript is for the automation of workflows. Many examples exist of AppleScript systems that automatically retrieve data and images from databases, and then format them for publication on paper (such as monthly real estate listings) or on other media (many television listings are produced in this way). Workflows might be repetitive tasks, but they also could be complex tasks involving a number of applications. In these cases, AppleScript scripts can be used to retrieve data from a FileMaker database, insert it into Quark XPress page layouts, print it, and so forth.

How AppleScript Works

AppleScript differs from some other macro and scripting tools in that it truly is a language: AppleScript doesn't automate mouse clicks in specific screen locations, but it interacts with the semantics of applications. (For example, instead of instructing AppleScript to click a Quit menu command, which you know will be located at a specific screen location, you can instruct it to send the Quit message to a given application—regardless of where menus or windows might be.)

Many applications are scriptable and, on Mac OS X, scripting is built in to a number of applications automatically. (Applications built with the Cocoa programming framework fall into this group—iPhoto is one such.)

Types of Scripts

Scripts come in four types:

- *Text scripts* can be edited and run from Script Editor or from Script Runner (both are part of Mac OS X in the AppleScript folder inside Applications).

- *Compiled scripts* can be run from Script Runner (or the script menu described later). They can't be edited.

- *Applets* are compiled scripts that can be double-clicked.

- *Droplets* are scripts onto which you can drag-and-drop files, folder, text clippings, images, and other items of that nature. They do something to the item that's dropped onto them.

In addition to scripts, AppleScript comes embedded in applications that you write with AppleScript Studio. Part of Apple's developer tools suites, AppleScript Studio combines Cocoa, AppleScript, Interface Builder, and anything else you can use on Mac OS X. Power users can quickly learn to create powerful applications with AppleScript Studio, and developers can provide one-off custom applications in the blink of an eye.

Automatically Running Scripts

Many programs enable you to attach scripts to specific events or conditions. In Mac OS X 10.2, the CDs & DVDs preferences let you determine how the computer responds to certain types of events, such as the insertion of blank CDs or blank DVDs, music or picture CDs, or video DVDs. You can choose for a certain application to be launched, for nothing to happen, or for a script to be run. You can write the script yourself, or it can be prepared by someone else. Because scripts can do almost anything, you can trigger an amazing range of events.

Automating Your Work with AppleScript

This section provides a brief overview of AppleScript—for more information, see *Mac OS X: The Complete Reference* (McGraw-Hill/Osborne, 2001). The section in this chapter is designed to give you a general idea of how scripting works but doesn't go into the detail that you need to write your own scripts.

AppleScript itself provides certain basic programming tools—the capability to create variables dynamically in which to store information, control mechanisms such as loops and if statements, and a host of arithmetic and other functions. In addition, applications provide their own functionality if they're scriptable.

NOTE *You can open most of the downloadable scripts described in this chapter in Script Editor to see how they're written. If you do so, you might find the code rather daunting. However, if you step through a few scripts, you'll notice the bulk of the code is similar. Large sections of code in droplets, for example, are devoted to identifying all the selected files that were dropped on the droplet. It's the same code in each case. The actual code that does the work of the droplet—resizing an image, for example—is usually brief, often amounting to only a few lines.*

AppleScript Components: Classes and Actions

An application's functionality consists of two parts: its *classes* and its *actions*. These are listed in its *dictionary,* which is viewable through Script Editor. Figure 8-1 shows the dictionary for Image Capture.

A dictionary is divided into *suites*; this dictionary has only one such suite. The first part of each suite lists its commands. Here, the commands available are open, scale, rotate, save, and close. A brief description of each one along with its syntax is provided. *Commands* are the verbs of AppleScript.

After the commands, the classes for each suite are listed. In this case, only one class exists, a *document,* which has two properties: width and height. *Classes* are the nouns of AppleScript.

Organizing AppleScript: Dictionaries and Suites

An AppleScript dictionary isn't separate from the application. The information displayed in Figure 8-1 is obtained from the application itself, and that same information is used by AppleScript in parsing and executing AppleScript commands. In other words, the dictionary is always available, and it always matches the functionality exactly.

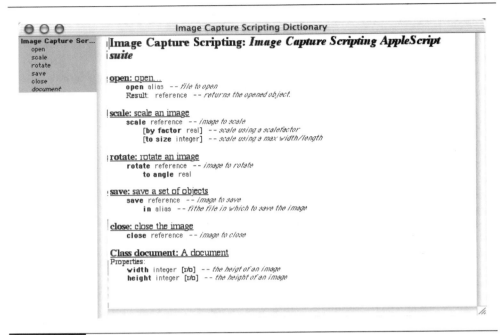

FIGURE 8-1   Image Capture dictionary

To view an application's dictionary, choose the Open Dictionary command from the File menu in Script Editor. If your application isn't listed in the window that appears, you can click the Browse button in the lower left to search for it. If you can't open it, that means it has no dictionary and that the application by itself isn't scriptable. (This doesn't mean you can't use AppleScript with it: the next section shows you how droplets can work with unscriptable applications.)

Many applications define their own suites. AppleScript itself defines a number of standard suites with commands and classes.

AppleScript Syntax

When you write a script, you combine the application's commands and classes with AppleScript syntax to create an executable command. A particularly important part of AppleScript is its capability to locate properties and classes using common words. Thus, AppleScript supports concepts such as *every, first,* and *last.* In addition, words that make the language more human-readable (such as *the*) are usable, but are optional.

Each line of AppleScript code is interpreted either by AppleScript itself or by a specific application. For example, if you want to create a variable and set it to today's date, you can do that with the following line of code:

```
set the_date to the current date
```

Every word of this line is an AppleScript word, with the exception of `the_date`, a variable you implicitly declare by using it. You could change `the_date` to `my_date` or to `currentday`, and the script would run equally well. Changing any of the other words—the AppleScript words—would prevent the script from running. AppleScript can interpret this entire line of code and, thus, can stand on its own. (If you type it into Script Editor, it will run successfully).

Telling an Application to Execute AppleScript Code

Most of your AppleScript code needs to be interpreted by a specific application. Thus, you enclose most code in a *tell block*. If you want to empty the trash from a script, you can write

```
tell application "Finder"
  empty trash
end tell
```

You need to direct the command to the Finder because AppleScript on its own doesn't understand the empty trash command. Because a single script can contain many tell blocks, you can switch from one application to another. And because you can copy information from one application to your own variables, you can pass that information among applications. In one tell block, you might write

```
set current_market_value to the price of the
  current_real_estate_listing
```

And then, in another tell block, you could write

```
set asking_price of current_product to current_market_value
```

`current_market_value` is an AppleScript variable you create. You set it in the first line of code from, perhaps, a database, and, in the second example, you place its value into what might be a field in a page layout program. The tell blocks are directed to different programs, according to the names you provide in the first line.

This is what AppleScript does, and now you've seen in very broad terms how it does it. Now it's time to look at what you can do with the scripts Apple has provided.

Using Droplets to Manipulate Files and Images

Droplets are compiled AppleScript applications onto which you can drag-and-drop files, text, images, and other items. When you do so, the droplet is automatically launched, and it takes the dropped item into its operations.

For example, if you want to turn a photo into a QuickTime movie with an audio track, you can use the Make Audio Card droplet to do so. (*Make Audio Card* is one of the iPhoto scripts: all are described later in this chapter.) Here's how you use Make Audio Card.

1. In iTunes, select a single track of music to use to accompany the audio card.

2. Drag any JPEG, GIF, PICT, or TIFF image onto the Make Audio Card droplet.

3. The droplet will launch and will construct a QuickTime movie with the image and the music. You'll be asked to name it, and then you can choose where to store it.

4. The droplet then opens the movie. In many cases, the image will be too big for your screen. You can watch as the droplet resizes the movie window to fit on the screen.

5. Finally, the droplet will play the movie.

Several points are worth noting about this process. The first, of course, is how wonderfully it integrates digital hub tools such as iPhoto, iTunes, and QuickTime—and how little work you have to do.

Next, consider Step 2 in the process described here. The droplet can work with JPEG, GIF, PICT, or TIFF images. These can be images displayed in a window (such as one of the iPhoto windows), or they can be files of those types. Thus, you can drag an image either from the Finder (a file) or from iPhoto (or an image editing program) onto the droplet and it will work.

This step is important in understanding how a supposedly nonscriptable application, such as iPhoto, can be scriptable. If you try to open an AppleScript dictionary for iPhoto, you won't be able to do so: none exists. iPhoto doesn't respond directly to the Apple events that underlie AppleScript, but its development framework (Cocoa) supports dragging images out of views and windows. You can do this to drag them into other types of documents or to place them on droplets.

> **NOTE** *If you're a programmer, investigate scripting support in Cocoa frameworks. A great deal of scripting now comes free. This is a significant change from older frameworks (such as PowerPlant and MacApp) as well as from earlier versions of Cocoa. These advances appeared in the May 2002 developer tools release.*

Toolbar Scripts

You can place AppleScript applets and droplets in the Finder toolbar. All you have to do is drag them into the toolbar, and they'll appear there in all your Finder windows. Figure 8-2 shows a Finder window with two such AppleScript components.

Resize and Browse are two of the digital hub scripts you can download, as described in the "iPhoto Scripts" section later in this chapter. You can resize a JPEG, GIF, PICT, or TIFF image by dropping a file or image onto Resize. You'll be asked for the new width, and the script will automatically resize it.

> **NOTE** *The Resize script uses the Mac OS X Quartz imaging mechanism to do this, and it's accessed through the Image Capture Scripting interface, as you can see if you examine the script. Because Image Capture is distributed with Mac OS X, these scripts all work right out of the box (as long as you haven't deliberately removed applications, such as Image Capture, that you think you won't need).*

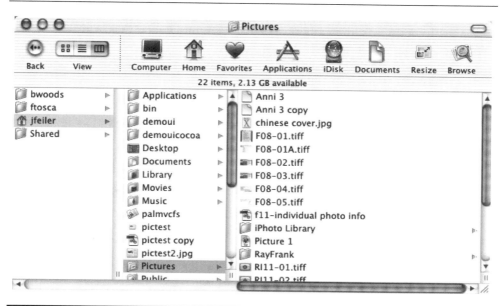

FIGURE 8-2   Toolbar with AppleScript components

Browse acts on an entire folder either dropped onto it or selected in a Finder window. If you click Browse (or drop a folder on it), it opens your default browser and displays an index of all the image files in that folder. You can then click any of them to display it.

Using the Script Menu

From the AppleScript site, you can download the Script menu, as shown here:

You drag it into the menu bar and it stays there, providing you with one-click access to scripts on your Mac. (To remove it, CONTROL-drag the icon from the menu bar.) By default, the Script menu contains all the preinstalled scripts. As you can see, though, you can add your own scripts to it by opening your Scripts folder. When the folder opens, drag any scripts you want into it, and they will then be available in your Script menu.

Any script can be added to your Scripts folder. AppleScript, Perl, and Shell scripts (from Terminal) can all be placed there.

Downloadable Scripts

Among the scripts you can download are the Toolbar scripts, as shown here:

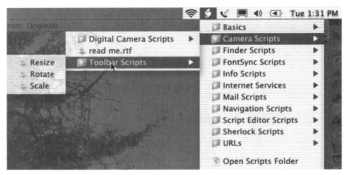

Resize, Rotate, and Scale are appropriate for adding to your Finder toolbar. As described previously, you can use them to manipulate images. You needn't add them to the toolbar, though. If you select a file in the Finder, you can then launch one of these scripts from the Script menu, and it will do the appropriate task. These scripts use the Image Capture software that's part of Mac OS X.

Some similar functionality is provided in the Digital Camera scripts shown here:

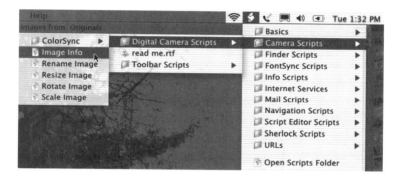

These scripts use Internet Explorer to display the images. One of the most useful of these is the Image Info script: you select images or drag them onto the script, and then you can view the information shown here:

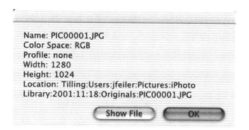

The reason this is so important is this: if you're browsing images in an application such as iPhoto that stores the files in its own filing system, you can easily find out exactly where a file is located. If you click the Show File button, the appropriate Finder window will open, as shown in Figure 8-3, so you can copy the file. (Remember not to move iPhoto files using the Finder.)

iPhoto Scripts

You can find a variety of scripts for iPhoto at **http://www.apple.com/applescript/ iphoto/index.html.** These let you select photos in iPhoto and email them simply by dragging them onto a droplet. Also, as described previously, you can create audio cards and QuickTime slide shows integrating images and iTunes tracks.

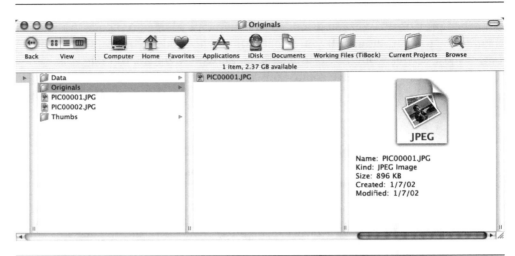

FIGURE 8-3   Image file shown in Finder

iTunes Scripts

You can find a variety of scripts for iTunes and iPod located at **http://www.apple.com/applescript/itunes/index.html**. These scripts let you move music into and out of iTunes, as well as perform a variety of tasks. One script even creates CD liners automatically in AppleWorks from an iTunes playlist.

Summary

This chapter provided an overview of AppleScript and the ways in which you can use it to tie together the tools of the digital hub, as well as the Finder itself and other applications. AppleScript enables you to automate workflows and to combine applications to accomplish a variety of useful tasks.

Many scripts are available for downloading at **http://www.apple.com/applescript**. You can add them to your Finder toolbars. You also can download the Script menu to organize your scripts further.

Droplets work particularly well with digital hub applications: you can drop images onto them and manipulate them in a variety of ways. These images can be dragged from application windows (such as iPhoto windows), or they can be files themselves.

As you experiment with Apple's scripts, you'll see how you can integrate your applications and make your work easier.

Chapter 9

Storing and Backing Up Your Digital Hub Files

In This Chapter...

- ■ Storage Issues. To start with, this section introduces you to the three basic storage and backup issues: backups, archives, and transfers.

- ■ Burning CDs and DVDs. Diskettes are pretty much gone from the picture today. CDs and DVDs are the main removable media on which you can write. This section shows you how.

- ■ Using the Internet for Storage. Beyond your computer is a world of storage that you can access. All of it provides the virtue of off-site storage, but it comes with concerns about reliability, access time, and security.

- ■ iPod For Backups. You may think that iPod is an MP3 player, but it's really a very fast FireWire disk. Here's how to access its disk functions.

- ■ Using Backup Software (Retrospect). The most widely used backup software on the Macintosh, Retrospect is an integral part of many people's lives. This is an overview of some of its main features and how to use them.

Although many people live dangerously without backing up their data files, even they generally agree they *should* do so—and *will* as soon as they get the time. They usually find the time and inspiration to back up their files after losing a significant number of them in a disk crash or other catastrophe.

Working with digital hub files increases the need for a serious backup strategy. Not only are many more files involved than in a typical word-processing project, but those files can be enormous. And, if you already have a backup strategy, the magnitude of the backup needs might overwhelm it and cause it to break.

This chapter looks at storage and backups for the files you need for movies, photos, music, and DVD projects.

Storage Issues

First, distinguishing among three related concepts—backups, archives, and transfers—is important. In each case, you copy data from your computer. The distinctions arise with regard to what you do with the data—whether you plan on keeping it temporarily or forever, or whether you're merely transferring it elsewhere.

Backups

Backups are copies of files you create to protect your work in the short term. If you lose a file today, you should be able to go to a backup copy of the file as it was yesterday. (File loss can include mistakes you make, as well as physical loss or corruption.)

The frequency of backups varies. For many people, this is daily, but others are satisfied with weekly backups. If you're working on an important project, you might make copies of your files manually (by selecting Save As from the File menu or by using the Finder to duplicate files). In such cases, you might have backups every 15 minutes.

You might save several generations of backups: yesterday, the day before, and the day before that. You normally start to reuse your backup media on a regular basis, however, limiting the length of time you can go back. A good practice is to keep some of your backups at a remote location. This protects against physical damage to the place where your computer and the backups are stored. For most people, a choice must be made between the convenience of having a backup close by in case you need it and the security of storing it offsite. One possible solution is to store this week's backups onsite and to store the previous week's backups offsite.

Backups can be done manually or automatically using products such as Retrospect from Dantz (discussed later in this chapter) or Apple's Backup program from .Mac. The most reliable form of backup is an automatic backup done on a schedule you create—perhaps at 2:00 in the morning. Because Mac OS X has energy-saving features (set them in System Preferences), leaving your computer on all the time isn't particularly costly.

You can also manually do backups to your hard disk, to another disk, or to removable media, such as ZIP drives, tape cartridges, and CDs or DVDs. Note, backing up to your hard disk rather than another disk or removable media is inherently dangerous. If the disk crashes or is stolen, both your original and backup are lost.

Backups are designed as just that—backup to your primary data files that remain on your computer. Because backups might never be used, checking to see that they're created properly is important (backup software does this). Furthermore, you should conduct periodic backup drills in which you attempt to restore files to your computer. Try this before you need to do it. When you're in the heat of the moment confronting the possible loss of files, you aren't in a good position to learn how to restore them to your computer.

Backups can be done using ordinary files stored on the same devices you use for other data files. You also can use backup software that stores files in a proprietary format. That software can use disk or CDs, as well as a variety of tape backup devices. Tape backup is attractive because it's generally cheaper than using disk. However, its access time is slower, which is why it is rarely used as an online storage medium.

Archives

Unlike backups, *archives* are designed to be replacements for your primary data files on your computer. In many cases, you create an archive at the end of a project, and then you remove those files from your computer. (To be prudent, you normally create at least two archives to provide added assurance.)

Archives are usually created at the end of a project or at specific points—such as the end of the year for an accounting archive. Because archives might be needed at some distant point in the future, you need to worry about the long-term storage issues discussed in the section "Long-Term Storage Issues."

NOTE *"Year-end" and "month-end" are normally used to refer to the data, not to the date on which the archive is created. Year-end accounts can reflect transactions through the end of the year, and they may be updated through the first month or two of the year. You can distinguish between "as-of" archives and period-end archives if you want to indicate the difference between the data files as they exist on a certain date ("as-of") or with certain data (period-end).*

Transfers

Finally, *transfers* are situations in which you move files from one location to another without the intention of returning them. (An archive is usually created with the intention of returning it.) A transfer is common when you send files to a duplication service. With DVDs, for instance, you can burn your own, or you can find companies to duplicate DVDs. If you need to create a DVD that will be produced in bulk (*replicated,* as opposed to *duplicated*), however, you typically send the data out on a tape cartridge. Such cartridges can contain a great deal of data, but they're relatively slow compared to a disk drive, and they're unusable for random access.

You also transfer data when you move from one computer to another. Yet another transfer scenario occurs when you prepare a set of files to be transferred to a class of students or other group of people who need a common set of data.

Burning CDs and DVDs to Store Your Files

You can burn CDs and DVDs directly from the Finder on Mac OS X. (In the first release, you needed additional software, but in Mac OS X 10.1, that was fixed.)

NOTE *This section refers to burning data discs: if you're creating a DVD with iDVD, you don't use these instructions. See Chapter 13 for more on iDVD.*

CD Formats

You need to know about two sets of CD formats. The first relates to whether the CD is write-once (CD-R) or whether you can write to it many times (CD-RW). CD-R is generally better for music; CD-RW is better for data in most cases. (The R in CD-R stands for recordable; the RW in CD-RW stands for rewritable.)

The second set of CD formats refers to the speed of the CD or its capacity. A common capacity today is 74 minutes of music, which turns out to be about 650MB of data. Look at your computer instructions or technical specifications to see what type of disc is recommended.

DVD Formats

Several DVD formats exist—more than the two primary ones for CDs. iDVD will create DVDs using the DVD-R format. You can buy these discs from Apple or from many office supply and electronics stores. DVD Studio Pro (and many other applications used for professional production) creates DVD-R discs, as well as DVD-RAM discs. Additional formats are supported by other computer and DVD-burning drive manufacturers. These will likely merge over the next few years. The DVD-R format can contain 4.7GB of data—more than seven times the storage capacity of a CD.

What you need to worry about is whether the DVDs you create will run on the devices you want to use. Typically, you want them to run either on your Macintosh (or someone else's) and on DVD players. Some early DVD players didn't support all formats but, today, most do support the discs you create with iDVD. For an updated list of supported players, look at **http://www.apple.com/idvd**.

Burning CDs and DVDs

The process of burning CDs and DVDs with data on them is basically the same. First, insert a blank disc in the computer. You may see a warning like that shown here:

Type in the name for the disc and choose the format you want to use. For data, the choice shown here is correct. If you are burning a CD-R to be used on an audio CD player, you can choose the iTunes/Audio CD option. Don't burn audio CDs onto CD-RW discs unless you are absolutely certain that your player will read the CD-RW format: most don't. The disc will appear in the Finder with the name you entered, and you can drag documents and folders to it as you would to any other location. (You can see the Documents folder being dragged onto the disc Wednesday Backup in Figure 9-1.)

When you're ready to burn the disc, you can choose Burn Disc from the File menu, as shown here.

FIGURE 9-1   Drag items to the disc in the Finder.

If you prefer, you can simply choose the Eject command for the disc, and the Burn Disc command will automatically be executed. You're asked to confirm that you want to burn the disc, and then the files will be transferred to it. Note, until you burn the disc, the files you dragged to the disc icon haven't yet been written.

Using the Internet for Storage

As you saw in Chapter 5, you can use your iDisk (part of .Mac) to store files. You can use it for backups or archives, and you can use your Public folder to transfer files. You can even use prepared HomePage templates to make downloading files easy for visitors to your Web site.

The Internet is viable as a storage medium only if you have a high-speed connection (or if your files are small). Because Internet storage is relatively cheap, however, it can be attractive. In addition, remember Apple is maintaining the iDisk files. Apple is doing backups of the iDisk files, and it's automatically providing you with offsite storage.

iPod as Disk Backup

If you have an iPod, you have yet another option for storing files. You can use iPod simply to store music, but it's a large (5 or 10 gigabyte) hard disk and you can use it as a hard disk.

iTunes (discussed in detail in Chapter 12) behaves like its digital hub partners—iMovie, iDVD, and iPhoto—in hiding file manipulation from you. But you can easily gain access to the disk. First, connect your iPod. If you haven't configured iTunes to open automatically, you need to launch it. Your iPod should appear in the list of sources at the left. Select it with a single click, and then click the iPod options button in the lower-right of the window, as shown in Figure 9-2.

The iPod Preferences window is shown to the right.

The key option here is Enable FireWire disk use. If you select it, your iPod appears in the Finder, and you can drag files to and from it, just as you would with any other disk. The one exception is your music: iPod and iTunes manage their files without making them visible to you.

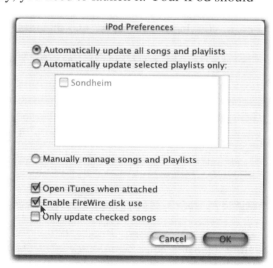

FIGURE 9-2   Open iPod options in iTunes.

If you selected this option, you need to unmount the iPod manually before disconnecting it. As with a digital camera, you select the iPod in the Finder and drag it to the Trash, or use the Eject command from the File menu or the contextual menu that appears when you CONTROL-click on the iPod icon. If you don't do this before you disconnect the iPod, you could lose data.

Using iPod to Store Your Contacts

iPod now lets you manage contact information. It has a folder named Contacts and, if you place address files with the suffix .vcf in that folder, they'll appear properly formatted on the iPod. You can export .vcf address files from applications such as Mail, Palm Desktop, and Outlook Express. This is a convenient way to get your contacts onto your iPod. Note, though, the transfer is one-way: you can't update from the iPod to your computer.

Other Disk Storage Options

You can also use disks on your own computer or on your LAN to back up files on either a permanent or temporary basis. The advantage of this is it simply involves copying files from one place to another. The disadvantage is local disk storage (or even network disk storage) is likely to be more expensive than storage on removable media such as CDs, DVDs, or the various types of tape cartridges.

You can combine the speed and convenience of disk backup with removable media by using drives, such as ZIP drives, which you can plug in as FireWire or USB drives. You then use removable cartridges or disks in the drive.

Long-Term Storage Issues

Backups are normally kept for only a brief period of time, but archives can be kept for quite some time. If you plan to keep data for a long time, you have some special issues to consider. Most important, make certain the storage location is secure: that normally means clean, dry, and cool. This also means knowing where the storage location is located. (This problem is quite common. In fact, many time capsules buried by civic groups and municipalities have disappeared because their location and existence have been forgotten.)

If you have valuable archives, check them periodically to make certain they can be read. Particularly in the case of tape cartridges, you need to make certain the tape itself, as well as the tape reader, is stored properly.

One great virtue of Internet backups is you aren't responsible for maintaining the storage media. In addition to .Mac, many ISPs provide online storage. Also, companies exist that specialize in secure storage for valuable data.

If you're storing data files, make certain you store the applications that can read them. Especially in the case of version changes, you could find yourself with an unreadable file format. And, if you're storing the application, you probably need to store the operating system under which it ran. Or, open the archived data periodically and resave it in the current version of the software (or a substitute product). Many people have five-year-old, carefully stored data files that for all intents and purposes are useless.

Using Backup Software (Retrospect)

Retrospect is the preeminent backup software for the Macintosh. It provides sophisticated backup processing, and it supports a variety of media ranging from ordinary disks and CDs to a variety of tape cartridges. Retrospect is available as a stand-alone product, but it also comes bundled with many backup drives.

The advantages of using an automated tool like Retrospect center around the fact that you needn't do anything except make sure you have a tape in your backup drive and leave your computer on. If you rely on manual backups, you'll quickly find you forget either totally or skip some files that need to be backed up. This section provides an overview of Retrospect and how you can use some of its features specifically with digital hub files. More documentation is provided with Retrospect itself. Also, Retrospect now provides EasyScript to walk you through the steps shown here.

NOTE *Other backup software is available as tools you can run from the command line. One such tool (included with Mac OS X) is rsync. Another backup strategy uses version control to allow multiple users and multiple copies of files to be managed. Project Builder, one of the developer tools from Apple, incorporates version control. See its documentation for more on setting up Concurrent Versions System (CVS).*

Scripting Your Backups

Retrospect enables you to create scripts, and then you schedule them to run at various times. Figure 9-3 shows a scheduled script. You can see a number of Retrospect concepts in the window. Retrospect has an EasyScript dialog that helps you create scripts like this—you answer questions and the script is created. Restrospect scripts—even those you create manually—aren't mysterious collections of words and phrases.

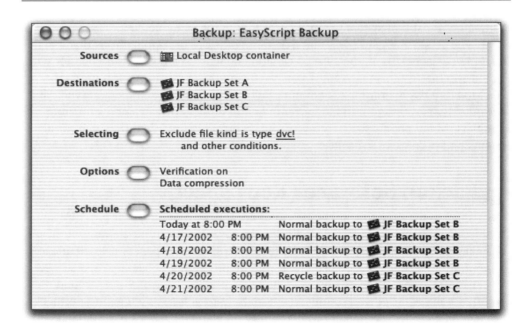

FIGURE 9-3   Retrospect script

Sources

First, you specify the sources for your backup. The most general is your entire computer, as shown here. Retrospect finds the mounted disks and backs them up.

Backup Sets

You back up files to a backup set. A *backup set* can be a single disk (or part of a disk) or it can be a tape cartridge. It can span several disks or cartridges: Retrospect will manage the logistics. If you're using an unattended backup (the best kind), you'll probably want to make certain your backup set fits entirely on a single cartridge or disk. Otherwise, Retrospect will stop and wait for you to switch media. (Some tape backup drives have cartridge changers, but they quickly run into substantial money.) Scripts normally contain a number of backup sets, which are rotated according to the schedule (described at the end of this section).

File Selections

In the next section, you can see that certain files were selected. This is described in the next section. Many people make no selections and simply back up all files.

Options

A variety of options are available, and the most important one is shown here—verification. After having written the data, Retrospect goes back and compares what was written to what is on disk. This gives you immediate verification that your backup is okay.

Scheduling

Finally, you can see the scheduling information. This script is scheduled to run daily at 8 P.M., as you can see. A normal backup (as is the case in the first four scheduled backups) copies those files that have changed. As you can see in the fifth backup, something new happens. Here, the entire backup set is erased and everything, changed or not, is written out to it. This is a common strategy. The full schedule for this script consists of recycling one of three backup sets each Saturday, and then doing normal (or incremental) backups from Sunday to Friday.

A single data cartridge usually holds this amount of data. Thus, each Saturday, one cartridge (*A, B,* or *C*) needs to be placed in the backup tape drive. After that, though, nothing needs to be touched until the following Saturday.

Looking at Backups

You can use the Retrospect Reports tab from its main screen to see the status of your backups. If you click Reports, you can see the status of your disks, as shown in Figure 9-4.

User/Volume	Elapsed Days	Errs	Date	Backup Set (Script)
▼ 📠 Local Desktop				
▼ 📄 Georgie				
	1	0	4/15/2002 8:47 PM	JF Backup Set B (EasyScript Backup)
	4	0	4/12/2002 9:40 PM	JF Backup Set A (EasyScript Backup)
	11	0	4/5/2002 8:12 PM	JF Backup Set C (EasyScript Backup)
▼ 📄 JFDeskDisk				
	1	2	4/15/2002 8:37 PM	JF Backup Set B (EasyScript Backup)
	4	2	4/12/2002 9:30 PM	JF Backup Set A (EasyScript Backup)
	11	1	4/5/2002 8:00 PM	JF Backup Set C (EasyScript Backup)
▼ 🌐 Backup Clients				

FIGURE 9-4   Report of disk backups

Here, you can see that for the disks on the desktop, each has been backed up to three different backup sets according to the schedule. Thus, if you need to go back to restore a file, you have almost three weeks' worth of data to retrieve.

Instead of looking at a disk to see where it was backed up, you can look at a backup set to see what it contains (use the Contents button in Retrospect's Reports tab). Figure 9-5 shows the result.

As you can see, individual entries are within each backup set for each time it was backed up. Here's how you get down to individual days of backups within the weekly backup set. Remember, these backups are incremental backups, so only a few files are backed up each day. If you scroll down to the bottom of the backup set, you'll see the first entry—the recycle backup—backs up many files (in this particularly case, over a quarter of a million!).

To find an individual file, double-click the particular backup you're interested in, and you'll see the display shown in Figure 9-6.

Also under the Reports tab is the log of backups, as shown in Figure 9-7.

Reviewing this periodically is useful. If you have verification turned on, you'll normally find a handful of files that fail verification because they have legitimately changed. If you're receiving email, for example, during the backup, you'll have changes to your mailbox. Files with the suffix .log are exactly that, logs of behavior, and they're the most likely files to fail verification (and not to require any action on your part).

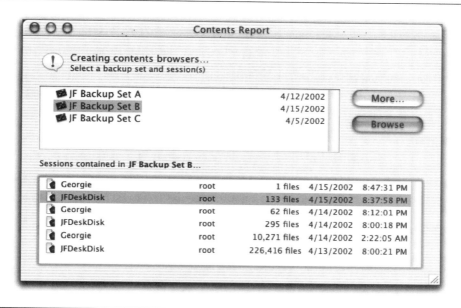

FIGURE 9-5   Report of backup set

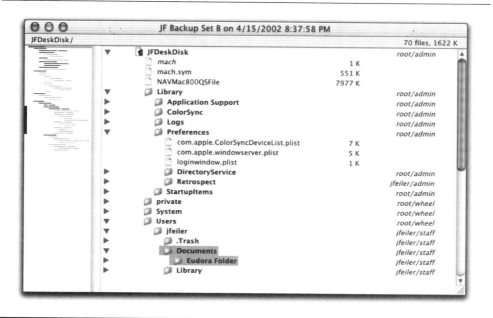

FIGURE 9-6   Locating an individual file to restore

Using Backup Software
(Retrospect)

```
●●●                    Operations Log
2588 lines, using 123 K on disk

+    Normal backup using EasyScript Backup at 4/15/2002 8:37 PM
     To backup set 🖺 JF Backup Set B…
*    Resolved container 🖩 Local Desktop container to 2 volumes:
          🖫 JFDeskDisk
          🖾 Georgie

-    4/15/2002 8:37:58 PM: Copying 🖫 JFDeskDisk…
     4/15/2002 8:45:57 PM: Comparing 🖫 JFDeskDisk…
>         File "Operations Log": different data size (set: 124,285, vol: 124,346), path: "JF
>         File "system.log": different modification date/time (set: 4/15/2002 8:36:17 PM, vol
     4/15/2002 8:47:31 PM: 2 execution errors.
          Completed: 133 files, 69.2 MB, with 0% compression
          Performance: 77.5 MB/minute (60.9 copy, 106.3 compare)
          Duration: 00:09:33 (00:07:46 idle/loading/preparing)

-    4/15/2002 8:47:31 PM: Copying 🖾 Georgie…
     4/15/2002 8:49:56 PM: Comparing 🖾 Georgie…
     4/15/2002 8:50:36 PM: Execution completed successfully.
          Completed: 1 files, 269 KB, with 0% compression
          Performance: 1.7 MB/minute (1.4 copy, 2.2 compare)
          Duration: 00:03:05 (00:02:47 idle/loading/preparing)

     4/15/2002 8:51:22 PM: 2 execution errors.
     Total performance: 66.6 MB/minute with 0% compression
     Total duration: 00:12:38 (00:10:33 idle/loading/preparing)
     Quit at 4/15/2002 8:51 PM
```

FIGURE 9-7   Backup log

Retrospect assembles these files into *snapshots* for each disk. Thus, if you simply want to restore a file from yesterday's backup, you can use the Immediate tab to do so using the snapshot of last night's files.

Selecting Files to Add to a Retrospect Backup

Retrospect enables you to specify files to exclude or include from backups, and this becomes an important feature with digital video. Digital video files are enormous, and backing them up can both quickly eat up even a large tape cartridge and take a long time. Remember, your digital video files already are copies: the original data is on the MiniDV cassette from your digital camcorder. While you're working on a project, if you keep the cassettes, there's no reason to back up the data files, because they're duplicates of the cassettes. (You can do the math for yourself to determine whether your MiniDV cassette is cheaper as a storage device than a tape cartridge or a CD-ROM or DVD. The calculation is different for everyone because you need to take into account the prices you actually pay for the media, the cost and complications of storing the media, and your own preferences. For many people, saving the MiniDV cassettes until the end of a project is simplest, particularly since you can—and should—label them with the date and time you used them.)

Note, however, your iMovie editing that's stored separately from the raw digital video might need to be redone if your disk copy of the digital video is destroyed. You can choose how much of a risk you want to take. As soon as you finish creating your iMovie, the resultant file can either be burned onto a DVD with iDVD or stored as a QuickTime movie. Whether you ever need to save the disk copy of the digital video is up to you. Many people find saving the MiniDV cassettes is easier and cheaper.

To skip iMovie files, use Retrospect's selection criteria, which is shown here.

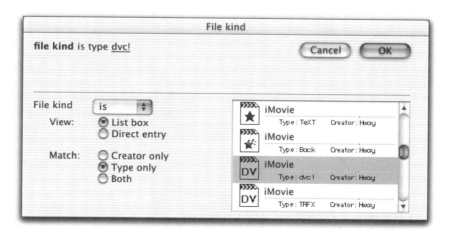

Use the Modify button to add new criteria, as shown here.

Using Backup Software (Retrospect)

As you can see here, the digital video files are excluded, but standard iMovie files (with your editing commands) are included in the backup.

Summary

All your work will go for naught if you lose your digital files. Proper storage and backups are essential. In this chapter, you learned the distinction among backups, archives, and transfers. The basics of burning data CDs and DVDs were also provided. (Remember, DVDs created with iDVD use a different process, which is described in Chapter 13.)

You have a variety of storage options beyond your computer—both on the Internet and with iPod.

Finally, Retrospect, the leading Macintosh backup software was presented. The cost to back up your files with Retrospect is relatively small, and the benefit can be enormous.

This chapter ends Part 1 of the book. By now you've seen the basics of the digital hub, and you've been introduced to photography, digital photography, connectivity, .Mac and other Internet features, printing, and AppleScript. Now that all this has been covered, you're ready to get to work to make movies, photos, music, and DVDs on your Mac.

Part 2

Making Movies, Photos, Music, and DVDs

Chapter 10

Making Movies with iMovie

In This Chapter...

- ■ The iMovie Workflow. This is the overview of the process involved in creating your movie, from initial planning and filming to distribution.

- ■ Getting Around iMovie. The iMovie interface is described in this section.

- ■ Importing Video. Getting video from your digital camcorder is simple. You learn how here.

- ■ Exporting Video. When you're finished, you generally want to export your video back to your camcorder (and possibly then to a VCR), or to QuickTime, or to iDVD. The steps are outlined here.

This chapter covers the basics of using iMovie. You'll find much more information in Part 3 of this book—particularly what you need to know about integrating photos from iPhoto and music from iTunes and other sources. iMovie makes it easy to add titles, transitions, and effects, and all those are covered in Part 3, too.

What you find here is an overview of how you use iMovie, what it looks like, and how to use it, as well as how to get your video into it and your movie out of it.

Moving to Digital Editing

Some of the most enthusiastic converts to digital editing (as found in applications such as iMovie, iPhoto, and iDVD) are professionals. Many of these converts started out dubious, to say the least. Journalist Susan Arbetter is the host of the popular Roundtable show on WAMC Northeast Public Radio, a network of ten National Public Radio affiliates covering upstate New York and western New England. She has worked in radio for 13 years, starting in Boston at WBOS-FM. Susan is the recipient of many awards, including a national Scripps-Howard Award for Excellence in Electronic Journalism; the National Press Club Kozik Award for Environmental Journalism; and numerous regional Murrow, New York State Broadcasters, and New York State Associated Press Awards.

Susan was voted the Women's Press Club's "Media Person of the Year, 1998," as well as 1998's "Best Voice of the Capital Region" by the Albany *Times Union* newspaper. In May 1999, the Albany *Times Union* voted Susan "Best Local Radio Talk Personality."

Susan and her on-air colleague, author Larry Sombke, were awarded the National Garden Writers' Association Award for Best Gardening Talk Show, 1999. Interestingly, Susan has no clue how to garden.

I asked Susan about her conversion to digital editing:

"Like most radio professionals, I hated digital editing when it first appeared on my desktop. For the ten years prior to computerized editing, I cut tape the way all old nicotine-stained broadcast veterans did: with tape, a wax pencil, and a razor blade.

"And boy was I good. In office gossip around the reel-to-reel machines, I was known as The Blade Runner. I could literally take someone's breath away from a sound clip.

"So imagine my despair when those very reel-to-reel machines that had been my canvas for a decade were ripped out of the studio to make way for a Freudian nightmare called "digital editing." No more tape. No more reels rolling along to the sound of your voice. No blood. The whole thing was, well, ambiguous. (Where did you put the sound in?)

"The station I worked for hired trainers, showed us videotapes, and gave us a month to get acclimated. It was the hardest month of my life.

"But little by little, I was getting more and more done. Instead of shlepping into the studio for every tiny cut, I could sit at my computer. Instead of guessing how an edit might sound, I could listen to ten editing variations in my headphones, and then decide how to proceed. Rather than ending up with a tangled web of useless tape at my feet (and wax pencil shavings in my lap), I had . . . nothing. It was almost seamless.

"I wish I could tell you there was a single moment when all the fine elements of digital editing emerged into my consciousness, but I can't. It was a slow, sometimes painful, shift in my attitude. But now I'm sold. I love it. Don't touch it."

The iMovie Workflow

The iMovie Workflow

If the term "workflow" sounds daunting, lay your fears to rest. *Workflow* is only the term used to describe the sequence of events you follow to create a movie. You have a number of tasks to do and a number of tools to use, but the process is no more complicated than making dinner. There, your work flow might involve chopping vegetables, cooking them, and combining them with other ingredients in a casserole, and then serving your guests or family.

Here are the steps in your movie-making workflow:

1. Plan your movie. This might be as complex as raising money for an hour-long video and then writing a script, or it could be as simple as grabbing your digital camcorder as you go out for a walk.

2. Shoot your video.

3. Import the video into iMovie.

4. Edit the video, adding transitions, removing bloopers, adjusting color, and creating titles.

5. Export the video so you and others can view it. You can export it back to DV format on your digital camcorder, and then you can move it to a VCR. You can export it to iDVD (see Chapter 13). Or you can create a QuickTime movie to burn onto a CD or post on a Web site (including your .Mac site). Subsequent marketing or publishing steps might exist for you to take.

And there's one crucial final step: look objectively at what you've done and evaluate its strengths and weaknesses. That way, your next movie will be even better.

You use iMovie for importing, editing, and exporting your movie. Your camcorder is used both for shooting the movie and for playing it on a TV or recording it onto a VCR. The iMovie parts of the workflow are generally called *postproduction* (sometimes just *post,* as in "We'll fix it in post.").

The extent of your work in iMovie depends on what you're trying to achieve and the time you have available. Nothing prevents you from importing the entire contents of a MiniDV cassette and immediately exporting the entire video to a QuickTime movie or as input to iDVD. But your work in iMovie can make all the difference in the world.

Filmmakers know the call "That's a wrap" at the end of shooting a scene is a long way from the end of the process. Purely mechanical issues must be addressed (color correction, for example), but also there's the long process of using the raw material of the footage to tell a story or to make a convincing argument. The following are some of the issues you should think about.

Don't Use Everything You Shoot

When you're shooting your video, a good idea is usually to err on the side of inclusion: When in doubt, shoot it. If you have a choice, shoot scenes more than once, perhaps from varying angles. Particularly when shooting outdoors, lighting is hard to match from one day to another and, if you have to go back to reshoot a scene, it might be hard to prevent the scene from appearing quite different.

In traditional movie-making, a *shoot-to-print ratio* of 5:1 is common. This means for one hour of finished film, five hours of film have been shot. And this, in turn, means for one hour of finished film, four hours are thrown away. Low-budget productions can't afford the time or the cost of such shoot-to-print ratios, and they might be forced to use less than optimal footage because that's all there is. On the other hand, some films (including many commercials) have much higher shoot-to-print ratios.

The cost of digital media is low, so stop trying to edit on your camcorder. Shoot, and then use iMovie to remove unneeded scenes. This might be a new way of working for you, but it can dramatically help improve your movies.

. . . But Make Sure You Shoot Enough

One of the common mistakes people make when shooting videos is not having enough footage. iMovie lets you create great transitions between scenes—transitions like cross fades from one clip to another. Transitions take time, and if your clip starts with someone talking right away, you might be unable to use a transition because it might obscure the speech. (If you want to make a satirical amateur movie, use no transitions and just put one talking head after another on your video. "Here's Aunt Jane. Look quick, that's George. Isn't the dog cute? . . .")

Filmmakers often start a scene with an *establishing shot,* which lets the audience know where you are. This can be as simple as a shot of the door through which someone enters, sits down, and finally starts talking. That sequence will give you plenty of footage to play with for transitions. And, if you don't need it, it will simply be part of the 80 percent of your footage that winds up on the digital cutting-room floor.

Projects and Media

iMovie creates a folder for your movie project. In this folder is a subfolder called *Media,* which contains a separate file for each of your clips. An iMovie file that contains your editing information is also in your folder.

You can use clips in more than one movie: don't copy them using the Finder. Instead, import them (as described in the upcoming section, "Importing Video and Other Files."

Getting Around iMovie

iMovie takes up your entire display when it's launched. If you had any doubt that the digital hub applications provided a new way of working by replacing the original Macintosh desktop metaphor, doubt no more: the traditional desktop is almost totally hidden while you run iMovie. iMovie even has its own Trash. (One part of the desktop, the Dock, is visible.) Figure 10-1 shows iMovie in action.

FIGURE 10-1   iMovie in action

The interface has three primary sections:

- In the top left is the *iMovie monitor,* which is where you can play back your movie and the clips you import or create. The iMovie monitor is also where you control importing.

- In the top right is the *shelf* for your movie clips: buttons at the bottom of the shelf let you vary the display in this area. In addition to Clips, you can choose from Transitions, Titles, Effects, and Audio.

- Across the bottom, two horizontal displays toggle between the clip viewer and the timeline viewer. (In Figure 10-1, the timeline viewer is shown.)

In addition, the amount of disk space available on your hard disk is shown between the shelf and the viewers at the bottom. The trash for iMovie—separate from the trash on your desktop—is also shown there.

Each of these components is described in detail here.

Clips

The video you import into your project consists of *clips*. You can click the Clips button at the bottom of the shelf to see clips, as shown in Figure 10-2.

You can import all or part of a DV tape as a single clip. You also can have iMovie import each scene as a separate clip. (A scene is registered by your digital camcorder when you go from standby into record, and iMovie can sense these breaks.)

FIGURE 10-2   Clips on the shelf

By default, iMovie imports video as separate scenes. These clips are placed on the shelf. You can control this using the Preferences command from the iMovie application menu. The Import tab is shown here:

Here is where you choose between scene-by-scene importing and importing the video as a single clip. This is also where you can decide whether to put the imported clips on the shelf or directly into your movie.

NOTE   *If you don't want to do any editing, turn off automatic scene breaks and choose to import clips into your movie, not the shelf. That way, everything will go directly into your movie as soon as you click the Import button (see the upcoming section, "Importing Video and Other Files").*

You can select clips on the shelf one at a time with the mouse. SHIFT-click to select multiple clips. (Note, this is different from the behavior in the Finder where SHIFT-click selects the beginning and end of a range of items, and COMMAND-click selects multiple items.)

You can eliminate clips by dragging them to the trash (just below the shelf). You can also drag them into your movie, using either the timeline viewer or the clip viewer at the bottom of iMovie. (These are discussed in the next two sections.)

When you select a single clip by clicking it, its first frame appears in the iMovie monitor. You can then play it or edit it with the scrubber bar, crop markers, and the playhead.

The length of each clip is shown at the top left. This is in the form minutes:seconds:frames. (The number of frames per second depends on the video format you're using. *NTSC,* common in North America, consists of 29.97 frames per second (fps). *PAL,* common elsewhere in the world, consists of 25 fps. If you crop or trim a clip, you'll see its length is immediately changed on the shelf.

Each clip is labeled automatically as it's imported. You can change those names and set Audio Fade options by double-clicking a clip to open the window shown here:

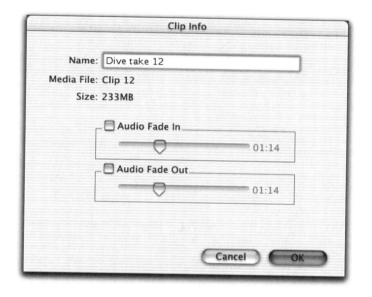

If you choose to fade the audio for a clip in or out, click the checkbox. You also can control how long the fade-in or fade-out lasts by adjusting the slider.

iMovie Monitor

The iMovie monitor is used both for importing video from your camcorder and for viewing the video you're working with in iMovie. Its two modes are controlled by the Mode Switch in the lower left of the iMovie monitor, which is shown here.

Here, the Mode Switch is in Edit mode (at the right). You can also click the small camcorder icon to move it to the left into Camera mode.

Working in Edit Mode

In *Edit* mode, the buttons at the bottom of the iMovie monitor let you control playback. As you play a clip, the *playhead* moves along and numbers show you exactly what frame is playing. The numbers indicate the minute, second, and specific frame number. In Figure 10-1, the playhead is about three-quarters of the way along, and the current frame is the 29th frame of the 6th second. (You have an option in Preferences not to display minutes until the clip or movie is over one-minute long.)

Moving the Playhead   You can move the playhead back and forth to position it manually. To move it, drag it with the mouse. You can also use the keyboard to move the playhead. The following table lists the keyboard commands.

Keyboard Command	Description
HOME	Move playhead to beginning
END	Move playhead to end
RIGHT ARROW (hold down to keep moving it)	Move playhead forward one frame
LEFT ARROW (hold down to keep moving it)	Move playhead backward one frame
SHIFT-RIGHT arrow	Move playhead forward ten frames
SHIFT-LEFT arrow	Move playhead backward ten frames

Using the Buttons   You can also control playback with the buttons at the bottom of the iMovie monitor. From left to right, the buttons, their purposes, and their keyboard equivalents are shown here.

Button	Description	Keyboard Equivalent
Rewind	Moves the playhead backwards. Click a second time to stop. (Don't hold it down continuously.)	COMMAND-[
Home	Moves the playhead to the beginning of the clip or movie.	HOME key
Play	Starts to play. The playhead moves along as the movie plays. The Play button changes to a Stop button while it's playing.	SPACEBAR (for both Play and Stop)

Button	Description	Keyboard Equivalent
Play Full Screen	The movie plays and takes up the entire display (subject to black areas that might be needed if the shape of the movie differs from the display). Click the full-screen movie to stop it and return to the iMovie interface.	None
Fast Forward	Moves fast forward. Click a second time to stop. (Don't hold down.)	COMMAND-]

Adjusting the Volume   To the right of the iMovie monitor buttons is a volume control for playback. Adjust the volume control with the mouse, or use the Up arrow to increase the volume and the Down arrow to decrease the volume. If you can't adjust the volume to the level you want, adjust the speaker or headphone volume using the volume control at the top of the numeric keypad or using Sound from System Preferences. (For example, if you set the Mute option in System Preferences, adjusting the iMovie volume control won't do you any good.)

Working in Camera Mode

When you connect a digital camcorder and turn it on, iMovie generally launches and switches to Camera mode. If iMovie is already running, it will switch to Camera mode. If this doesn't happen, turn off the camcorder, and then turn it on again. Also, check that the connections are firm and tight.

NOTE   *When a digital camcorder is attached to a FireWire port, it doesn't appear in the Finder the way most digital cameras attached with USB connectors appear.*

In Camera mode, the buttons at the bottom of the iMovie monitor control the camcorder, not the display in the iMovie monitor (although when the camcorder is playing, the image from the tape cassette is shown in the iMovie monitor). You learn more about Camera mode in the upcoming section, "Importing Video and Other Files."

Scrubber Bar

In Edit mode, the *scrubber bar* at the bottom of the iMovie monitor not only enables you to position the playhead, it also lets you use it to select parts of the movie.

Getting Around iMovie

When you hold the mouse over the hatch marks at the bottom of the scrubber bar, two small triangles appear:

These are *crop markers,* which you drag back and forth along the scrubber bar to the beginning and end of a section of the movie. That section will be highlighted in yellow in the scrubber bar. Instead of dragging the crop markers with the mouse, you can click a crop marker, and then move it to the left or right one frame at a time with the LEFT ARROW or RIGHT ARROW key. Holding down the SHIFT key makes one press of the arrow key move ten frames at a time. (*Scrubbing* refers to the action of moving film or tape back and forth repeatedly as you edit it.)

Once you select part of the clip with the crop markers, you then have two choices.

Action	Description	Command
Cropping	This deletes everything outside the selection, that is, everything before and after the selection.	Crop from the Edit menu or COMMAND-K
Trimming	This deletes the selection, that is, it leaves everything before and after the selection.	Clear from the Edit menu (no COMMAND-key equivalent)

You can take yet another editing action: you can split the clip into two. You don't use crop markers for this. Instead, you position the playhead where you want to split the clip, and then you choose Split Video Clip at Playhead from the Edit menu (or use the keyboard-equivalent, COMMAND-T).

Trimming

Trimming saves your selection and eliminates everything else. Use trimming to delete the material you know you definitely won't ever want. For example, if you followed the advice given previously in this chapter, you have extra footage at the beginning and end of each clip. The part with the sound of your voice saying "Whenever you're ready" or "Action" can safely be trimmed away. Likewise, the end of the clip where someone can be heard saying "Whew!" or "Great" or "That's a wrap" can go.

Cropping

If something in the middle of a clip is useless, you can crop it out. This might be a blooper or a section of tedious talk. *Cropping* provides a way of deleting it forever. You might have jumpiness when you play back the clip as the sections before and after the cropped part butt up against one another, but that might not matter. More likely, you'll solve that problem by splitting rather than cropping.

Splitting

By *splitting* a clip, you can manipulate each of the split parts separately. You might find that splitting a clip into three parts and removing the middle parts gives you two usable parts. If you play them back-to-back, a jump will occur where the middle part was. You might be able to use them with a transition, though, or in two different places as you assemble your video.

In practice, you often combine these commands. In the case of a clip with an unusable middle, you can crop it out, and then split it into two parts: this has the same effect as splitting the clip into three parts and tossing away the middle one.

Clip Viewer

A pair of viewers run across the bottom of iMovie. You can switch between them by clicking the tabs at the left. The viewer at the top (with the eye) displays the clip viewer. The lower one (with a clock) displays the timeline viewer. Both viewers let you look at all the scenes in your movie sequentially. A scrollbar across the bottom of the viewers lets you move from the beginning to the end of the movie.

The *clip viewer* lets you look at each clip in turn. The clips are represented by the same images you see in the clip viewer. Each is the same length in the clip viewer, but the time of each clip varies when you play it.

Add clips to your movie by dragging them from the shelf to one of the viewers. You can place a clip anywhere in the movie—iMovie automatically moves existing clips aside. You can also rearrange clips in the clip viewer. If you decide against using a clip, you can drag it back to the shelf from the clip viewer. You can also use Clear from the Edit menu to remove it, but that doesn't put it back on the shelf—it's gone.

When a clip is selected in the clip viewer, it appears in the iMovie monitor, and you can play it. If you select more than one clip (with SHIFT-click), they're all displayed in the iMovie monitor. You'll see small vertical lines indicating the breaks between the clips. (You can experiment with this easily. Select a clip in the clip viewer. Then, while watching the scrubber bar, SHIFT-click an adjacent clip in the clip viewer. You'll see the change.)

Getting Around iMovie

Timeline Viewer

The *timeline viewer* shows you the clips in your movie, but it's scaled to time: a clip that's twice as long as another takes up more space.

As with the clip viewer, you can rearrange clips, drag them to or from the shelf, and delete them. You have control over the display of the timeline viewer. Choose the Views tab from Preferences in the iMovie application menu, as shown here:

The timeline viewer has three tracks: from the top down, they are the video track and two audio channels. The audio portion of your video starts by being part of the video track. So for your basic editing, you can ignore the two audio tracks. (See Chapter 15 for more on using audio.)

Along the bottom of the timeline viewer are three sets of controls.

Zooming

At the left, a *zoom control* lets you set how the timeline viewer is displayed. At the default setting (Auto), the timeline viewer scales the clips, so the entire movie can be seen without scrolling. You can see the timeline in greater detail if you can select other settings. (Use this for editing and synchronizing when you want precise results.)

Speed

The *speed slider* lets you control the speed with which the select clip is played (or several clips, if several are selected). You can quickly see the results: select a clip, change the speed slider, and then click the Play button in the iMovie monitor. You can create clever effects in this way, and you can often combine speed adjustments with reversals of clips. Select one or more clips, and then choose Reverse Direction from the Advanced menu.

Audio Fading

At the right, just as in the Clip Info window, you can set a fade out or fade in. Here, however, you can adjust those settings for more than one clip at a time. Also, you can adjust the volume.

Importing Video and Other Files

Getting your video into iMovie is simplicity itself. Importing clips from other movies, as well as importing various other types of files, is also easy.

Importing from the Camcorder

Connect your digital camcorder to a FireWire port on your computer. Turn it on and set it to the VCR, VTR, or playback setting (the terminology varies among different camcorders). In iMovie, click the Mode Switch to the left to Camera mode (this might be done automatically for you).

You can use the controls at the bottom of the iMovie monitor to play back, fast forward, or rewind the tape in your camcorder. To import, start playing just before the section you want to import, and then click the Import button. Video will be imported until you click the Import button again, click Stop, or the tape runs out. Depending on how you set your Import preferences (see Figure 10-3), you'll get either one long clip or a series of clips based on the scene breaks in your camcorder.

Troubleshooting the Camcorder Connection

If this doesn't work, here are some things to check. If the camera isn't recognized at all, check to see if all the connections are tight. Some connectors need a little extra push to snap into place, and a common problem is that the connectors aren't pushed in all the way. (No known connector for this type of equipment requires anything like a hammer blow, so simply check with firm hand pressure.)

With all connections snug, turn the camcorder off and then on again. Check to see if the camcorder is in VCR, VTR, or Playback mode. (Another way of putting this is you shouldn't be able to record at this point.)

You can also take two rather extreme additional steps. You can restart your computer with the camera turned on. Occasionally, this causes the camera to be recognized at last. (The restart, in this case, will often fix whatever the problem was, and you won't have to go through this again.)

If you have access to another Macintosh, try plugging your camera into it. Or, if you have access to another digital camcorder, try connecting it to your own computer.

Support for iMovie is available through Apple's support pages at **http://www.apple.com/support**. You can check out discussions and search the Knowledge Base. Try using your camcorder's brand name as a keyword. Also, look at **http://www.apple.com/imovie**, the iMovie page. A list of camcorders with known issues is on that page, and it's kept current.

Trouble Shooting iMovie/Camcorder Controls

Another set of issues emerges if the camcorder is recognized, but the buttons in iMovie monitor don't control it properly. You can check the Apple sites listed previously for more information. However, you can use the camera's own controls to reposition the tape and to play it. The only iMovie control you absolutely need is the Import button.

Preserving Your Battery

Importing movies can be a big drain on camcorder batteries. Not only do you have to play it, but you might be rewinding, fast-forwarding, and so forth. Your camcorder should have an attachment that lets you connect it directly to a power source (often to a connection on the battery charger). Plug it in there, and you'll save your battery.

Importing Files

In addition to importing video from a camcorder, you can import files from elsewhere on your computer or on any network or disk to which you have access. Choose Import File from the File menu and navigate to the file you want to import.

NOTE   *If you aren't familiar with opening files from within applications, see Chapter 4, "Working with Files," in* Mac OS X: The Complete Reference *(Osborne/McGraw-Hill, 2001).*

You can import three types of files: DV streams, graphics, and audio.

DV Streams

These are the clips you see on the shelf. To import a clip from another iMovie project, use the Import File command from the File menu, and then navigate to that project and select the clip you want. The clip will appear on the shelf along with your other clips, and it'll be copied into the Media folder of your project. It will remain untouched in the other project. (You can also import QuickTime movies as DV streams, but you need QuickTime Pro. The process is described in Chapter 13.)

It might make your life easier to go into the other iMovie project, select the clip, and rename it by double-clicking it. This way, you're certain to get the right clip. Remember, never rename clips in the Finder!

Graphics

You can import graphics as clips. They can be useful as titles, or with voice-over narration, graphics can be an important part of your movie. File formats supported for importing are PICT (a Macintosh format), GIF, and JPEG (Web-based formats supported by most graphics software), Photoshop, and BMP (a Windows bit-mapped file format).

Audio

Finally, you can import audio files. Both MP3 and AIFF file formats are supported. With MP3, you can use your iTunes library as a source for background music. Unlike DV streams and graphics, audio files are imported into a track in the timeline viewer, not on to the shelf.

A Caution About Importing Files

Be careful about importing copyrighted files. The definition of fair use of copyright media is changing rapidly. New copyright laws are proposed and enacted frequently.

Exporting Video

Just as you can import files, you can export them. When you finish creating your movie, unless you want to play it only in iMovie, you need to export it in one format or another. Your choices are three:

- ■ Use QuickTime to create files that can be shared with Macintosh and Windows computers that have QuickTime. You can also play QuickTime movies through many Web browsers.

- Use DV to export the movie back to your camcorder and record it on a cassette. You can then play that cassette on your camcorder, or you can connect the camcorder to a VCR and record it on a cassette. You also can connect your camcorder to a television and play it back there. (Instructions for connecting your camcorder to a VCR or television should come with the camcorder.)

- Use the DVD option to prepare your movie for inclusion in a DVD you create with iDVD.

To export your movie, choose Export Movie from the File menu. Choose the type of export you want from the pop-up button at the top of the window.

To QuickTime

If you choose QuickTime, you'll see the window shown here:

You have a variety of different formats available. A big difference exists in the size of the QuickTime file, depending on how big the playback will be, so make certain you choose carefully. It might be worthwhile to export the movie in several different sizes for several different purposes. And, if you keep your iMovie project available (or backed up on an archive of one sort or another), you can always reexport it.

If you choose the Expert settings, you can manually adjust the QuickTime parameters, as shown in Figure 10-3.

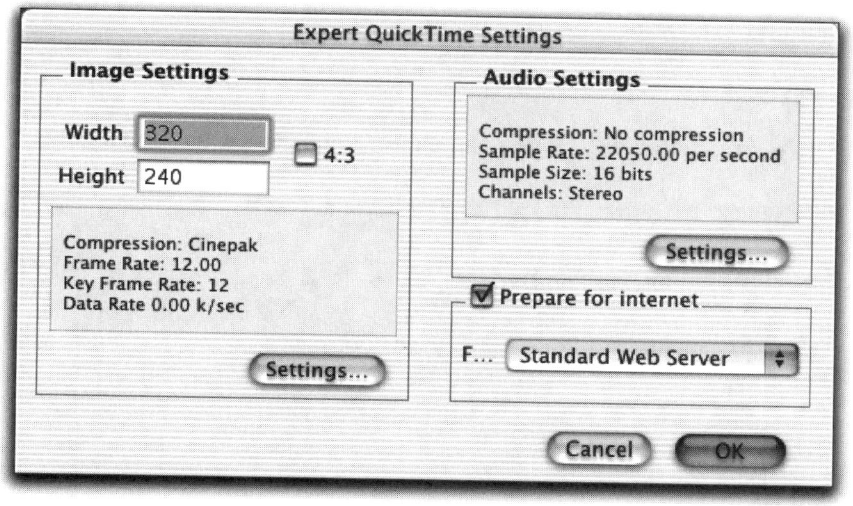

FIGURE 10-3   QuickTime Expert export settings

To DV

If you export your movie back to your camcorder, set the options shown here:

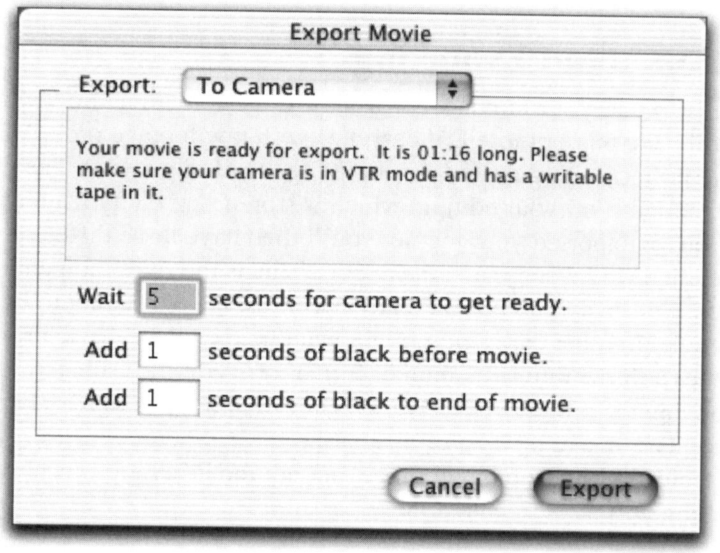

Generally, a good idea is to export the movie to a different cassette than the one you used to shoot it.

To DVD

Finally, to get ready for iDVD, you can export your movie, as shown here:

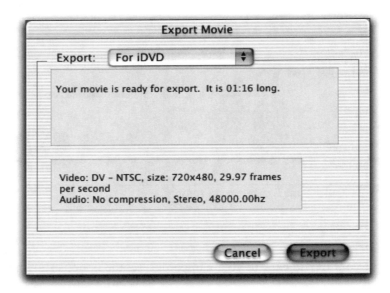

A Question About Exporting

You normally export your movie when you're finished with it. Now what? You probably will have one or more DV cassettes with raw footage on it. You'll have your iMovie project with that footage copied to the Media folder. The iMovie project also contains all your editing, which is stored separately from the media.

When you've exported your movie, you'll then have three different versions: the cassette, the iMovie copy, and the export. This is the right moment to decide what to keep. For many people and many purposes, the only thing to keep is the exported movie. In other cases, you might want to keep the iMovie project, so you can either reexport the movie in another format or reedit it. If this is your choice, consider copying the project to a CD or DVD in data mode or to a backup cartridge. iMovie projects can take up a lot of disk space.

If you decide to keep the raw footage, but not the iMovie project, remember, all your editing will have to be redone.

The iMovie Trash

The basic paradigm of iMovie is the clips are saved in the Media folder and all your editing commands are saved in the iMovie project. So when you trim or crop clips, the underlying clips are preserved on disk.

The trash icon just beneath the shelf shows you how much disk space is accounted for by the footage that's been removed from your clips (and how much disk space is accounted for by clips you removed from the shelf without placing them in your movie). You can select a clip and choose Restore Clip Media from the Advanced menu: your edits for that clip will be restored.

You can use Empty Trash in the File menu, however, to make all your edits final. The copies of the clips on disk will be modified at this point. You need never empty the trash: in that case, your disk-based clips will be the raw footage. Emptying the trash can reclaim a lot of disk space, but this is at the cost of being unable to go back to your preedited versions.

The choice is yours.

Summary

This chapter provided you with an overview of digital editing with iMovie. If all you've done before is to shoot video and show it, the iMovie workflow with its editing and shooting of far more video than you finally need to use might be new to you, but it can help you to create more interesting and useful movies.

Inside iMovie, your main controls are the iMovie monitor and the scrubber bar, the shelf, and the clip and timeline viewers. Each was described here and, with them, you should be able to perform powerful edits of your movies.

Importing from digital camcorders and exporting to QuickTime and DVD were also covered, along with the basics of importing graphics and audio.

If you can, take some time now to explore your digital camcorder and iMovie. Make a disposable experiment: film a chair or a tree—and tape it over and over. Try the editing tools until you become comfortable with them. There's more on making movies in Part 3, but these are the basics.

When you're comfortable, move on to the next chapter: photos.

Chapter 11

Using iPhoto

In This Chapter...

■ Getting Around iPhoto. The iPhoto interface is simple and compact. Here's an overview of what you can do and how to do it.

■ Importing Photos. You can import photos into iPhoto from your camera, from disk, and from memory card readers. This section shows you how.

■ Organizing Photos with Albums. iPhoto lets you create albums for your photos. You can organize them, label them, and do everything you would do with a traditional album (and more: photos can be in more than one album).

■ Editing Photos. iPhoto lets you do many of the basic photo editing tasks you would do in a darkroom, as well as some of the advanced editing chores you would do with an application such as Photoshop. These features are described here.

■ Making a Book. You can create an actual book of photos along with text. As you see later, you can automatically order a printed and bound copy from Apple.

■ Printing Photos. You can print to a printer from iPhoto. Be certain you set the printing options described in this section for highest quality.

■ Making a Slide Show. You can have your Macintosh automatically display photos and even play music. This section provides that information.

■ Sending Photos via Email. iPhoto can create an email message using your default email application and include selected photos as attachments.

■ Ordering Prints. iPhoto provides a simple interface to Apple's photo printing service.

■ Ordering a Book. Here's the information about ordering a printed and bound copy of the book you created.

■ Creating a Page for Your .Mac Web Site. A version of the HomePage software from .Mac is part of iPhoto. This automatically creates a Web page for you and uploads it to your .Mac site.

■ Setting a Desktop Picture. With one click, you can select a photo to use as your desktop background.

■ Creating Screen Savers from Photos. iPhoto is integrated with the Screen Saver pane of System Preferences and it can automatically set up a slide show to fill your screen during idle time.

■ Exporting Photos. You can export photos as files, as Web sites (your own—not your .Mac Web site), or as a slide show in QuickTime. All those options are described here.

■ iPhoto Preferences. Finally, here are some of the customizations you can select for iPhoto. (Note that some of the behaviors described in this chapter are subject to preferences settings, so your version of iPhoto might behave a bit differently if your preferences are different.)

Just as iMovie is the postproduction tool you use after you shoot your video, iPhoto is the tool you use after you shoot your still photos. Use iPhoto for correction and editing, as well as for publishing.

Getting Around iPhoto

Figure 11-1 shows the iPhoto interface. It uses an Apple interface design called *metal,* which resembles a brushed metal surface. Some of the traditional interface elements (such as a title bar) aren't shown in the standard way. And an addition to typical Mac OS X behavior is provided in applications that use metal. You can drag the window from any part of it with the metal background.

The Photo Library, Last Import, and Albums

At the left, several collections of photos are provided for you. By default, iPhoto keeps all photos in the *Photo Library,* the first item at the top left of the iPhoto window. When you click the Photo Library once, the photos in it are shown in the main pane of the window.

Directly beneath Photo Library is a special collection of photos called Last Import (it's the one with the icon of a roll of film). The photos from your last import are shown here, as well as in Photo Library.

Beneath these two standard collections, you can create other collections of your own: these are called *albums*. (You find more about creating albums in the section, "Organizing Photos with Albums and Keywords," later in this chapter.)

FIGURE 11-1   iPhoto at work

The Info Pane

An Info button is located at the bottom of this section; it is the third button from the left in the row of buttons, and is shown here.

Click the Info button once and you see some basic information about the album—or individual photo, if you selected one in the main pane.

This information is obtained automatically from the photo or the album. The name of the photo or album is changeable: Album titles can be changed by selecting them in the list of albums, and photo titles can be changed by selecting a photo and changing the title in the title field at the bottom of the Info pane. In Figure 11-2, you see the name of the selected album (Trip Highlights), the dates of the various photos (May 3–May 20, 2002), the number of photos (12), and the amount of space they take up on disk (25.2MB).

Click a second time and more information is revealed: Figure 11-2 shows the results of a single click (a) and a double click (b).

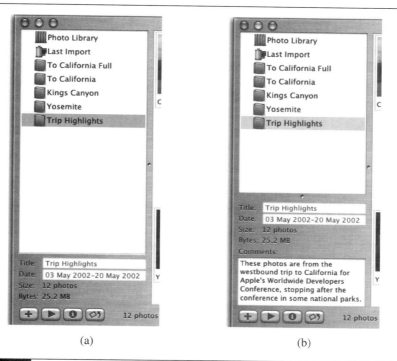

(a)   (b)

FIGURE 11-2   Information about photos and albums

The comments in this part of the Info pane are yours, and you can enter them directly here. For example, here you can see a description of the contents of the Trip Highlights album.

The rest of the iPhoto window is described during the course of this chapter. The main set of controls you work with is the set of five buttons in the lower center of the window:

- Import
- Organize
- Edit
- Book
- Share

Importing Photos

The first step in using iPhoto is importing your photos into it. You have four separate sources for photos:

- You can import them directly from your camera with a USB connection.

- You can remove your camera's memory card and put it in a small card reader attached to your computer.

- If you have image files on disk (your own hard disk, a networked disk, or a CD-ROM, such as a PhotoCD), you can import them from disk.

- Finally, if you have prints or slides from film, you can scan them in.

Importing from a USB Connection to Your Camera

If your camera's fairly recent, it probably has a USB connection to use in moving photos to your computer. If your camera has a USB connection, plug it in and turn the camera on. (If it's already turned on, you might need to turn it off, and then on again.) In most cases, the system will sense the camera and launch iPhoto. If it doesn't, launch iPhoto yourself. Normally, the Import button is selected automatically. If the Import button isn't selected, click it.

NOTE   *The cameras that support iPhoto are listed on Apple's Web site at* ***http://www.apple.com/iphoto/compatibility****. The list is updated periodically, and you'll note the newest cameras tend to be on the list. If your camera has a USB connection and isn't on the list, you'll probably need to launch iPhoto manually as described here. Another source of iPhoto-compatible cameras is the Apple Store at* ***http://store.apple.com****. Here Apple offers various third-party products (including cameras) for sale. Typically, the cameras at the Apple Store are compatible with iPhoto. You can buy them there or from other vendors.*

When the camera is connected and you've clicked the Import button (or the system has done it for you), you'll see the display shown in Figure 11-3.

At the bottom left, an icon shows a connected camera. It will identify the camera and show you how many photos are in it. (This information is automatically sent over the USB connection.) Click the Import button at the lower right to import the photos automatically into the camera.

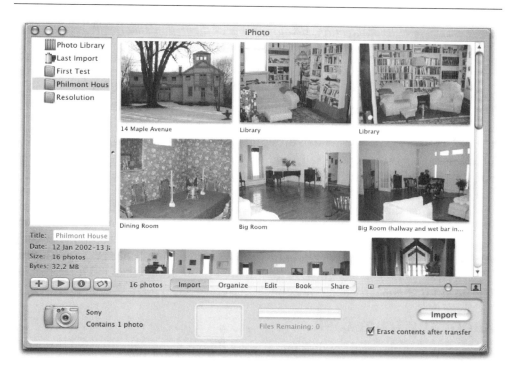

FIGURE 11-3   Connected camera in iPhoto

The checkbox in the lower right lets you choose whether to erase the photos automatically from your camera's memory. In most cases, you want to do this.

The photos will be imported into your Photo Library. You can also see them in the Last Import collection. From here, you can go on to edit and adjust photos, to organize them, and to share them. Those topics are covered in the next section of this chapter.

When you finish, click the Computer button in the toolbar of a Finder window. Most cameras are mounted as removable disks and appear that way in the Finder. When your import is complete, select the removable disk icon and choose Eject from the File menu (or from the contextual menu you see when you click the disk icon while holding down the CONTROL key). Or you can drag the removable disk icon to the trash.

Once you eject the removable disk icon, you can turn the camera off and disconnect it.

Importing Photos

A few cameras don't show up as removable disks when they're connected via the USB connection. If yours is one of them, don't worry about ejecting the removable disk icon before disconnecting it.

Importing from a Card Reader

If your camera doesn't have a USB connection, you can buy a card reader that does have a USB connection. Card readers exist for each type of removable memory (some accommodate two different types of memory). *Card readers* are relatively inexpensive (under $50), and they enable you to remove the memory card and place it in the card reader. At that point, the card reader appears as a removable disk in the Finder.

You can use this technique even if your camera does have a USB connection, but most people prefer to use the USB. This is the technique to use if you have an older digital camera that isn't supported by iPhoto. (If you want to make certain your card reader is supported, you can check at **http://www.apple.com/iphoto/compatibility**.)

The next section shows you how to import a photo from disk, and it applies to the "disks" that appear when you connect card readers.

Importing from Disk

You can import photos from disk into iPhoto. iPhoto recognizes JPEG, TIFF, and PICT files. You can get them onto your disk in many ways: you can download them from the Internet, you can create them with drawing or editing programs, or you can scan them (as described in the following section).

Once you have a photo on disk, import it into iPhoto using the Import command from the File menu. (If the file is grayed out, it isn't a data type iPhoto recognizes.) When you import a file from disk in this way, it's copied into your Photo Library and appears inside iPhoto in the same way a photo downloaded from a camera does.

Importing from a Scanner

If you have prints or slides made from film, you can import them using a scanner. For prints, follow the scanner's instructions to create a JPEG or TIFF file on your hard disk. If you have a 35mm slide, you can buy an attachment for many scanners that lets you scan directly from the slide. (Together with such an attachment, you'll probably be spending a little more than $100 for such a scanner.) These attachments work by shining light through the slide or negative, so the image is focused on the scanner's glass. From there, the image is scanned exactly as if it were a paper image. More expensive slide and negative scanners (around $1,000 or so) create higher-quality scans from slides or negatives using a more sophisticated technique.

NOTE

If you have a good-to-better (but not best) scanner and if you have a collection of photos or slides, such as your family archives, you might want to have them scanned professionally with the highest-quality equipment. Not only does this give you the best images possible, but it also gives you a digital archive that won't be subject to further deterioration of ink or paper.

Where the Photos Are on Disk

iPhoto stores its photos in a folder called iPhoto inside your Pictures folder. Everything inside this folder belongs to iPhoto. Keep out of this folder! If you want to add new photos, use the Import command from the File menu or import them from your camera. If you want to remove photos, select the photo(s) you want to remove, and then choose Cut or Clear from the Edit menu. Or, you can select a photo and press the DELETE key.

As noted in Part 1 of this book, the Finder has a smaller and smaller role to play in applications such as iPhoto. In fact, Apple repeatedly stresses in its documentation that you *must not* use the Finder to add or remove photos.

What happens inside the iPhoto folder is this: iPhoto copies every photo you import. (iPhoto copies them from your camera, but it might remove the original. It copies them from your disk, but never touches the original.)

Once iPhoto has imported and duplicated your photos, it stores them along with the editing you perform. Thus, if you cropped a photo or changed it from color to black-and-white, it still has the original version to revert to if you want to remove your edits.

For this to work, iPhoto must be able to connect the edits (stored in one file) with the original photo (stored in another). That's the main reason for you to keep out of the iPhoto folder.

Because iPhoto always duplicates photos, importing a large number of photos can use up a lot of disk: you might have a set on your hard disk and a duplicate set in iPhoto. (This situation doesn't apply if you're importing from your camera.)

If you're running short of disk space, copy the originals to a CD-ROM or a backup device. Continue working with the iPhoto copies.

Organizing Photos with Albums and Keywords

To the right of the Import button, the Organize button lets you organize your photos. You have two basic types of organization: photo albums and keywords.

Creating Albums

 You create albums by clicking the plus (+) icon at the bottom left of the iMovie window.

The new album appears in the previous list. You can rename an album by clicking its name in the list and typing the new name. To add a photo to an album, first make sure it's visible in the main pane of the window. Most often, you'll move photos from Photo Library or Last Import. Select either one and scroll the photo you want into view. Then drag it into the album where you want it.

Inside each album, you can choose to display photos by date or by import (film roll). First, select the album in question from the list at the left. You can select one of these from the Arrange Photos submenu of the Edit menu. If you choose to arrange the photos within an album in either of these ways, all photos in the album will be arranged that way. You also can arrange them manually, a third choice in this submenu. (Arranging photos by date and film roll is available for albums, Photo Library, and Last Import. Arranging photos manually is only available for albums.)

NOTE   *Before you go overboard arranging photos manually within albums, make certain you read "Making a Book," later in this chapter. This section shows you a different and more convenient way of arranging photos.*

Using Keywords and Comments

After you choose the Organize button, a search pane appears at the bottom of the iPhoto window, as shown in Figure 11-4.

To assign comments to a photo, select Assign at the lower left, and then select the photo. Then type the words you want to apply to it (you can apply as many as you want). When you finish, press RETURN. In this figure, the Sea Lion photo has the words Newport and Oregon attached to it (this is where the photo was taken). Then, when you want to search for a photo, click the album you want to search, select Search at the lower left, and then type the word(s) you're interested in, as shown in Figure 11-5.

Figure 11-5 illustrates several aspects of searching. As you can see, the word "oregon" was typed as a search term. It appears in the titles of two photos, so those are shown. Oregon is also in the keywords for the Sea Lion photo, so that one also appears. Finally, note that capitalization doesn't matter for searching.

If you type several words, iPhoto will look for photos that have all those keywords assigned to them. You might want to start with a broad search (for

FIGURE 11-4   Comments organizer

example, one word), and then refine your search down to a manageable number by adding more words.

You can also use keywords to categorize your photos. (Use preferences, described at the end of this chapter, to switch between free-form comments and structured keywords.) If you use keywords, you can use those provided by Apple or you can add your own. Then, for each photo, simply check the keywords that apply. The keyword mechanism is shown here:

Searching for comments

Editing Photos

The Edit button lets you do basic, but powerful, editing of the images. The Edit controls, shown at the bottom of the windows after you have selected the Edit button, are shown here:

The main edits are

- Rotating
- Cropping

- Setting brightness and contrast
- Color changes
- Enlarging and reducing image size

Remember, iPhoto is saving the original of your photo and storing the changes you make with these edits separately. Use Revert to Original in the File menu to eliminate all changes. To delete only the most recent change, use Undo at the top of the Edit menu.

Rotating

At the bottom left is the Rotate button, which rotates the image 90 degrees in a clockwise or counterclockwise direction. (You select the direction in Preferences.)

Cropping

To *crop* an image, simply use the pointer to draw a rectangle around the part of the photo you want to keep. As you draw, iPhoto will keep that rectangle displayed fully, but the rest of the photo will appear slightly shaded. If you don't like the rectangle you've drawn, click and draw another one elsewhere.

You can constrain your drawing to certain standard shapes and sizes such as 4×6 or square, as shown in the pop-up menu. This is useful if you're cropping photos to be printed on certain types of paper.

To undo a selection or crop, click anywhere in the photo. If you click and move the pointer, a new rectangle will be drawn.

Setting Brightness and Contrast

The two sliders in the center of the editing tools let you adjust brightness and contrast in the photo. These adjustments apply to the entire photo, not only to a selected area. These controls give you an opportunity to revisit settings you determined (or your camera determined) when you were taking the photo. The adjustments you make here have similar, but different, effects, as do the shutter speed and aperture settings at exposure time. Experiment with both sets of controls to see how you can modify photos. In general, the better the original adjustment (that is, at photograph time), the better the image.

Color Changes

You can apply two types of color changes. The first type reduces the red-eye effect caused by flash. To use the red-eye reduction, draw a rectangle around the area you want to work with (usually a person's eye). Then, click the red-eye button. Try to minimize the area to which you apply this affect. While reducing red-eye is good, changing legitimate colors (which can happen if the effect is applied too broadly) is not.

Your digital camera probably has a red-eye reduction option. This works by firing the flash a fraction of a second before the picture is taken. That first flash causes the eye to adjust to the bright light, so when the actual picture is taken, the flash doesn't hit an enlarged and reflective pupil. Generally, better results are obtained by preventing red-eye in this way using the camera. But, if you haven't been able to do so, use iPhoto to undo the damage.

The second type of color change in iPhoto is the capability to make all or part of the photo black-and-white. Select the rectangle to which you want the effect to apply (or nothing, if you want to convert the entire image), and then click Black & White.

Enlarging and Reducing Images

Finally, you can use the size control at the lower right to enlarge or reduce the image as you're editing it. Note that this is used to help you more accurately construct the areas for cropping and red-eye reduction. This doesn't affect the actual size of the image. You can use the zoom slider together with the scroll bars to resize and recenter the image.

Making a Book

One of the most popular features of iPhoto is the capability to make a book or photo album from your photos. You can order a printed and bound copy directly through iPhoto, and it will be returned to you in a few days. This section shows you how to make a book.

Start from an Album

You start by selecting an album from the list at the left. You can use an album you already created, or you can create a new album just for this purpose. Remember, iPhoto manages its photo files efficiently. If you create a new album and put some of your photos in it, you won't be creating new files on disk because iPhoto maintains references to its photos. (You do create duplicate files the first time you import files from disk into iPhoto but, thereafter, iPhoto works totally off its set of photos without further duplication.)

Each album can have one—and only one—book associated with it at a given time. You can change the format of that book, and you can order printed copies of any of those books you create—but only one at a time. In other words, format a book, organize its contents, order a printed version, and then start over, reformatting another book for the same album.

When you create your album, place the photos in the order you want them to appear in the book. Once they've been flowed into the book, you can then move pages around. If you have four photos, and decide to put two on each book page: photos one and two are on page 1, and photos three and four are on page 2. You can then move page 2 ahead of page 1, and the sequence will be photos three, four, one, two. But you won't be able to put photos one and three next to one another unless they're adjacent to one another in the album. As you play with iPhoto, you'll see how this works.

To get started, click the Book button at the bottom of the main pane in the iPhoto window. The photos from the album will be flowed into a book displayed across the bottom of the main pane of iPhoto, and you can begin to customize the book and individual pages.

Book Themes

After you select the Book button, the book tools are displayed across the bottom of the iPhoto movie. You can choose from a variety of themes using the pop-up menu at the left. These then apply to the entire book, and individual pages can have a variety of formats. Themes such as Picture Book let you put one or more photos on each page (with no text).

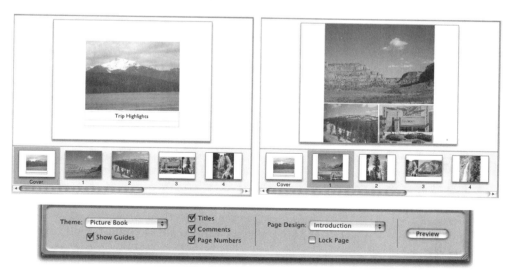

Other themes, such as Catalog and Story Book, let you combine photos with text.

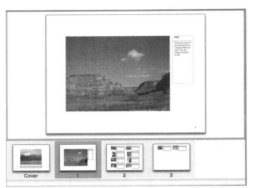 

Some themes, such as Year Book, are designed for specific uses.

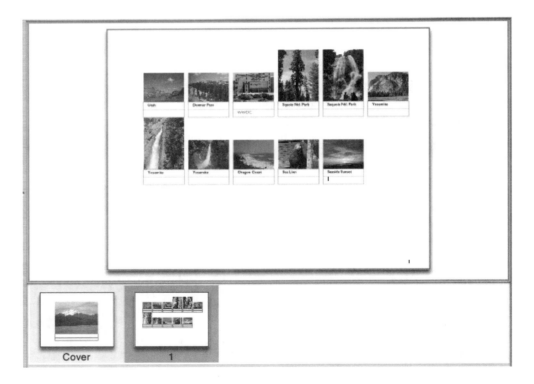

QuickTime Pro lets you make a number of adjustments to your movie before you export it.

Within each theme you can select from various page formats. For instance, in the Picture Book theme, although the photos appear on pages without text, you can type a lengthy introduction.

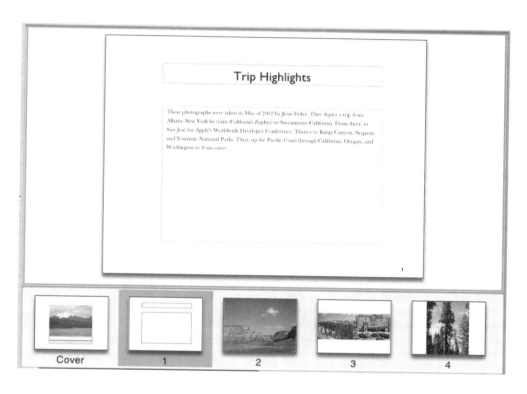

Page Designs

The pop-up menu in the lower right lets you choose the design for each page.

You can choose from different designs for different books. For example, a Year Book lets you choose from page designs with anywhere from one to thirty-two photos per page. A Picture Book allows anywhere from one to four photos per page.

Most book themes have at least two special pages. The Cover is printed on the front cover of the book (oddly enough!). The Introduction is the first page. Some themes, such as Story Book, also have an End page.

Titles, Comments, and Page Numbers

Next to the pop-up menu for selecting your book's theme, three checkboxes let you choose whether to have titles, comments, and page numbers. Titles are brief titles for each photo. Comments are lengthier descriptions, often placed below or next to titles. These checkboxes are next to the book themes because they apply to the entire book—all of its pages. (Note that some book themes don't have titles or comments on interior pages.)

Locking Pages

When you're happy with a page, you can lock it with the checkbox marked Lock Page. A small padlock appears. At this point, the contents of the page are locked and you can't change the page design. To unlock a page, simply click the checkbox again to deselect it.

Previewing a Book

If you want to see how your book will look, click Preview, and your book will open in its own window. You can use arrows in the window (or the arrow keys on the keyboard) to browse through the book. You can't print this preview, but you can order a printed and bound copy of the book. This is one of the choices available when you click the Share button.

Printing Photos

The fifth button at the right of the set of five below the main pane in iPhoto lets you share your photos in a variety of ways. These ways are described in this and the following sections.

Use the Print button at the left (or the Print command from the File menu) to print your photos. Depending on your printer, you'll find advanced choices in the Print pop-up menu, as you can see in Figure 11-6. (The name and content of advanced choices vary by printer.) Make certain to select the correct paper for an ink jet printer: results depend on the paper and printer settings. Certain formats require that the image be printed upside down or sideways so that the final result will appear properly, and iPhoto will do this for you.

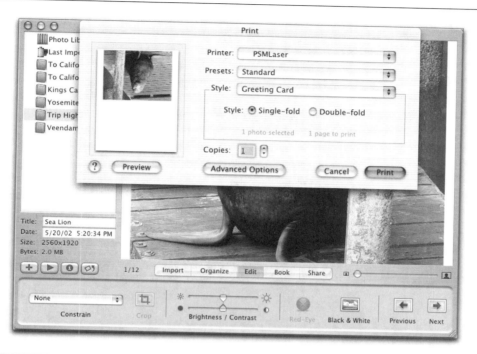

FIGURE 11-6   Set print settings for your paper.

Making a Slide Show

You can create a slide show from an album or from selected photos. Either select the entire album by clicking its name in the list at the left or select individual photos from an album by COMMAND-clicking them. Then, click the Slide Show button below the album list.

The slide show will play over and over until you click the window to stop it. To set slide durations, use the Preferences command in the iPhoto application menu. You also can choose music to play in the background. You can use iPhoto suggestions or you can use any of your iTunes music. (See Chapter 12 for more about iTunes.)

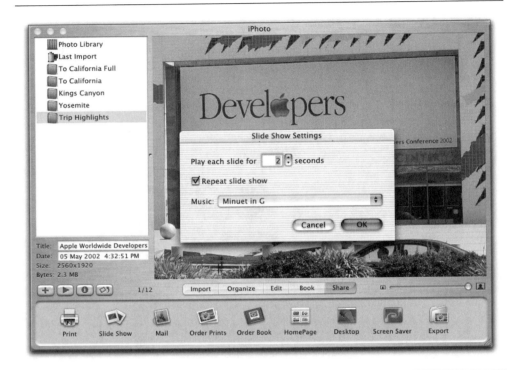

FIGURE 11-7   Slide show music and preferences

You can also create a slide show as one of the Share button's features. Click Share, and then click Slide Show. You can then set the slide show music and display characteristics, as shown in Figure 11-7. (When you use the Share button and the Slide Show button rather than the Slide Show button below the album list, you don't have to use Preferences to set these choices.)

Sending Photos via Email

If you select one or more photos, you can send it (or them) in an email message. Simply click the Mail button under Share and you'll see the dialog shown here:

You can choose from various sizes and resolutions. Note, the dialog shows you how big the photos will be in the email message. If your friends and colleagues all have high-speed Internet connections and don't mind receiving large attachments, you might not have to worry. As noted previously in this book, however, sharing snapshots for viewing on the computer's display doesn't require the highest resolution. Sending a small photo is always possible and, if a larger version is wanted, you can resend it. (iPhoto uses the default Email program you have set in System Preferences using the Internet preferences.)

Ordering Prints

The Order Prints button sends an order to Apple to produce high-quality prints of the photos you selected in the main pane of iPhoto. Start by selecting the photos you want. Use COMMAND-click to select various photos. If the photos you want are all together, you can SHIFT-click the first and last photos. (If you want them all, use Select All from the Edit menu—COMMAND-A).

NOTE *You need an Internet connection to order prints.*

As you can see from Figure 11-8, a variety of choices are available in terms of size. iPhoto warns you if you attempt to order a print that might be of dubious quality. You also can order multiple copies of each print. (Note, the sizes and prices shown in this figure could vary over time.)

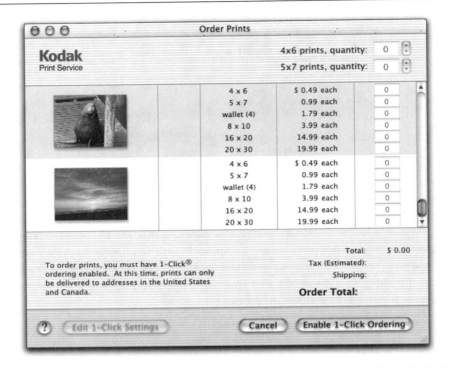

FIGURE 11-8 Enter your print order in iPhoto.

iPhoto relies on the 1-Click ordering you set up with Apple through its Web site. If you haven't set this up, you'll be prompted to set it up here. You need to select a password.

Then, you provide some basic identification.

Create an Apple ID

Apple ID:	jesse feiler	Enter your email address
Password:	••••••••••••	Must be at least 6 characters
Validate:	••••••••••••	Retype your password

Enter a question and answer that you can easily remember
to help us verify your identity in case you forget your password.

Question: Name of your best friend?

Answer:

Please enter your date of birth.

Month: [▼]   Day: [▼]

☐ I would like to receive Apple news, software updates, special offers, and information about related
products and services from other companies.

(Privacy Policy)

Finally, you provide billing information.

Enter 1-Click Billing Information

Apple uses industry-standard encryption to protect the confidentiality of your personal information.

First Name: Jesse   Last Name: Feiler

Address:

City: PHILMONT   State/Province: NY

Country: United States [▼]   Zip/Postal Code: 12565

Phone 1: 518   Phone 2:

Credit Card: ○ *VISA*   ○ MasterCard   ○ DISCOVER   ◉ [ ]

Card Number: XXXXXXXXXX2000   Expires: [4 ▼] / [2005 ▼]

Preferred Shipping Method: ◉ Standard   ○ Express

Ordering Prints

Your photos will be printed and shipped to you, using the shipping request you select.

Ordering a Book

You can also order a book you created. Select the album for which you created a book, and then click Order Book under the Share button. (If you haven't set up 1-Click, you'll be prompted to do so, as described in the previous section.)

NOTE   *You must have an Internet connection to order a book.*

Figure 11-9 shows the book-ordering window. You can select colors for the cover, types of shipping, and so forth. Note, the book pricing is based on a certain minimum number of pages (ten, at press time). You'll be warned if your book will be shorter than this because you'll still pay the ten-page minimum. Additional pages are charged individually.

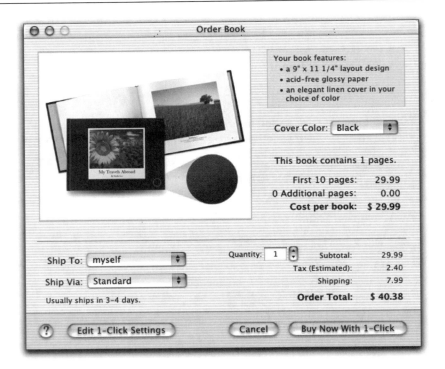

FIGURE 11-9   Order a book through iPhoto.

Creating a Page for Your .Mac Web Site

The HomePage button lets you create a Web page automatically for your .Mac Web site. (If you don't have an .Mac account, you need to create one from Apple's Web site before you continue. Click .Mac at the top of **http://www.apple.com** to create your account.)

NOTE *To use HomePage, you must have an Internet connection.*

The photos you selected are automatically flowed into a Web page. You can type a title and overall comment for the page, and you can add text for each photo. (By default, the photo name is used.)

Across the bottom of the HomePage window (shown in Figure 11-10) are several themes for the page. You can experiment with them by simply clicking each one in turn.

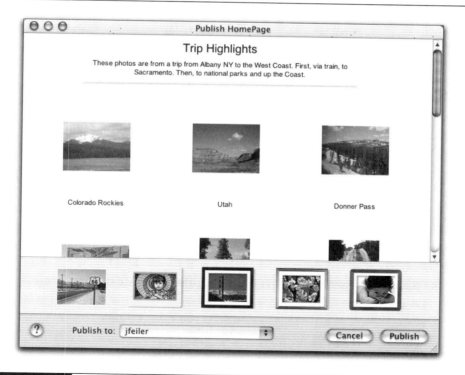

FIGURE 11-10　Create a Web page through iPhoto.

Note that the placement of the photos on the page that's generated is controlled by HomePage. You can control the order (by rearranging them in your album), but their placement depends on HomePage, as well as on the browser someone is using to view your page.

If you have more than one site, a pop-up menu at the lower left lets you choose to which site to publish this page. When you're ready, click Publish, and everything is done for you: the photos are automatically moved to the Pictures folder in your iDisk and the page is created.

NOTE *To edit pages on your site, log on to .Mac at **http://www.apple.com**. You can edit your pages there, and you can remove them, if needed. To remove photos from your Pictures folder, log on to your iDisk (choose iDisk from the Finder's Go menu) and delete them from the Pictures folder. Do this only after you remove Web pages in which they're displayed.*

Setting a Desktop Picture

Because iPhoto is integrated into Mac OS X, using one of your photos as a desktop picture is as simple as selecting it, and then clicking Desktop under the Share choices. The photo is immediately set as your desktop picture.

Creating Screen Savers from Your Photos

Screen savers can extend the life of computer displays. They also can personalize your computer environment. The screen savers you create from iPhoto slowly loop through all the photos in a single album. When you move the mouse or press a key, the screen saver disappears and your standard desktop reemerges. Click Screen Saver under the Share choices, and you'll be asked to select the album you want to use. (You can create one especially for this purpose and drag photos into it. Remember, you're not creating duplicate files—only duplicate references—so there's little overhead associated with having a photo in several albums.)

Once you select the album to use, another button on that dialog lets you adjust the screen saver preferences, which are shown in Figure 11-11.

Note that for flat-panel displays, you can prolong the life of the display by using Energy Saver to dim the entire display rather than using a screen saver.

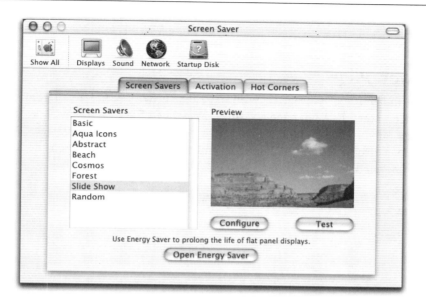

FIGURE 11-11   Set screen saver preferences directly through iPhoto.

Exporting Photos

Finally, you can export photos using the Export button or the Export command in
the File menu. Start, as always, by selecting the photos you want.

File Export

The first tab, File Export, is where you can specify the types the files created, as
well as the resolution to be used. The File Export tab is shown here:

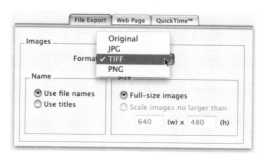

As noted in Chapter 3, you might want to export high-resolution photos in small formats, depending on their use. Your high-resolution photo stored in the Photo Library will remain available for future use.

As a Web Page

You can automatically create a Web page, as shown next. This differs from HomePage in that the Web page and all its associated files (the images) are created in a folder on your disk. You can then move that entire folder to your own Web site (or someone else's). Use HomePage for publishing on your .Mac Web site. Use the Export command and this dialog to publish on other sites.

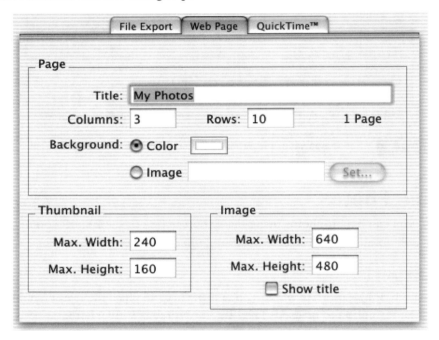

As a QuickTime Movie

Finally, you can create a slide show as a QuickTime movie, as shown next. You can then post that movie on a Web site, or use it for promotional purposes or as entertainment. The movie will contain the images, so you don't need your iPhoto originals on the computer that displays the QuickTime movie.

iPhoto Preferences

iPhoto is a simple yet powerful application. The only feature that hasn't yet been covered in this chapter is iPhoto's preferences. These are shown in Figure 11-12.

The preferences are mostly self-explanatory, and a number of them have been referred to already in this chapter. Note, in Figure 11-12, the option controlling a double-click on a photo: here, the action chosen is to open the photo in Photoshop. You can choose any application to which you have access as the editor, or you can choose to open a double-clicked photo in its own window in iPhoto.

Summary

This chapter has provided an introduction to iPhoto: how to use it, how to import photos, how to edit photos, and how to assemble them into albums, Web pages, books, and prints. The iPhoto tools are simple but powerful. As you use them, you'll see how you can improve the quality of your photos and how you can share

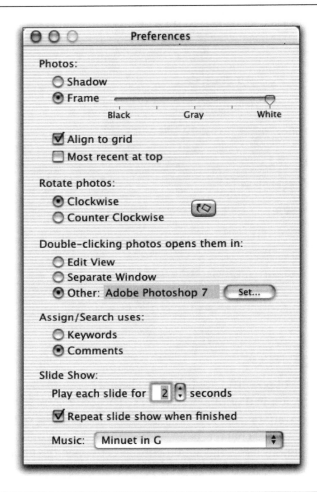

FIGURE 11-12   iPhoto preferences

these photos and display them in the best way. (You'll also probably learn how to improve the photos you take as you look at them carefully and see what you can do better next time.)

Chapter 12

iPod and iTunes: Music and Portable Disk

In This Chapter...

- The Digital Hub: A Case Study with iPod and iTunes. Chapter 1 provided a conceptual overview of the digital hub. This chapter shows how two products (iTunes and iPod) take advantage of those technologies to create a powerful application process for you.

- Getting Around iTunes. iTunes is simple. One window lets you browse music, manage playlists, and control playback. iTunes is shown here.

- Getting Around iPod. iPod is even simpler. This brief section shows you what's on the iPod—and how the standard plug and play protocols and FireWire make power cords unnecessary.

- iTunes Preferences. If you're going to do anything more than just play CDs, you should familiarize yourself with these preferences. Most people set them and forget them, but you probably need to make certain your initial settings are okay.

- iPod Preferences. iPod preferences—controlled from the iPod button in iTunes—let you use iPod as a disk.

- iPod as a Disk. When your iPod triples as a music player, contact manager, and portable disk, you get your money's worth. This section touches on the disk issues and shows you how to add contacts to your iPod.

- Using iTunes Music. Finally, you can use your MP3 music from iTunes in movies and DVDs.

If you think iTunes and iPod are toys, think again. These are sophisticated devices. Maybe your taste runs more to Mozart than to rock: it doesn't matter. Digital is digital and music is music. iTunes and iPod don't care what you listen to. Apple's great iPod advertising notwithstanding, an awful lot of people use their iPod for opera, classical music, Broadway, and jazz.

NOTE   *This chapter focuses on iPod. You can use other MP3 players with iTunes, and the behavior is similar. With iPod, though, you have additional functionality (such as contact information).*

The Digital Hub: A Case Study with iPod and iTunes

Perhaps nowhere is the concept of the digital hub clearer than in the case of iTunes and iPod: software and hardware that use the technologies described in Chapter 1 to "just work." iTunes lets you import music into a library on your Macintosh. Able to read a variety of input formats, iTunes stores music in three preferred formats: MP3, WAV, and AIFF.

You organize your music in any way you want, and you can play it using your Macintosh speakers. But if you add an iPod, everything changes. The iPod uses a FireWire connection to synchronize its contents automatically with the contents of your iTunes library on disk. The basic form of synchronization couldn't be simpler: plug in the iPod. (You don't even need to turn it on. Its FireWire connection senses iPod and computer, turns on the iPod, and launches iTunes on the computer.)

In fact, not only does iPod use the FireWire standard, its storage is also quite standard. iPod is simply a disk (introduced at 5GB, and then upgraded to 20GB). Although iTunes focuses on music, and while the iPod is billed primarily as a portable music player, the use of standards allows you to add all sorts of new features.

For example, in the first revision of iPod (spring 2002), a contact manager was added. You could download contacts from your hard disk to the iPod. This, too, is totally standards-based. The contact information is, in fact, *.vcf files,* a standard format for contact information used by many applications (including Mail). Applications that don't store their information in .vcf format can, nevertheless, often export to it. (Eudora is one such application, as is Palm Desktop.) So, using the standard format (.vcf), the standard connectivity (FireWire), and a standard hard disk, you automatically synchronize contact information on your music player.

There's more. When connected to your computer, the iPod can appear as a hard disk. (When connected using default settings through iTunes, iPod isn't visible in the Finder, but you can change that.) Nothing prevents you from dragging files to and from your iPod. This means you have automatic synchronization of the files it manages (iTunes and contact information). You have manual synchronization and transport of files using iPod, as you would any removable or portable disk.

For the final achievement, Apple is using the FireWire feature that allows it to send power, as well as data, over the connection. Thus, the iPod has no connector for power: it has a FireWire connector that provides both data and power. (If you want to recharge the long-lasting iPod battery, you can connect it—via FireWire to your computer. Or, you can connect it—again, via FireWire—to a power adaptor you can connect to your standard household current.)

Another aspect of the digital hub is shown in iTunes, as it was in iPhoto and, to a certain degree, in iMovie. The Finder is less and less important. Move and rename files with the application , not with the Finder. Also, leave them where iTunes (and the other applications) puts them.

Getting Around iTunes

You can launch iTunes directly or you can have it launch automatically when you connect an MP3 player or an iPod. The iTunes window is shown in Figure 12-1.

In the upper left are the basic controls to play music on your computer. (The iPod controls are on the iPod.) The central button toggles between Play and Stop. The adjoining buttons are Rewind and Fast Forward (to the next track). Below these is a volume slider.

Music is played through the speakers or headphone that you've connected to your Macintosh. See Sound in System Preferences to select and adjust these devices.

FIGURE 12-1   iTunes in action

Across the top is a pane that displays information about the current track. A diamond moves along a time line as it plays, and you can drag it ahead or back to Play from a different location.

At the upper right is a button that controls what's happening. You also can click it to toggle between two display modes in the browser in the center of the iTunes window. The display shown in Figure 12-1 can be sorted by clicking any of the column titles. An alternate display (obtained by clicking the Browse button) shows a list of artists, a list of albums, and then a smaller version of the display shown here. You can select individual items, artists, or albums to move them.

The scrolling list at the left of the window displays the various sources of music you can deal with. You have a *Library* of music, which contains all the music you imported. You also can have an iPod—this shows up only if it's connected. And you probably will have a *Radio Tuner* icon, which lets you browse Internet radio broadcasts and play them. If you click Radio Tuner, the central display changes to a list of types of radio stations: you can open each one by clicking the disclosure triangle to the left. Then, select one you're interested in and click Play in the upper left of the window. The Radio Tuner display is shown in Figure 12-2.

FIGURE 12-2   Radio Tuner

You can create any number of *playlists,* which appear in the scrolling list at the left, in iTunes. You can create a playlist by choosing New Playlist from the File menu. Then, drag any songs you want into that playlist. The songs will continue to be stored in your Library, but references to them will be put into the playlist. (This is why you mustn't move or rename iTunes files with the Finder—it will break these links.)

Because playlists contain references (not the complete files), you can have any number of playlists with any number of duplicate songs in them.

Another way of creating a playlist is to select a number of songs from the Library or to select another playlist. Then, choose New Playlist from Selection from the File menu, and you'll automatically have them stored in a playlist.

You can rename playlists by clicking their names in the Sources view and renaming them (just as if they were Finder files). You can also rename songs. If you rename them in the Library, they're renamed everywhere. If you rename a song in a playlist, it's renamed there, but its name from the Library appears elsewhere.

NOTE   *To create a playlist consisting of one or more CDs, import them into your Library. Then, you can sort the Library using the Albums column (click at the top), and you can select all the items in that Album so you can create a new playlist with New Playlist from Selection in the File menu. Another way is to use the iTunes browser. Create a new playlist with New Playlist, and then drag the album name or artist name into the playlist. All the songs from the browser will be brought in.*

Getting Around iPod

Getting around iPod is simple: few controls exist. The most basic functions are managed for you automatically. As noted previously, there's no on/off switch. iPod comes to life when you touch a button or plug it in. And iPod goes to sleep when you haven't used it for some time.

Furthermore, the single cable provides both power and connectivity. When you plug the cable in to your Macintosh, files are automatically synchronized. Note, your iPod synchronizes to a specific Macintosh. If you want to synchronize it to another Macintosh, you're asked if you want to switch to that Macintosh. If you do, you'll erase the contents of the first Macintosh from the iPod. Data for music and contacts flows from the Macintosh to the iPod. No data transfer occurs from the iPod to the Macintosh, unless you use it in Disk mode (see the upcoming section, "iPod as a Disk").

The only controls on the face of the iPod are four buttons surrounding the dial. A single button is also in the middle. A simple diagram comes with the iPod, but most people find they can navigate through without any difficulty, without even looking at the diagram.

iTunes Preferences

If you choose Preferences from the iTunes Application menu, the window shown next opens. Tabs across the top let you set a variety of preferences.

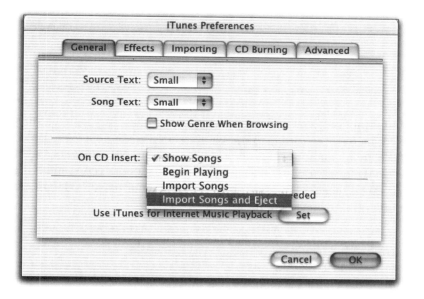

The two most important preferences here are toward the bottom. The first preference determines what will happen when you insert a CD. If you normally use iTunes to play CDs (that is, not to store music in a library or to transfer it to an iPod), you don't want the Import Songs and Eject option. If you want to choose what to hear, you want Show Songs. Or if you want to play a CD as if it were in a CD player, you want Begin Playing.

At the bottom, you can choose to make iTunes your standard player for music over the Internet.

The Effects preferences shown next let you customize playback. Note, if you set the crossfade playback to 0 seconds, songs will play without interruption.

iTunes Preferences

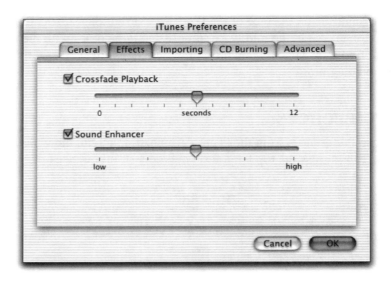

The Importing preferences let you control how importing is done. Important settings here include the format. Your choices are the MP3 encoder, WAV, and AIFF. These are all audio format supported on various MP3 players. If you use iPod, MP3 is the one for you. Other players might support WAV and AIFF, and they might save space with those formats. Look at your player's documentation to see which format you should use.

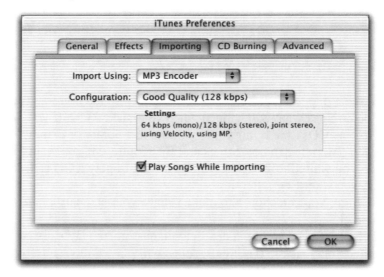

Also, depending on the sensitivity of your ears and the device you use to play back your music, choose the quality you want. As is so often the case, a trade-off exists: more quality takes more disk space. Don't waste space for higher quality you can't hear.

CD-burning preferences let you set up how you'll burn CDs (if you have a CD burner in or connected to your computer). You record on CD-R discs. CD-RW discs are for data. CD-R disks are write-once discs, so it's useful to set up a playlist in iTunes to collect what you want to burn and then, perhaps, to play through.

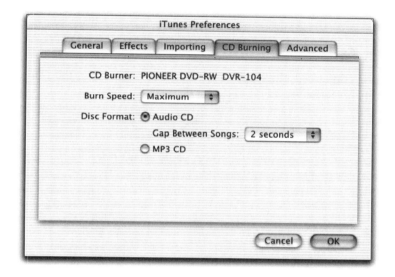

Finally, Advanced preferences are shown here:

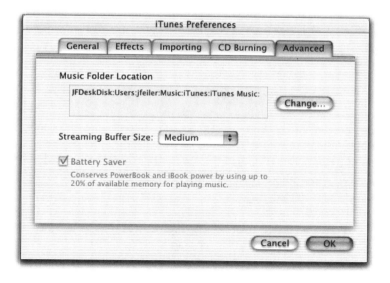

You can change the location of your iTunes folder here. If you plan to move your iTunes folder (not a good idea in most cases), you need to change this preference. Remember, the iTunes folder is mostly self-contained. Your Library contains the music, and the playlists refer to it.

You can also import music into iTunes, using the command in the File menu. This imports a reference to music located outside the iTunes folder. If you move files around, you'll probably break these links, so be careful.

iPod Preferences

If your iPod is connected, the iPod button in the lower right of the iTunes window lets you set its preferences:

The two preferences shown here—automatic update and automatic opening of iTunes—are the most common. They make everything "just work."

If you want to use your iPod as a FireWire disk, select Enable FireWire disk use. The window shown here then appears:

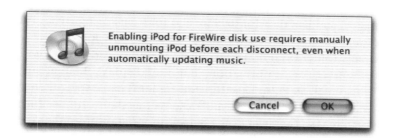

iPod normally doesn't appear in the Finder. When it's in Disk mode, it does appear, though, and you must manually dismount it (or drag it to the Trash).

iPod as a Disk

Figure 12-3 shows part of a Finder window displaying folders and files on an iPod.

The two iTunes folders contain your music and are managed by iTunes. The Contact folder contains contact information: you manage it.

You can create any other folders you want on your iPod. It behaves like—and, in fact, is—an external FireWire disk. Your iPod is fast and fairly big. Furthermore, it's bus-powered through the FireWire connection (there's no separate power cord).

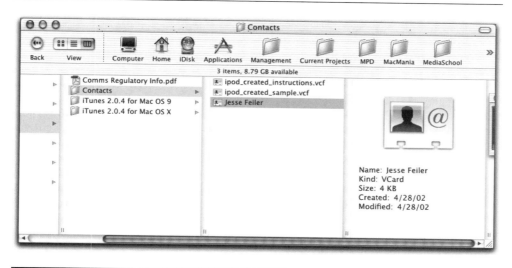

FIGURE 12-3   iPod in the Finder

Your iPod makes an ideal disk for backup and for transferring files. (And it's particularly great as an extra disk for an iBook or PowerBook.)

The Contacts folder on iPod is designed to contain .vcf files. These are standard files with contact information, and iPod displays them appropriately. Many programs (such as Palm Desktop and Eudora) can export their data as .vcf files. Other programs (such as Mail) use .vcf as their primary format.

If you're using Mail, you can drag contact information from the Address Book application into the Contacts folder of a connected iPod. Locate the address card you want in the address book, and then drag the entry into Contacts, as shown in Figure 12-4.

Using iTunes Music

iMovie and iDVD can read MP3 files, including those in your iTunes library. You can use them to import music as background for your movies and DVDs. As usual

FIGURE 12-4   A .vcf card in Mail

with the architecture of these applications, the music is copied into your movie or DVD project once you complete the import.

Summary

This chapter provided an introduction to iTunes and iPod. Both are easy to use, in large part because they rely on the standards found throughout the digital hub. Also, as you've seen, the iTunes interface and behavior is similar to that of iPhoto (playlists are a lot like albums). This similarity makes moving from one to another easy.

In the last few chapters, you've seen how to make movies, photos, and music. Now it's time to put them all together with DVDs, which is the topic of the next chapter.

Chapter 13

Getting Started with iDVD

In This Chapter...

- iDVD Terminology. The preceding chapters have dealt with technologies that are scarcely new (movies, photos, and music). DVDs are new, and iDVD is a new type of authoring tool for many people. This section introduces you to the features and terminology involved.

- The iDVD Workflow. Just as a workflow exists for movies, a workflow also exists for creating DVDs. The iDVD workflow is just as simple, although you have more possibilities for content.

- Getting Around iDVD. iDVD has a single, simple window, just like iPhoto and iTunes. Here's how to use its controls.

- Creating a Slideshow. You can build slideshows from graphics into your DVD. This section shows you how.

- Working with Themes. Apple provides a number of themes ("looks") for your DVDs. In addition, you can create your own by customizing the Apple themes. Here are the features and commands.

- iDVD Preferences. As always, you can set preferences so the iDVD application works the way you want it to. Preferences are described in this section.

- Importing Content. Content can come from a variety of sources. Some can be imported directly, while other content (such as QuickTime movies) needs to be converted to digital video. This section shows you how to do that.

- Using the Project Info Window. You can manage your project with the Project Info window as shown here.

- TV Safe. The TV safe feature of iDVD lets you keep track of how your DVD will play on TV screens.

Many people think of DVDs as long videos (some DVDs can store several hours of video; those you make with iDVD can store up to 90 minutes). Others think of DVDs as videos you don't have to rewind. Still others—the ones who get it—understand DVDs are a brand new medium. True, they can store enormous amounts of data and video, but they also have an interactive element (their menus), which lets users easily navigate through them.

For a Hollywood movie on a DVD, this means you can click one item to play the movie or click another item to play individual scenes. Extra material fills the enormous space on the DVD—trailers from the theatrical release, outtakes, interviews with directors or stars, alternate endings, and the like.

You can create a DVD like that, but the real opportunity for DVDs comes in combining video, still graphics, text, and other media in an interactive and involving experience. Part 3—particularly Chapters 16 and 17—explores some of the new frontiers of DVDs. This chapter focuses on the basics.

NOTE   *Two points are important here. The first is that iDVD is now in its second major release (iDVD 2). Many of the features described here weren't present in the first version of iDVD. If you have the original iDVD, you can buy and download an upgrade from the Apple Store (**http://www.apple.com**). Also, iDVD only runs on computers with the SuperDrive from Apple, which lets you burn DVDs.*

iDVD Terminology

iDVD terminology consists of two important iDVD concepts (projects and folders), as well as some basic DVD issues.

DVD Terminology

A number of formats exist for DVDs, just as a number of formats with varying degrees of compatibility existed at the beginning of the age of CD-ROMs. The Apple SuperDrive uses DVD-R and the General uses media format. These discs can be played in most DVD players and on computers that can play back DVDs.

In recent times, some vendors (such as Sony and Technicolor, which are the two largest DVD replicators in the United States) began to provide services to replicate DVD-R discs. If you use another vendor, you need to create a master of your DVD's data to provide to the replicator. This master can be on a DVD created by a tool such as Apple's DVD Studio Pro, or it can be on a tape cartridge, also created by such a tool.

For small runs, you can burn individual copies of your DVDs directly from iDVD. It's up to you to decide if that's feasible. Creating a DVD requires encoding the data. A lot of data exists, and the encoding takes processor time. If you have a high-end Macintosh, that's not a burden. When you create your first DVD, you get a sense of how long it will take to burn each subsequent DVD of that size. If you need a handful of DVDs, burning them yourself on your Macintosh might make sense. (Thanks to symmetric multiprocessing and multiple processors on high-end machines, you can do other things. You could also take the time to do other tasks such as cleaning your office, planting a garden, or reading a novel.)

> **NOTE**   *DVD formats are in a state of flux. Check the documentation of your computer's DVD drive, as well as the discussions and Knowledge Base articles at* ***http://www.apple.com/support*** *for the latest information.*

DVD Menus

A *DVD menu* is a screen with a number of buttons on it. On a computer, you can click the button representing the sequence you want to play. With the remote control of a DVD player, you use the forward and back arrows to highlight different buttons in turn. When you have the one you want highlighted, you click the center (Play) button.

Figure 13-1 shows a DVD menu screen constructed in iDVD. As you can see, an onscreen controller lets you use it as if it were the remote control of your DVD player.

This is a basic and standard interface. Within iDVD, you're limited to six buttons per DVD menu (but you can get around that, as you see in the "Folders" section that follows).

How iDVD Manages Your DVD Projects

Just as iMovie works on a single movie at a time, iDVD works on a single project at a time. Projects can be stored anywhere on your computer's disk. Unlike the other digital hub applications, a project stores references to content, no matter where it's located on your disk (or network disk). That content isn't moved into the project folder. In part, this is because the content can be so enormous. You can move the project folder around but, if you move content around, you're likely to break your iDVD project—iDVD won't be able to find the files it references if you moved them.

You can name your project anything you want, and you can store it wherever you want. While iDVD doesn't copy the media for your project into the project folder, nothing prevents you from doing so. If you make a nice, self-contained folder that contains your photos, slides, and raw DV footage (that output from iMovie), you can move it around and copy it successfully from one computer to another.

The disadvantage to this approach (and one of the reasons iDVD doesn't do it automatically) is this: if you're using a movie for two DVDs or for a DVD as well

FIGURE 13-1   DVD menu and controller

as a separate QuickTime project, that movie might wind up being stored twice on your computer—and these files can be extremely large.

Think about how you want to organize your content before you start your iDVD project. Once you start the project and begin adding content to it, reorganizing your files and folders on disk is much harder than if you do so before you start. The two big questions to consider are if you'll wind up duplicating files and whether you have enough disk space in one place for the media that will go into your iDVD project. Note that this issue is only of concern as you're creating your iDVD project. Once it's complete, you'll burn your DVD, and you can archive (or even destroy) the project and media files.

Folders

iDVD limits the number of buttons on a DVD menu to six. If you need more, you create a folder button. You can then add up to six buttons (slideshows or movies) to that folder. And so on. For example, in the previously shown Figure 13-1, four buttons exist.

- How We Met
- Planning the Wedding
- The Big Day
- Thanks to All

If you click How We Met, you might then be presented with four more buttons:

- His Story
- Her Story
- His Mother's Story
- The Truth (According to Her Sister)

When you click the Folder button in the lower left of Figure 13-1, a new Folder button appears, as shown here:

If you double-click the folder, you can add additional folders, slideshows, or movies to it. Note a small return arrow automatically placed in the window. This is to enable users to move to the higher level of the DVD menu within which you placed the folder. The arrow is shown in the lower left of your screen:

The iDVD Workflow

Because you're dealing with such large volumes of content when you create a DVD, having an idea of the workflow is more important than ever. The following steps are involved in the workflow, and the order of these steps varies to a certain extent. You always start by planning, and you end by burning a DVD. You might work on all your photos first or, as suggested here, you can work on acquisition and editing of photos, movies, and scanned images all together.

■ *Plan.* As you see in Chapter 16, you can plan projects and stay on top of them in many ways. For now, think about what you want to accomplish with your DVD and how you want to do it. Also, in planning for the content you'll collect, remember to get copyright clearances long in advance of your deadline.

■ *Acquire and Edit Photos.* If you're going to use photos, collect and edit them ahead of time. The easiest tool to use is iPhoto. You might want to assemble the photos for your DVD in a single iPhoto album. (Because the album only contains references to the folders, you needn't worry about wasting disk space this way.) When your DVD project is complete, you can remove the album.

■ *Acquire and Edit Movies.* Here's where iMovie comes in. You create and edit movies, just as you normally do. At the end, you export them for inclusion in iDVD. Note that because DVDs are interactive, you might consider using shorter movies with which people can interact. Instead of working on seamless transitions from scene to scene, maybe the user can click a DVD button to choose the next scene.

- *Acquire and Edit Scanned Images.* Any graphic can be placed on a DVD. If you need scanned images, collect them.

- *Acquire and Edit PDF Documents.* With Mac OS X, any document that can be printed can be saved as a PDF file in the Print dialog. And that PDF file can then be inserted into a DVD. This means any document you can print can wind up on a DVD without any effort from you.

- *Acquire and Edit Other Images.* You might have images that you draw, and you might have images created by programs such as PowerPoint. Collect these, too.

- *Create an iDVD Project.* Using iDVD, create a project and import all the content you have acquired and edited. You can test the project from inside iDVD.

- *Burn a DVD.* When you're happy with your project, burn one or more DVDs and distribute them.

Getting Around iDVD

iDVD is powerful in large part because it's so simple. (In some ways, iDVD is reminiscent of *HyperCard,* Apple's popular multimedia authoring tool from the late 1980s, for this reason.) You only need to know about two sets of tools: the main window and the Status display.

The Main iDVD Window

The iDVD main window is shown in Figure 13-2. When you launch iDVD, this is what you see.

The drawer at the left has three tabs (Themes, Customize, and Status), which are discussed later in this chapter.

In the main window, you can see the DVD you're creating, and you can play it. To add movies and other content to your project, simply drag them into the main window.

FIGURE 13-2   iDVD main window

Project Organization Controls

The controls at the lower left have the following functions:

- **Themes**   This toggles the drawer open and closed.

- **Folder**   This adds a folder to the DVD. You can move the folder around by dragging it once you add it. You can place up to six movies or slideshows into this folder.

- **Slideshow**   This creates a slideshow and adds a button to the DVD. Again, you can drag it to the location you want. A slideshow can contain any number of graphics—including one. (See "Creating a Slideshow" in the next section.)

Getting Around iDVD

Project Editing Controls

Three controls are at the lower right of the iDVD window:

■ **Motion button**   This toggles motion in your iDVD preview window. This controls whether movies in buttons play and whether a background image plays. Don't confuse this with the Preview button.

■ **Preview button**   This starts to play your DVD. A small onscreen controller provides the same buttons your users see on their DVD monitors (a computer or television).

■ **Burn button**   This burns your DVD.

Here's the controller when you're in Preview mode:

Checking Status of Space and Encoding

If necessary, click the Themes button to open the drawer. Then click the Status tab to see your project's status, as shown here.

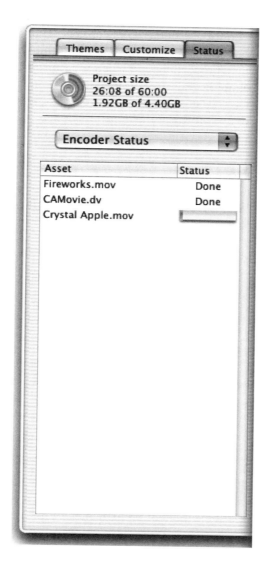

The *Status pane* shows you how much space is used up on your DVD. It also shows you the status of each element of the project. Some elements (known as *assets*) need to be encoded for use in the iDVD project. This encoding is done in the background while you're doing other tasks (such as thinking), and the Status pane shows you how that's proceeding and when it's finished. Most of the time, you don't notice this going on at all. If you're adding a large asset to the project and iDVD becomes somewhat unresponsive, however, look on the status pane to see if encoding is in progress. If it is, relax until it's done.

Creating a Slideshow

Slideshows can contain one or more graphics, as well as optional narration or other soundtracks. To add a slideshow to your DVD, click the Slideshow button, which is found at the lower-left corner of your screen.

If you double-click the slideshow, you open the window shown in Figure 13-3.

Drag files (graphics or PDFs) into the slideshow and drag them to rearrange them. The buttons at the bottom let you add arrows to the screen if you want. (If people will be using your DVD on a TV and operating it with a remote control, the onscreen arrows could be distracting, but they might be essential for computer users who view your DVD.) Other buttons let you create an auto-playing slide show. You can also drag an audio file (perhaps from your Music or iTunes folder) into the audio well, so it plays during your slide show.

That's all there is. If this seems like a cursory overview, it isn't. There isn't that much to creating a slideshow with iDVD. Of course, creating a good, interesting, and usable slideshow requires some thought. See Chapter 16 for some issues to consider.

FIGURE 13-3   Customize your slideshow.

Using Themes to Customize Your DVDs

Apple provides you with a number of themes for your DVDs. The Themes pane in the Themes drawer lets you select from them. Some themes have video in them—a video plays in the background behind the DVD buttons. Others have audio.

A pop-up menu lets you choose among the different types, as shown next. (Motion themes have a small icon indicating a person walking in the lower right.)

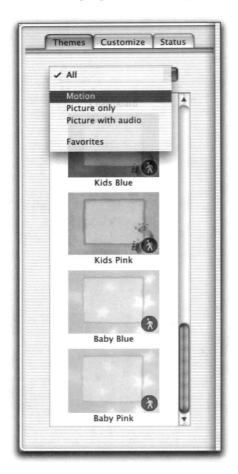

Themes are the "look" of your DVD. You can customize them in many ways to make your look different from that of other iDVD users. You can also use themes for portions of your iDVD project. In that way, you can give your users hints about where they are in the DVD.

You can use the Apply Theme to Project and Apply Theme to Folders commands in the Advanced menu to select where your themes are applied—to the project as a whole or only to the selected folder.

Creating and Customizing Themes

Use the Customize tab at the top of the Themes drawer to customize a theme. If you want to reuse it, click Save in Favorites at the bottom, and it will be available for future use. As you can see next, you can supply your own video or audio, select a variety of text styling options, and even select the default frames for buttons.

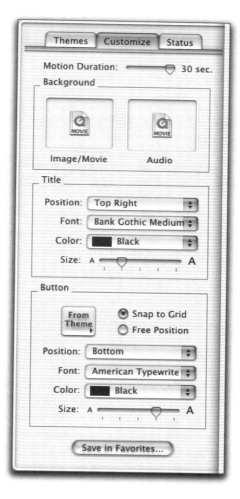

Setting iDVD Preferences for Video Formats and Watermarks

Preferences can be set from the command in the iDVD application menu, as shown here:

The watermark is a small translucent Apple logo that appears on each frame. Apple would be happy for you to use it, so people can see you've used an Apple product in creating your DVD, but it's up to you. Here's where you turn it on and off.

NTSC is the video format used in the United States and Canada. *PAL* is the video format used in most of the rest of the world.

Importing Content for Your DVD

When you're building a DVD, you can import content using the Import command in the File menu. You can choose from Audio, Video, Background Video, and Images. Simply select the file you want and it will be imported. iDVD will *render* it (convert it to DVD format) in the background as you work. You can see the status of your imported assets in the Status tab of the Themes drawer.

You can't drag iMovie files into iDVD, but you can drag QuickTime or DV movies in. You can create these either in iMovie or with QuickTime Pro. (If you have the basic version of QuickTime, you can purchase an upgrade using Preferences in the QuickTime Player Preferences.)

Converting a QuickTime Movie to DV Stream Format Using QuickTime Pro

To convert a QuickTime movie to DV Stream format, choose Export from the File menu in QuickTime Pro. You can name the exported file and choose its type. As shown next, choose DV Stream.

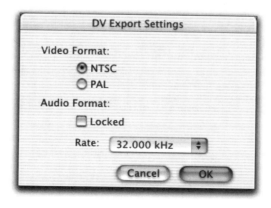

If you want to modify the settings, click the Options button in the lower right of that window. The Options window shown next will open. These settings are optimized for most purposes, and you rarely need to change them.

The Use pop-up menu located beneath the Export pop-up menu (in which you selected DV Stream) lets you customize the encoding, as shown next. The numbers in this pop-up menu are the sampling rate—the higher the better. Again, if you don't know what these settings are, use the default.

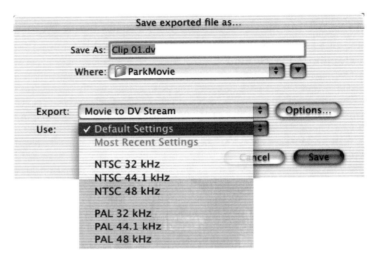

Using the Project Info Window to Check Status and Rename Your DVD Disc

You open the Project Info window, shown next, by using the Project Info command from the Project menu.

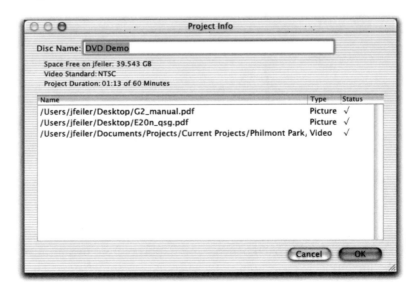

Here you can see the status of all your imported files. You can see their location on disk, and a checkmark is at the right if the imported file has been rendered into DVD format.

NOTE *The name of your DVD is at the top of this window. This is in an editable field, and you can change its name here.*

Create DVDs That Will Work on All TVs

One concern to remember is this: the size of displays varies. An area known as a *TV safe area* exists in which you're assured your DVD images and buttons will be displayed on all devices. Choose Show TV Safe Area from the Advanced menu to show that area. Your display will be similar to that shown in Figure 13-4. (The grayed-out area around the margins of the display is not in the TV safe area.)

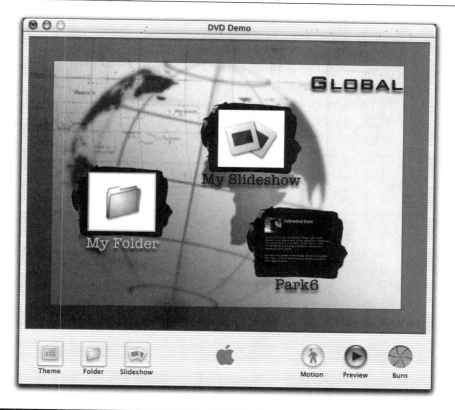

FIGURE 13-4 TV safe area

Create DVDs That Will Work on All TVs

Note that the area beyond the TV safe area is still visible in iDVD, it's just dimmed.

Adding Other Content to Your DVD in a DVD-ROM Partition

You can create a DVD-ROM section on your DVD for any files that you want to place on it—just as you would place files on a CD. Thus, you can add documents and applications to your DVD. To add files to the DVD-ROM section, use the pop-up menu on the Status tab of the Themes button to choose DVD-ROM contents rather than encoder status. Then, just drag the files into the list. Remember: to add content to your DVD movie, drag it into the main part of the iDVD window or use the Import command; to add files to the DVD-ROM section, drag them into the DVD-ROM contents section of the Status pane.

Summary

This chapter provided an introduction to iDVD. DVD technology is simple and powerful—and far more than simply video. You saw the basic terminology of DVD and iDVD, as well as the basics of the DVD authoring workflow and the iDVD window.

Beyond the basics of the iDVD window, you can create elaborate DVDs. These rely on themes, as well as on slide shows, to incorporate images and PDF files. Importing content is quite simple: the only trick is converting QuickTime movies to DV streams. Finally, Project Info window and TV safe area were discussed.

And with this chapter, the basics of *Making Movies, Photos, Music & DVDs On Your Mac* were described. There's one more basic issue to touch on, though. So much of your equipment is portable, it's worth thinking about how to travel with the digital hub. And that's the topic of the next chapter.

Chapter 14

Traveling with the Digital Hub

In This Chapter...

■ Time and Time Zones. Dates and times are used to organize your photos and movies. Here's how to keep your computer's clock correct.

■ Documentation. You can find portable, electronic documentation to carry with you. It's easier than lugging manuals around. Here's what you need in terms of manuals and other documentation.

■ Spare Parts, Cables, and Power. Far from home, you might be unable to find missing components. Or you might not want to waste time searching out electronics stores. This section is a checklist of what you need to take.

■ Using Other Equipment on the Road. When you travel, you might be using projection devices and other equipment in offices and conference centers. Be prepared for what you'll find.

■ On-the-Road Internet Connections. For most people, traveling means using alternate Internet connections. You should take some steps before you leave home to make your life easier. Here's what to do.

■ On-the-Road Storage. You might not have as much backup storage when you travel as you have at home. You can use that iPod as a portable, battery-powered hard disk to store your photos and video until you get home.

One of the great joys of digital hub technology is traveling with it. Whether you take a laptop along with a digital camera and camcorder or you only take your camera with you to bring back photos later to edit at home, everything should work seamlessly. That, at least, is the idea. This chapter can help you travel with peace of mind and your digital hub.

Time and Time Zones

Your Macintosh, like your digital camera and camcorder, has settings for the date and time. The Macintosh enables you to set the time and time zone separately. That way, when you travel, you can change only the time zone. Doing this allows the internal clock to manage the time at which things happen. Events don't appear to happen out of order when the internal clock stays the same and only time zones (or daylight saving time) change.

To set the time or time zone, launch System Preferences (from the Apple menu), and choose Date & Time. Click the Time Zone tab, as shown in Figure 14-1.

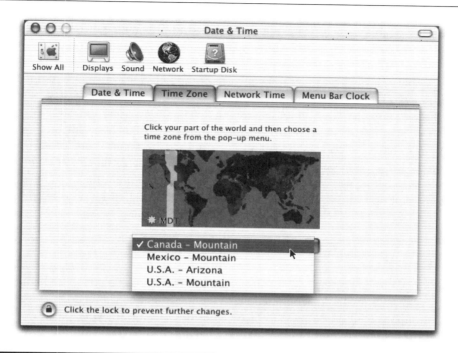

FIGURE 14-1   Setting time zones

The Digital Hub at Sea

Neil Bauman is founder of Geek Cruises, sponsor of (among others) the Mac Mania cruise. Here's how he handles Internet connectivity at sea:

"In 1999, I started Geek Cruises (**www.GeekCruises.com**)—the first company to combine career development and networking opportunities for technology professionals with the amenities of a luxury cruise. In January of 2002, we recorded another milestone: installing the first floating wireless computer network, which provided unlimited, around-the-clock Internet access for attendees. We have several routers placed throughout the ship and connected to the satellite dish that handles all onboard communications.

"We have several wireless access points (WAPs) placed throughout the ship. One of the WAPs is plugged into the fiber-optic backbone, which gets our traffic directly to the ship's satellite dish that handles all onboard communications."

Click the map at approximately your location. A pop-up menu appears at the bottom and enables you to select the specific world time zone you want. (To set the date or time itself, use the Date & Time tab. Also, consider using the Network Time tab to synchronize your computer with a network time server, such as the one at Apple. This enables you to keep your computer clock correct without worrying about it.

When it comes to your digital camera and camcorder, you might or might not want to keep your time and time zone correct. It's important for your Macintosh computer to have the correct date and time, but the camera and camcorder needn't be correct. Depending on how difficult it is to change the settings, you might want to leave them alone as you travel. iPhoto and iMovie use them for display when you import photos and movies, but the programs rely on the Macintosh clock and time primarily.

Documentation

If you're crossing international borders, you might need to be concerned about proving your ownership of your electronic devices. On entering a country with new equipment, you might need to prove your devices are for your personal use and not for resale. On returning, you might need to prove your equipment was acquired at home and not purchased while you traveled (if it is purchased while you traveled, customs duties could be owed).

On the other hand, if you're acquiring equipment while away from home, you need documentation to prove you have done so and what price you paid for it. (Note, customs duties needn't be based on the purchase price. They can be based on the value of the equipment.)

Documentation is also needed in case you lose your equipment or if it's stolen while you're traveling. Thus, you typically need two sets of documentation: one set to carry with you (copies) and another set at home (originals) to use in case you need to file an insurance claim.

NOTE

As noted previously, your insurance might or might not cover you while you're traveling. Even if your insurance does cover you, it might not be helpful. If you're giving a presentation to a client or a doting grandparent, you need your iBook. If you're going to a wedding, you need your digital camcorder. Knowing your insurance policy will cover a replacement— sometime—might not help much. See the following section, "Spare Parts, Cables, and Power" for some suggestions.

A critical form of documentation consists of the instruction books and manuals for your various devices. Today, almost all manufacturers post their manuals on their Web sites in PDF format. Preview, an application that's part of Mac OS X, can read PDF files. Thus, in preparation for your trip, you might want to visit the Web sites of the makers of your digital camera and camcorder (and any other devices you have). Download the PDF versions of the manuals and then place them in a folder on your iBook or PowerBook. Call it "Manuals," so you'll know what's in it. They'll all be there when you need them.

One reason this is such a good idea is that, far from home, you're likely to encounter conditions and situations you haven't met before. Perhaps you've always wondered how to use that macro button (you know it's for extreme close-ups, but until you poke your nose into that special clematis blossom, you might not care). Low-light, predefined focus, and other features of your digital camera and camcorder might suddenly matter a lot. Worse, if something that looks like an upside-down rabbit appears in your viewfinder, you could waste a lot of time and battery power trying to figure out how—and if—you should get rid of it.

Spare Parts, Cables, and Power

You have to decide how much spare equipment to carry. If you're going to a wedding or if you're giving an important business presentation, you might want to go so far as to have two of everything. If, however, you're going on a picnic with a group of friends you meet with each weekend, you might not care so much.

The most frequently lost or missing items are cables and batteries. When it comes to cables, you have one simple solution: wireless. As the cost of wireless is coming down (both AirPort and Bluetooth), you might want to consider whether it's worthwhile to add a wireless card to your computer—and digital camera or camcorder, if possible.

If you're not wireless, then you need to have one of each type of cable you'll need. Check *both* ends of the cables. Both FireWire and USB cables might have custom connectors at the camera or camcorder. Plug in your devices *using the cables you'll be traveling with* before you leave home and make sure everything works.

If you have more than one digital device, you're likely to have quite a few cables. To keep them organized, you might want to consider buying a few open-mesh bags, such as those sold for washing small items in washing machines. Not expensive, these bags let you put a single cable into them, and the bag keeps various cables from tangling themselves up (which they do in the darkness of suitcases and backpacks—it's their only joy in life).

Don't put cables in sealed plastic bags and don't tie or wrap them in rubber bands. They need to be kept reasonably loose and uncrimped—just the condition for prime tangling, unfortunately.

Batteries and power were discussed in Chapter 4 in the context of your home or office. When traveling, some additional issues need to be considered. In the case of power supplies that convert current from the wall to your computer or digital device, you need to check that input to the power supply will work if you're traveling in an area that uses different voltage. In the case of most Apple computers, the power supply will work with varying voltages: it will sense the correct one. For these power supplies, you might need to take converter plugs, so you can plug the power supply into the local outlet, but you don't need a voltage adapter. The device's documentation will specify the current it requires. This might also be on the back or bottom of the device.

For other power supplies, you could need a voltage adapter. (These are sold in electronic stores, as well as in shops catering to travelers, such as luggage shops.) These typically come with an assortment of plugs you can use. Read the label on the power supply to see what its input settings are. If you're in doubt, contact the manufacturer of the digital device (preferably through the Web—you might find a section on power or traveling that can answer all your questions). Get to know your rechargeable batteries. Some recharge quickly, while others might take a while, but hold a charge for quite some time. A digital camera with a battery that has enough power to take 50 photos could be fine for a full day of sightseeing for you.

If you need more power, consider buying a backup battery that can be recharged while your main battery is in use. The best batteries are expensive, but they're worth it if you're going on a once-in-a-lifetime trip.

NOTE
If you have friends with similar cameras or camcorders, find out what their battery situation is and what their life is like. If you need a spare battery for a weekend, you might be able to borrow one from a friend who has the same camera and who plans to spend the weekend planting hydrangeas.

Using Other Equipment on the Road

If you're giving a presentation while you're traveling, it's your responsibility to make certain everything works. Ask for a copy of the specifications of equipment that will be available for you. Watch out for some particular areas.

Projection devices can display your computer's image on a screen. They typically have a VGA connector you'll need to plug into your laptop. VGA connectors have

3 rows of 5 pins each, for a total of 15. They aren't the typical display connectors for most Apple displays, but the PowerBook has them built in and the iBook ships with a connector.

If you need a converter, buy it in advance. (You can buy them over the Internet through vendors, such as **http://www.macwarehouse.com** and **http://www .macwarehouse.com**. If you're uncertain what you need, call their toll-free numbers. Their customer service assistants are used to this question and, as long as you can describe the connector on the computer you're looking at and what connector you'll need, they can usually help you.)

As you can see, you must know the device(s) to which you'll be connecting. Most hotels and conference centers have a single page they can send you that details the equipment you'll find. Business offices that have many presentations also have such documentation.

You should arrive with everything except the equipment explicitly promised to you. This means cables, charged batteries, and presentation software are your responsibility.

NOTE *Experienced speakers know that while it's a good idea to be nice to everyone, it's a really good idea to be nice to the A/V staff. They're not servants—and if you treat them like servants, you're sure to have a broken cable and need to rely on them to bail you out.*

Check to see if you'll be expected to provide handouts. Sometimes, you can send a PDF file on ahead to be printed and distributed. If not, arrive with your handouts, not with a plaintive bleat to borrow a photocopy machine.

On-the-Road Internet Connections

Using Mac OS X to set up alternate Internet connections when you're traveling isn't hard, but because this is something you might not do frequently, this section provides you with some tips and hints.

Remember these two important points:

- First, don't change your home (or office) settings when you travel. Copy those settings if needed, and then modify the copy. The worst-case scenario is one in which you can't get the traveling Internet connection to work and you've screwed up your home-base connection, too.

■ Make sure you have an Internet service provider (ISP) lined up. If you have dial-up access at home (or at your office), you typically can use the same provider. All you need is a telephone number for your new location. Find this number from your ISP's Web site (or from customer service) before you go. If you use a nondial-up provider (such as cable or DSL), you'll need either a similar connection or a dial-up provider to use on the road.

NOTE *Today, more and more hotels are providing some kind of broadband, nondial-up service. You might want to check in advance with your hotel or hosts.*

If you need a dial-up ISP for relatively few occasions, consider purchasing a minimal plan. Most ISPs have a plan that costs only a few dollars a month, which provides you with minimal service—perhaps only a few hours—but you can pay additional for the hours you need. If you don't have frequent use for such a service, this could be worthwhile. Check on an ISP's Web site, particularly national ISPs that might have coverage in areas to which you'll travel. These plans aren't heavily promoted because many consumers see them as a "come-on"—the promise of cheap Internet service, but the gimmick of few connect hours. If you understand the terms and if those terms are useful to you, these plans are quite valuable.

Creating a New Location for on-the-Road Dial-Up Access

This section shows you how to create a dial-up connection to use when you're on the road. The following connection provides the information you need for an on-the-road nondial-up connection.

First, launch System Preferences from the Apple menu. Then, choose the Network pane, as shown in Figure 14-2.

Begin by adding a new location from the pop-up menu at the top of the window. You can start from scratch but, most of the time, you copy an existing location. From the bottom of the pop-up menu, choose Edit Location, and then select the location to edit or duplicate, as shown here:

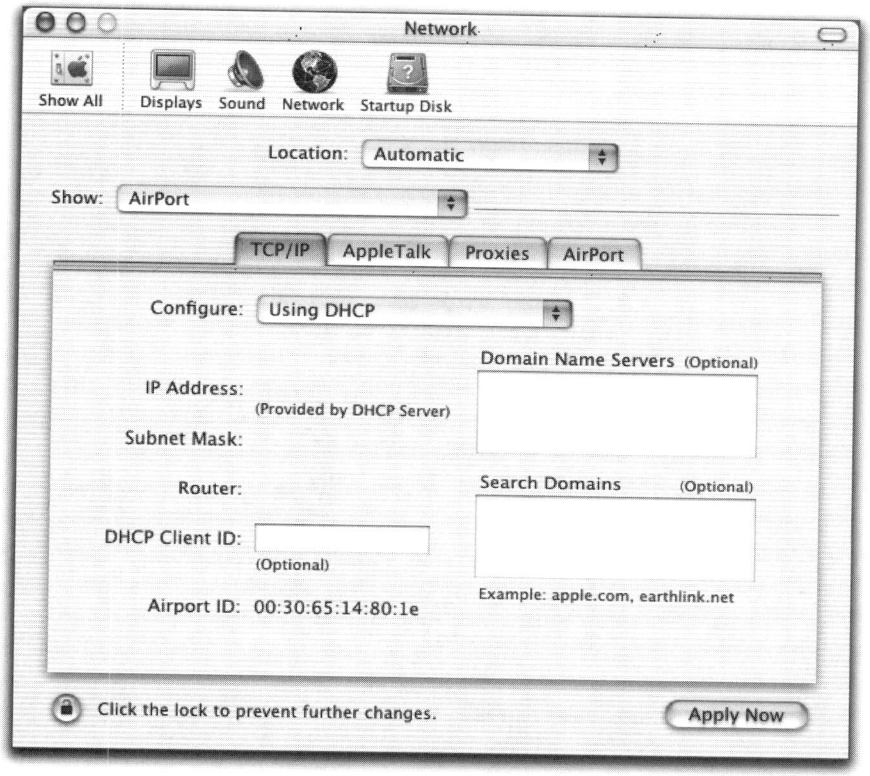

FIGURE 14-2   Network preferences

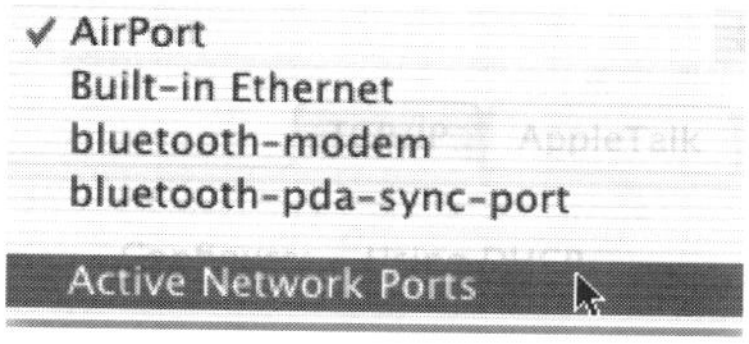

From the second pop-up menu, select the port or modem. If the port or modem isn't visible, select Active Ports, as shown here.

✓ AirPort
Built-in Ethernet
bluetooth-modem
bluetooth-pda-sync-port
Active Network Ports

Click the Internal Modem checkbox (or whichever port or modem you want to use), as shown in Figure 14-3. Also, if you want to disable certain other connections, you can uncheck those boxes. Remember, this applies to the new location you're creating.

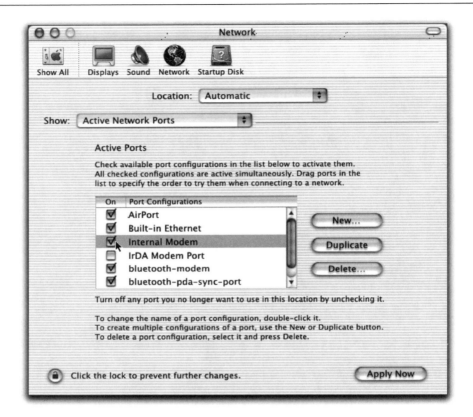

FIGURE 14-3   The modem needs to be active.

Return to the Internal Modem choice in the second pop-up menu, as shown in Figure 14-4. (If your modem was already in this pop-up menu, you won't need to go to Active Ports to activate it.)

Enter the ISP name for your own reference (it's not used in connecting). The user ID, password, and phone number are used. Set these up before you leave. Pay

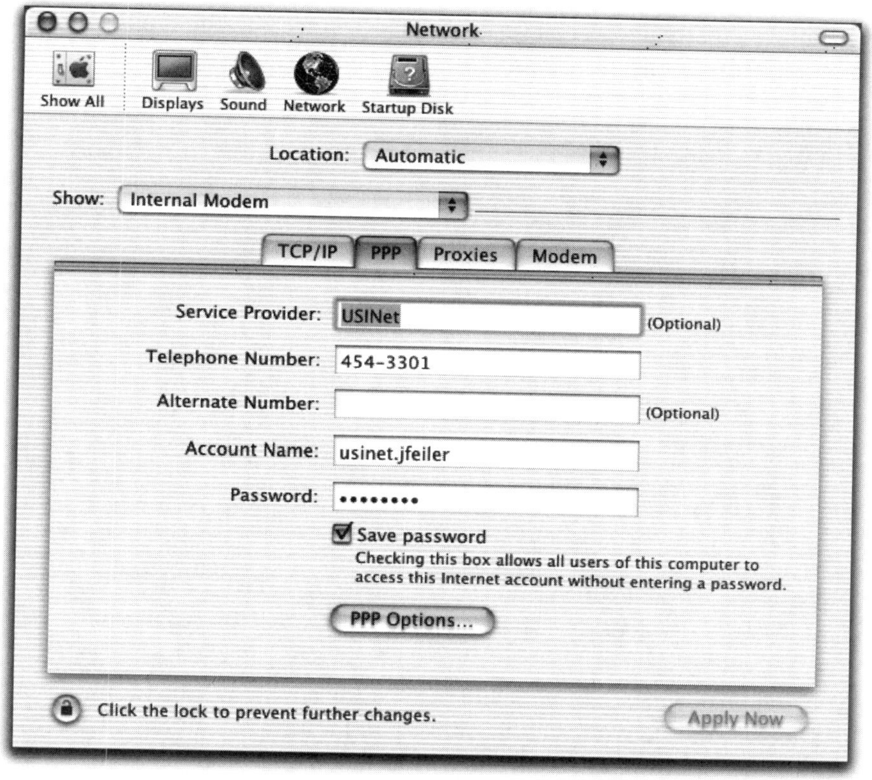

FIGURE 14-4   Enter new location dial-up values.

particular attention to the password. Your standard Internet connection might have its password stored in it. If you typed your password in years ago, you might not have a clue as to what it is. Some ISPs can tell you what your password is, but in other cases, they need to verify your identity, and this could take several days. (At least one ISP will only send you a new password via mail—not email.)

To connect with your new location, change your location (in the Apple menu) to the location you created. Then, use Internet Connect (in the Applications folder) to make the connection, as shown here:

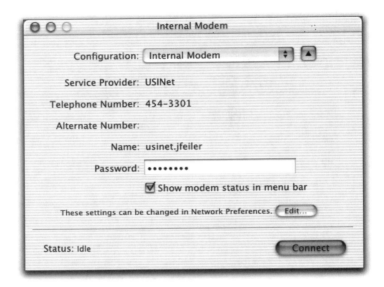

If you want to connect automatically to the Internet, you can set an option in the PPP pane of your network settings in System Preferences for the location you chose. Click the Options button to display the sheet, as shown in Figure 14-5.

The first option (Connect automatically...) launches Internet Connect and dials up whenever you need a network connection. If you're used to an always-on connection, you might not want to use this option. The reason is your computer (and you) are now used to connecting constantly for various purposes. Doing so with a dial-up connection might be annoying—and expensive—so you might want to choose to make the connection deliberately with Internet Connect.

Connecting a New Location for on-the-Road Cable, DSL, or Network Access

This is basically the same process as creating a dial-up connection. The only difference is, instead of choosing Internal Modem from the second pop-up menu (Show, which shows the available ports), you choose AirPort or Built-in Ethernet, as shown in Figure 14-2. Built-in Ethernet should always be available. If it isn't available or you need AirPort, follow the same steps to activate those ports, as shown previously. Then, configure the network connection.

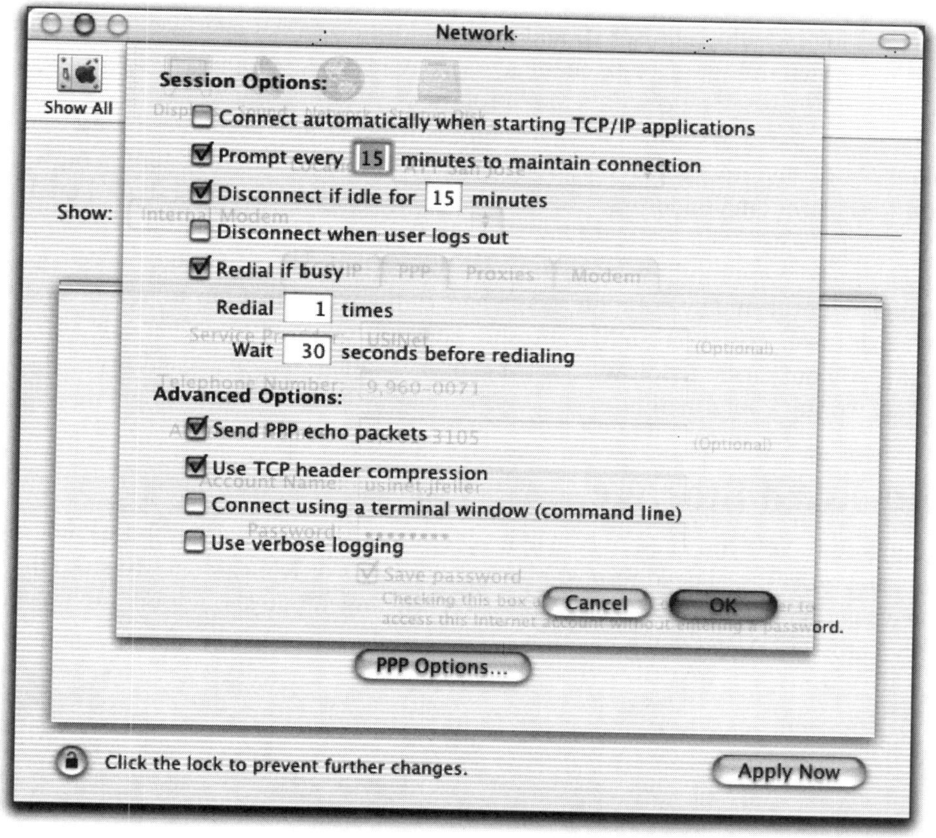

On-the-Road Internet
Connections

FIGURE 14-5   PPP options

NOTE *You can learn more on configuring network and dial-up connections in Mac OS X: The Complete Reference.*

Web-Based Email

Many people use programs such as Mail, Eudora, or Microsoft Outlook Express to manage their email. Others use free, Web-based mail services, such as those provided by Hotmail and a variety of other providers. You can also use your .Mac email account both with a mail program or with Web-based mail.

To access your .Mac email account over the Web, go to **http://webmail.mac .com** and log in with your user ID and password for .Mac. An interface reminiscent of Mail, shown in Figure 14-6, enables you to read mail, compose and reply, and do everything else you do with a mail program.

This accesses your .Mac email account. However, your computer-based address book and mail folders are separate from the Web-based system. You will need to transfer email addresses (or just save them as you read Web-based mail) if you want to use your address book.

The reason you might want to use Web-based mail is you can then access your email account from any computer anywhere in the world that has a Web browser. (It doesn't even have to be a Macintosh.) Thus, if you go into a cyber café in Tahiti, you only need to know your .Mac user ID and password to start reading and answering your email.

On-the-Road Storage

When you travel, you need to consider several storage issues. For digital cameras and camcorders, you need removable memory cards or DV cassettes to store the images and video you shoot. Depending on how much you shoot, you might need spare cards or DV cassettes.

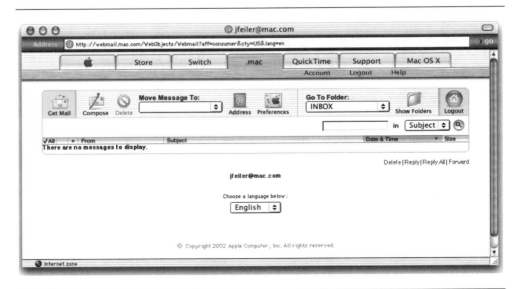

FIGURE 14-6   The basic interface to your .Mac Web-based email

You can transfer photos and video to your computer when you travel (as long as you have the cables). In the case of photos, that can often solve your traveling storage problems, as long as you cleaned off plenty of disk space in advance.

Video is another issue. Its demands for disk space are so large you might need an alternative strategy. Here are two:

- The cheapest strategy could be to buy additional DV cassettes and to do no video editing until you return home.

- The other strategy is to import your video into iMovie on the road. To do so, you need several gigabytes of free space on disk before you start. Rather than fully editing your movie, use the import to discard—permanently—clips or parts of clips you know you'll never use. These include blurred clips, things that seemed a good idea at the time, or severely duplicative clips. Then, you can either export the video back to your camera's DV cassette, or you can leave it on your computer. You can also burn it onto CDs for later use.

You can also travel with a portable multigigabyte hard disk to use for temporary storage. This, of course, is a description of the iPod in FireWire mode. (See Chapter 12 for more information.)

Summary

This chapter has covered the basics of working on the road with your digital hub. Many of the software features you need, such as time zones and alternate network connections, are built into Mac OS X. You access them primarily through Software Preferences in the Apple menu.

Other issues you need to concern yourself with are documentation (proofs-of-ownership, as well as user manuals), cords, and power supplies. You also might need to work with A/V people in office and conference centers where you make presentations. There, the rule is simple: be prepared, ask for little, and be nice to the support staff.

You learned how to create alternate network locations for use, as well as how to handle the issues associated with storage space on the road.

This chapter completes Part 2, the basics of using the digital hub. Part 3 moves on to advanced topics, helping you make better movies, photos, music, and DVDs, whether at home or on the road.

Part 3

Making Better Movies, Photos, Music, and DVDs

Chapter 15

Advanced Movie and Photo Techniques

In This Chapter...

■ **Making Movies Look Better.** In Chapter 10, you saw the basics of how to create movies with iMovie. Here, you find information and tips to make your movies look better with titles, transitions, special effects, and audio.

■ **Integrating Photos.** Movies don't have to move: here's how to add still images to your movies.

■ **PowerPoint in Your Movie.** You can integrate PowerPoint presentations or slides into your movie in several ways. This section shows you how and why to do so, and it also helps you decide on which approach to use.

■ **Making Photos Look Better.** Chapter 11 introduced the basics of iPhoto. Here, you find more advanced ideas for image manipulation with iPhoto, as well as with Photoshop.

This part of the book helps you move beyond the basics of creating movies, photos, music, and DVDs on your Mac. Whether you're thinking about creating professional-looking presentations, digital artwork, or simply the best personal remembrances you can, the chapters here can help you understand what's available, what you can think of doing, and how to do it.

Just as desktop printing brought the power of typography and graphics to hoards of people, so the digital hub brings new possibilities to unimagined millions (literally) of people. However, the technology doesn't automatically bring with it an understanding of the issues involved in creating digital media. Many of those issues (starting with the most basic—how to tell a story) are covered in this section.

NOTE   *One general tip applies to all the technologies described here: less is more. Attributed to twentieth-century designers, such as the great Dutch architect Mies Van der Rohe, it appeared more than a century before that in a poem by Robert Browning. And the concept has been well-known to artists and designers for centuries (with the exception of the Baroque era, which went off the more-is-more deep end). Choose the elements you'll use in your photos, movies, music, and DVDs. Select a variety of elements that make sense to you and help you create the work you want. Use them—and reuse them in a variety of ways. By limiting your repertoire of elements, you unify your work. You can see a contra-example of this in the onscreen presentations many people create. Slide transitions vary from slide to slide—dissolves, wipes, and a variety of other animated transitions appear with no apparent logic. Sooner or later, the audience waits, not for the next slide, but for the next transition. What will it be? (PowerPoint even provides a setting called Random Transition to make creating such a nightmarish presentation easier!)*

Making Movies Look Better

Many of the features of iMovie are available to you when you use the timeline viewer at the bottom of the iMovie window. (You switch between the clip viewer and the timeline viewer with the two icons at the left of the viewer.) This section shows you how to get around the timeline viewer. The chapter then focuses on some of the advanced techniques you can use, which include transitions, visual effects, adding audio, and using titles.

Using the Timeline Viewer

The timeline viewer is visible at the bottom of the iMovie window, shown in Figure 15-1.

FIGURE 15-1   iMovie window with timeline viewer

Tracks

Three tracks are in the timeline viewer:

- The *video track* (across the top) shows each clip. The length of the clips is proportional to their time. The video track contains your digital video—including its audio track.

- Two *audio tracks* (labeled 1 and 2) record audio here or add music and other sound effects in either of the tracks. You can also extract the digital video audio and place it in one or the other of these tracks. As with the video tracks, audio clips are proportional to their timings.

You can turn any of the three tracks on or off using check boxes at the right of the timeline viewer.

Time

Time markings are shown across the top of the timeline viewer. As you can see in Figure 15-1, the scrubber bar also provides some of the information shown in the timeline viewer: small vertical marks indicate the boundaries between clips. The total length of the movie is shown in the upper left of the timeline viewer (11 minutes, 16 seconds, and 23 frames in this figure). In the scrubber bar, the elapsed time is shown (3 minutes, 31 seconds, and 6 frames in this figure). Note, as you play a movie, the scrubber bar and timeline viewer are updated. You can see the elapsed time in the center top of the timeline viewer.

If you select an individual clip in the timeline viewer, it alone is shown in the iMovie monitor, and the scrubber bar reflects only that one clip's timing. Figure 15-2 shows a single clip selected. Note, the time in the timeline viewer and in the scrubber bar is 3 minutes, 31 seconds, and 6 frames.

You can rearrange clips by dragging them. You can also remove them by dragging them back to the shelf or by selecting one or more clips and pressing DELETE.

Splitting Clips

The playhead in the timeline viewer is synchronized with the playhead in the scrubber bar. Thus, any commands you can use that affect the playhead in the scrubber bar can also be used from the timeline viewer. So you can move the playhead (in either the timeline viewer or the scrubber bar) and split a clip at that point. You can also create a still image from the video at that point. (Both commands are in the Edit menu.)

FIGURE 15-2 Single clip selected in the timeline viewer

Working with Transitions

When you shoot a video, one clip follows another with no transition: You turn the camera off, and then turn it on again. (Or you go from Pause to Record mode.)

Transitions are the effects that ease the viewer from one clip into another. Many of these transitions have evolved over decades. If you watch the earliest silent movies, you'll see few transitions. Those that existed in the early days were quite basic: they consisted chiefly of fade-outs in which the entire screen gradually went black or of effects in which the image shrank to a small circle, and then winked out.

Inserting a Transition

Use the Transitions button on the shelf to see a list of the available transitions, as shown in Figure 15-3.

FIGURE 15-3   Using transitions

Drag the transition you want into the timeline viewer (or clip viewer). Existing clips move aside for the transition. You can preview and customize the transition before you add it: See "Modifying Transitions" later in this chapter.

Types of Transitions

When you work with digital media, transitions and other effects can be created dynamically by the computer. All you need to do is to select the ones you want. Remember the caution at the beginning of this chapter and try to avoid turning your movie into a movie about transitions. Think about the types of transitions you want to use, and use them wisely. Experiment with them (that's one purpose for iMovie)! Some transitions, such as *cross dissolves* and *overlaps*, emphasize continuity (you can see the end of one clip and the beginning of the next together on the screen for some time). Others, such as *fade in* and *fade out*, emphasize beginnings or endings as the screen becomes black or goes black. Still others, such as *push* and *scale down,* emphasize the break between scenes: one scene continues to play as another appears to bump it off the screen or to take over the screen. No overlap of images occurs.

Figure 15-3 shows one of the iMovie transitions in action: this is the Scale Down transition, in which the image playing continues to play in a scaled-down version (a picture-in-picture). It gradually shrinks, leaving the new image playing on the full screen.

Using Still Images in Transitions

Sometimes you want a transition to or from a still image—a black screen, perhaps, or a title screen with text on it. To do this, you place the still image into your movie (either via the timeline viewer or the clip viewer), and then you insert the transition before or after that still image.

NOTE   *To create a black screen, drag existing clips aside in the timeline viewer. A blank screen is then created in the "hole" you made. You can also create a black graphic and insert it, but this method is faster.*

Modifying Transitions

The *transitions pane* lets you modify transitions in a variety of ways. The slider at the top lets you choose how long the transition takes to be completed. Be aware, though, if you choose a relatively long time for the transition, you must have sufficient footage to implement it if that footage is used in the transition. (Fade in and fade out require no footage, but cross dissolves require both clips to be played simultaneously during the transition.)

Some transitions—*push*, for example—can be modified with regard to the direction they use. Use the four arrows at the left of the transitions pane to select the direction from which a new clip appears to push the old clip out of the way.

Finally, use the *Preview* button to see what the transition will look like. When you're satisfied, drag the transition into the timeline viewer or the clip viewer. Until you drag it into the viewer, it's not part of your movie.

Adding Titles

The *titles* pane (shown in Figure 15-4) lets you add titles to your movies.

A variety of title formats are available, and you can modify most of them with varying fonts, colors, and sizes. If you click a title, you can see it displayed in the preview window at the top of the title pane.

For some people, a big temptation exists to create silent movie titles—captions that announce what will happen, comments on what has happened, and the like. Remember, movies are primarily a visual medium. Titles should be used sparingly.

One frequent (and necessary) use of titles is to identify people or locations shown in a movie. The *Stripe Subtitle* format, shown in Figure 15-5, is particularly useful for this purpose.

FIGURE 15-4   Titles pane

FIGURE 15-5   Stripe subtitle in action

Adding Effects

The *effects* pane lets you modify one or more clips selected in the timeline viewer or clip viewer. Effects apply to an entire clip: if you want to apply an effect to only part of a clip, split it into two (using the command from the Edit menu).

Figure 15-6 shows the effects pane. You can choose from a number of effects that change the colors of the clip. Some enable you to set values, while others (such as black-and-white or sepia) have no such parameters. You can control the speed at which the effect appears and disappears.

NOTE   *The brightness control lets you create a totally white or black image. You can do a fade to white or black without a transition by using an effect.*

The best way to learn what the effects look like is to experiment with them. Use a single clip and try each effect in turn. You'll quickly find a few effects you're interested in, and then you can continue to refine your investigations.

Making Movies Look Better

FIGURE 15-6   Using the effects pane

Adding Audio

Your imported DV stream video has audio associated with it. You can use two audio tracks for additional sound. You can also remove the sound from the imported clip and place it in an audio track.

Preserving Existing Audio

To take the audio from a clip and place it in an audio track, select the clip, and then choose Extract Audio from the Advanced menu. The audio will be extracted and placed in the first audio track, as shown in Figure 15-7.

The reason for doing this might not be immediately obvious. Figure 15-5 shows one classic example. In the iMovie monitor, you can see the clip that's playing is a train schedule board in a railroad station. The clip's audio consists of the station master's voice announcing the train's arrival and the stations at which it will stop. The audio is interesting, but the static image of the train schedule board isn't too interesting after a few seconds.

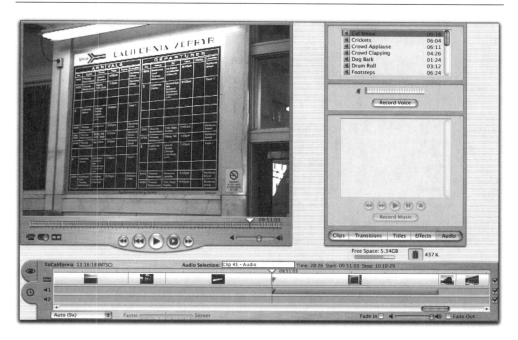

FIGURE 15-7   Extracting audio

Thus, the audio is removed from the clip. You can then move other clips in the movie—images of the train, views of the station, glimpses of passengers, and the like. The audio will play underneath all these. This is what's been done in Figure 15-8. Note, the selected audio runs underneath a number of clips.

Notice in Figure 15-8, the audio and the original video clip both show little push-pin icons. This indicates the audio is locked to the start of that clip. You can use the Unlock Audio Clip command from the Advanced menu to free the audio. Once you do that, you can move the audio elsewhere in your movie, independently of the clip.

You might want to start the station master's announcement during the previous clip, for example. You can unlock the audio clip, and then move it earlier in the timeline. You can then use the other audio commands in the Advanced menu to lock it to specific positions in other clips.

Experiment with the Advanced menu audio commands to see how they work. In doing so, take a clip that has some differentiated audio (this usually means words, not music or ambient sound). That way, you can tell what's happening.

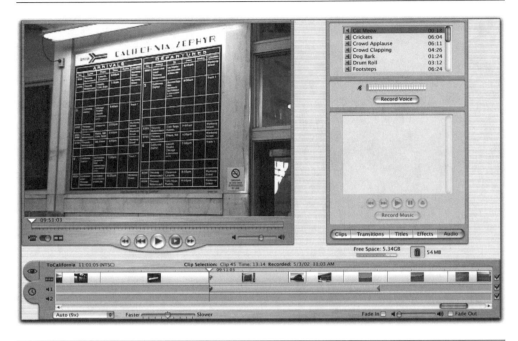

FIGURE 15-8   Extracted audio running under several clips

USB Microphones

You can record audio directly into iMovie using your computer's built-in microphone (if it has one) or a USB microphone you plug in. (Most iMac, iBook, and PowerBook computers have a built-in microphone. Other desktop models generally don't have them.)

To start recording, press the Record Voice button in the audio pane (as shown in Figure 15-8). When you finish, click the same button (now labeled Stop). Your recorded audio will be placed in audio track 1 automatically. It will overlay (not replace) existing audio in that track. (You wind up with the combined sounds.) You might want to clear space in audio track 1 by dragging existing audio down into track 2, so your newly recorded voice stands on its own. When you play the movie, the two tracks play together, but this makes managing the audio easier.

Voice-over narration is a wonderful way of building a movie (see more on this in Chapter 16). If you're shooting your own video, you can concentrate on the video, and then you can add the voice-over later. The alternative is to worry about shooting the video and speaking the voice-over at the same time.

NOTE *This technique is appropriate for adding voice-overs. You can play the movie as you record your narration. If you want to add music or more complex audio, see "Importing iTunes and CD Music" later in this chapter, as well as Chapter 16.*

Using Built-In Audio

A number of built-in audio clips are available in iMovie. Effects such as a dog barking, applause, and footsteps can simply be dragged into your audio track from the audio pane.

Importing iTunes and CD Music

Finally, you can use your iTunes and CD music in a movie. To use iTunes (or any MP3) music, choose Import File from the File menu, and then choose the file to import. The music will be placed in audio track 2 at the playhead.

If you want to import all or part of a track from a CD or DVD, insert the CD. The playlist will appear in the lower portion of the audio pane. You can use the forward, reverse, and play arrows to navigate to the place you want to start recording. Press Record Music, and the music will be recorded and placed in audio track 2 at the playhead.

NOTE *Be careful about importing copyright-protected music. The ease with which you can import music has nothing to do with whether it's legally permissible to do so.*

Integrating Photos

You can add still images to your movie easily: use the Import File command in the File menu and select the file you want to import. iMovie can import a variety of formats, including PICT, GIF, JPEG, Photoshop, and BMP. As described in Chapter 10, use the iMovie Preferences Import tab to specify how long each imported image should be played.

You can use still images for great effects, not only with transitions but also with narration and sound from your video. One particularly striking effect (although one that might be overused) is to take a still image and change it to black-and-white or sepia. Then, the image can come to life as you change it to color and video.

For this effect, start with a still image that's taken from the video. Position the playhead at the beginning of a clip and use the Create Still Clip command from the Edit menu to create a still. Place the still in your movie and change it to black-and-white (using the effects pane). Then, create a transition—perhaps, overlap—between the black-and-white still and the colored video. Drag that transition into the timeline viewer and play the sequence. An interesting experiment is to try the reverse: freeze a video and convert it to black-and-white or sepia. The process is identical (but backwards).

NOTE   *In Chapter 13, you saw how to create a slideshow in iDVD. If you're going to create a DVD, what's usually best is this: create a short movie in iMovie, put your still images in an iDVD slide show, and then place more movies from iMovie onto the DVD.*

PowerPoint in Your Movie

You have two reasons for using PowerPoint slides in your iMovie. The first is

if you want to display all or part of a presentation. The second is if you want to use PowerPoint's formatting tools to create titles that are more complex than you can create with iMovie. (You can use other tools, such as Photoshop and AppleWorks, to do this, too.)

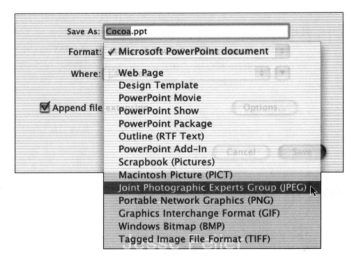

The fastest way to export PowerPoint slides as images is to use the Save As command. First, choose the format you want from the pop-up menu, as shown here. (JPEG, GIF, or BMP will work.)

Then, click the Options button, and choose Save Every Slide, as shown here:

You can then import the exported slides into your iMovie.

If you're creating a DVD, you can have PowerPoint export its slides as a QuickTime movie, which you can then import directly.

Making Photos Look Better

The first part of this chapter considered design issues to make your movies look better. This section considers photos. In fact, the first set of points in this section applies both to photos and movies. These are simple concepts that were mentioned before, but they bear repeating.

First, to make your movies and photos look their best, start with the best images possible. This means all the basics, such as keeping images focused and well-lit. This also means taking many more photos (and filming many more video clips) than you could ever possibly need. Make sure you have a selection of images from which to choose.

Second, get used to editing on your Macintosh. With your digital camera or camcorder, concentrate on the image clarity, focus, and light. Cropping images (particularly still images) is what you can do with plenty of time on your Macintosh.

Adjusting Image Quality with iPhoto

When you select a photo in iPhoto and click the Edit button, you can make a number of changes to the photo. (You can also double-click the photo, and then open it in its own editing window if you set that preference in iPhoto preferences, as discussed in Chapter 11).

The editing tools available to you in iPhoto (across the bottom of the window) are shown here:

You can change the size of the image with the pop-up menu at the left. Two of the buttons work only if you already made a selection inside the photo by dragging with the mouse: the Crop button and the Red-Eye button work on the selected area. The brightness and contrast sliders, as well as the Black & White button, work on the entire image. These sliders and the Black & White button work exactly as the effects controls work in iMovie.

If you open a photo in an editing window, a slightly different set of controls is provided at the top of the window in a toolbar. You can customize these controls using the Customize button at the far right of this toolbar, as shown in Figure 15-9. Drag the controls you want into the toolbar and rearrange them. Drag the ones you don't want out of the toolbar. This customized toolbar is then used for all future editing windows—until you change it again.

Using Photoshop

Photoshop is the major image-manipulation application on the Macintosh (and on other platforms). You could need its features—or you might be quite happy with the limited but powerful set in iPhoto. This section describes two of the Photoshop tools and is designed to give you a sense of some of Photoshop's capabilities and help you determine if you should pursue this program further.

The examples shown in this section both start from the same photo, as shown in Figure 15-10.

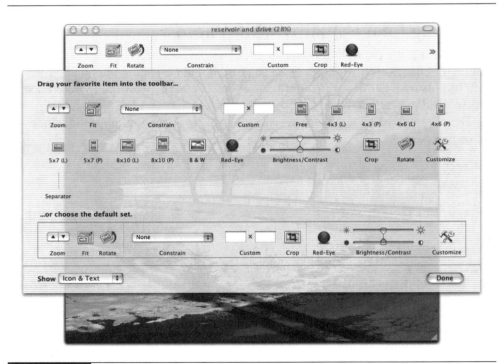

FIGURE 15-9   Customize your iPhoto editing window toolbar.

FIGURE 15-10   Original photo

Taken from a moving train, this is a clear image of a street sign, but the image is taken from the side and it's crooked. Photoshop can help you correct these problems. A fire hydrant is also in the image. Photoshop provides tools to let you easily select and extract parts of an image, such as the hydrant.

NOTE

A number of versions of Photoshop provide varying sets of functionality. Some versions are bundled with equipment (such as scanners). Others are available as entry-level products that are comparable to iPhoto or a bit more advanced. The full version of Photoshop provides tools such as those demonstrated here. Note, too, the choice of features to demonstrate in this chapter has been determined, in large part, by the constraints of a black-and-white book. Photoshop has sophisticated color correction and manipulation features. Photoshop also enables you to do fine touch-ups of images, and these kinds of features aren't easily shown using the printing process of a book such as this. Fortunately, two powerful (even awe-inspiring) features do reproduce well here.

Cropping and Adjusting Perspective

To straighten the sign, you start by selecting the Crop tool from the Tools palette.

Crop tool ────────▶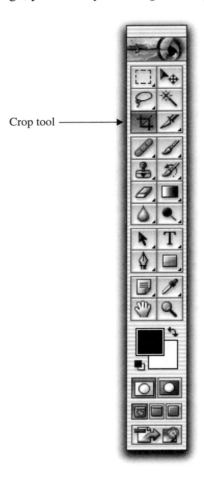

For each tool, the Options palette lets you make adjustments.

Sometimes the Options palette changes, depending on what you've done with the tool. In this case, select the Crop tool, and then select a rectangle in the image, as shown in Figure 15-11.

When you select something with the Crop tool, as shown in Figure 15-11, the Options palette changes.

FIGURE 15-11   Select the portion of the image to crop and adjust.

At this point, make certain the Perspective check box is checked (it's located at the right of the Options palette). Then, drag the corners of the rectangle so they follow the nonrectangular borders in the image of what you know to be a rectangle. Figure 15-12 shows how this is done.

Press RETURN. The image will be cropped and the perspective adjusted, as shown in Figure 15-13.

Photoshop does a lot of complex mathematical processing to make this happen. If you do this—particularly if the image is large and your computer isn't speedy, you might wait quite some time for the image to be adjusted. The first time you do

FIGURE 15-12   Adjust the rectangle.

FIGURE 15-13   The cropped and adjusted image

something like this it might seem like magic and, in some ways, it is. Only when you see the possibilities of digitally adjusting images can you understand what you do need to control with your camera or camcorder, and what you can deal with later on in your digital darkroom.

Manipulating Images in Photoshop

You're probably used to using the mouse for selecting images or parts of images to act on. Photoshop enables you to select images intelligently—using colors to select objects your brain recognizes. Here's a demonstration of this technique.

Start by selecting the Magic Wand tool in the Tools palette.

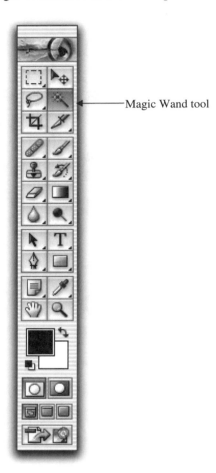Magic Wand tool

You can now click a colored part of the photo, and everything close to that color will be selected. Figure 15-14 shows the hydrant selected in this way, although, as you will see, more than one click is necessary.

In fact, what usually happens with photos of objects in the real world (as opposed to computer-generated images) is the lights and shadows cause an object with a single color to appear as having several colors. Clicking the hydrant initially might leave out a section that's in shadow (thus, a different color from most of the hydrant).

Using the Options palette for the Magic Wand, you can control the sensitivity of the tool to color variations. Use the Tolerance setting to type in the difference in

FIGURE 15-14 Select an object with the Magic Wand.

color (or shades of gray) you'll accept as being the same for the Magic Wand. The smaller the number, the closer the color must be. The larger the number, the less sensitive the tool will be. (If you set the number too high, clicking a red object might wind up selecting blue or even green objects.) Trial and error can help you. Rest assured, the process, though repetitive and possibly tedious, isn't lengthy or difficult.

When you're satisfied you've selected the entire object, you can use Cut from the Edit menu to remove it from the image, as shown in Figure 15-15.

FIGURE 15-15   Remove a selected object.

You can then paste the object into another image or save it on its own, as shown here:

The purpose of these demonstrations isn't to teach you how to use Photoshop. Using Photoshop isn't that hard, but it does require a little more than these few pages. Instead, the purpose has been to show you the sorts of digital manipulation possible with a powerful computer and a sophisticated digital editing program.

Summary

This chapter leads off the third part of this book, which moves beyond the basics of creating bare-bones movies, photos, music, and DVDs into the realm of advanced issues. You saw how to use transitions, titles, visual effects, and audio to create sophisticated movies with iMovie. You've also seen how to add still images to your movies as well as PowerPoint slides and entire presentations.

In the world of still images, you saw how to move beyond the basics of iPhoto to adjust brightness and contrast, size, and how to reduce the red-eye effect. Beyond even that, Photoshop provides powerful digital editing, and you've had a taste of the possibilities that provides.

It's time to stop for a while and get things organized. The next chapter shows you how to plan your digital projects.

Chapter 16

Planning Your Project

In This Chapter...

■ Setting Objectives. Whether you're preparing a fictional movie, a persuasive DVD, or a photo album for the grandparents, know what your goal is.

■ Working from Existing Media. It's easy to import photos, movies, and music, but the world didn't start with digital media. Here's how to work with legacy images.

■ Fixing It After the Fact. This section raises the issues you confront when you have digital media—but not the shots you want. (Yes, it's possible to recover if you missed "I do" at the wedding—if you're the videographer. It's not quite so easy for bride and groom.)

■ Preparing Shots. If you're taking as much footage and photos as recommended previously (maybe five times as much as you need), you need to be able to identify the shots you have.

■ Keeping Track of Things. Digital media takes up space—lots of it. You should confront these retention issues before you run out of disk space (and backup tape space, and CD space, and DVD space. . . .)

The previous chapter helped you make your movies and photos look better. This chapter addresses still more issues that can make your project better and, unlike the previous chapter, which dealt only with visual media, this one applies to all the media you'll use with the digital hub.

Planning your project doesn't necessarily mean creating a bureaucracy and an organizational hell for yourself and others (although it certainly can mean that). Planning a project doesn't always mean work you do before you start. As you'll see in the next section, "Setting Objectives," many cases exist in which you start to plan your project in midstream. Sometimes this is a recognition that things are out of control. Other times, it's an understanding that the tools at your disposal go so far beyond the box Brownies of yore and the out-of-focus home movies you might have grown up with, that you can—and should—manage and plan your projects with as much sophistication as you bring to your movies, photos, music, and DVDs.

A Little Respect, Please

I'm lucky to count the great actress Uta Hagen among my friends. She starred on Broadway with the Lunts (in *The Seagull*) and with Paul Robeson and José Ferrer (in *Othello*), she created the part of Martha in *Who's Afraid of Virginia Woolf?*, and she has received three Tony awards (including one for lifetime achievement). Uta encounters a crowd every time she leaves the theatre after a performance. One evening I met Uta after the show, and a young acting student asked for an autograph. The girl was shy and giggly, and self- consciously invited Uta to come see a play she was doing in a church basement somewhere. "Of course, you probably wouldn't think it's any good," said the girl. Uta looked directly at her and said, "If you don't have respect for your work, how can you expect anyone else to respect it?" The giggles stopped and, in a totally different (and much more mature) tone of voice she said, "Thank you, Miss Hagen." She walked away with her head held high.

Now don't confuse respect (and organization, planning, and seriousness about your endeavors) with dullness or a lack of humor. Comedy, in fact, sometimes takes more effort than tragedy. And don't think you can't have fun with these tools. The woodcrafter who takes weeks to carve a blue jay is organized and has fun. The members of a community chorus who rehearse once a week for months to prepare for a concert have fun—and they certainly are organized.

Setting Objectives

This section addresses the overall issues of projects. One of the biggest mistakes people make when they start to work with iMovie and iDVD is to underestimate their organizational needs. Don't worry: if you do that, as you'll see, you can still recover.

The Project Goal

Some projects are clearly defined—you're asked to make a commercial, you have a job creating a keepsake of a wedding, a group of which you're a member needs an advocacy video or DVD. Other projects appear clearly defined, but are not.

Knowing you're interested in digital media, your boss might invite you to make a promotional video for your company. Is the promotional video for stockholders? For potential new employees? For customers? For the zoning board that's being asked to approve a new facility in the town?

Still other projects aren't defined at all. Perhaps you're going on vacation and you plan to return with many photos and video clips. Somehow, you'd like to assemble them both as a keepsake for yourself (the unedited version) and as gifts for friends (the highly edited and polished version). But what the shape or look of this project is could well be unclear to you until you return from vacation.

Some projects materialize by themselves. Reviewing your photos and movies, you might discover interests you hadn't realized you had. Perhaps you realized you're more than casually interested in urban planning, and you go back to school to study it more extensively. Going back over those travel photos and videos, you could find a large collection of videos showing how people behave in public spaces. Voilà, a new project.

As you see, you can set the goal in advance, as you're working on the project, or long after you've shot the images. Whenever you set the goal, make certain it's as clear as possible. Whether as a friend, neighbor, colleague, or employee, beware the generic, "Why don't you make a video?" request. Narrow down that request: About what? Who for? How long? By what date? What's the budget? If you don't have an understanding at the beginning, you could fail or have an unpleasant relationship with the other people on the project.

NOTE *The digital hub applications from Apple make it easier than ever to create one-person projects. These are sometimes the hardest to organize because you "know" what you're trying to do. Cross-examine yourself in at least as much detail as you would someone else so you know what you're attempting to do. If you don't, you'll wind up with a project that consumes your time and never completely satisfies you.*

Stay Flexible (but Organized)

If you're preparing a Hollywood extravaganza, your project planning should precede your production, and it should be extremely detailed: a great deal of money is needed to make the extravaganza, market it, and distribute it. If it succeeds, that money will be made back, but if it flops, there's little recourse.

Most people aren't preparing Hollywood extravaganzas, so the financial stakes aren't that high (although for a small business, they could be proportionately even higher). The flexibility of the digital hub tools, combined with the power and flexibility of management tools on your Macintosh, make it possible to make changes during your project—changes that could even include changing its objective.

In fact, the project's objective can be viewed as existing over time: at any given time, you should know what you're aiming for, but that goal can change in many cases. Don't adhere to a rigid plan when that plan is no longer useful. Consider this one important tip as you refine your project goals: if you find yourself changing the objective to one you had and discarded previously, stop everything and reconsider your status. One or two dead ends in a project are legitimate, but if you keep going round and round as to the objective, you're probably spinning your wheels.

Working Habits

If yours is a one-person project, you can adjust to your own work habits. If other people are involved in the project, however, it's important to set some common work habits (without becoming a tyrant). One of the most common complaints is about wasting time. If people are meeting at your house or office to shoot or edit video, or to brainstorm a story line, having coffee could get the creative juices going. But if that's what you plan, have the coffee ready. (This might seem a basic point, but particularly in projects involving volunteers, it's an important one.)

Choosing Styles, Themes, and Points of View

Once you decide on your project goal, set the styles, themes, and points of view. These include everything from the look of photos and video to the transitions in iMovie and the menus and themes in iDVD. The objective of your project, together with its intended audience, can help you with this. A project designed to teach natural history to school students should have a different look from a memorial DVD about your grandfather.

You can set these styles before using the digital hub applications: you aren't limited to their themes and graphics. In fact, a good idea is to list your choices on paper. This way, when you're editing your movie or DVD, you can easily see which of the provided effects and transitions fit into your design.

Keeping Things Simple

Many people minimize the number of effects, styles, and themes they use. If you use a limited and consistent palette, your audience will quickly understand (often at a preconscious level) what you're trying to do. For example, in a movie you might choose to use one transition for the basic scenes. Another type of scene (flashbacks in a work of fiction, additional information in a documentary) could be introduced with a different transition. If you adhere to that rule, your audience can understand what you're doing and follow your movie easily.

Working from Existing Media

The world didn't begin with digital media. People have lots of legacy images, video, and movies they'd like to use with the digital hub applications. Some of these are digital, but others are older analog media.

You have several choices if you want to convert legacy media. Service bureaus will convert 35 mm photos (from prints, slides, or negatives), video, and movies to digital versions. If you have a JPEG or TIFF image, you can drag it into iPhoto. If the service bureau converts videos or movies to QuickTime, you can convert the QuickTime movie to a DV Stream and import it into iMovie. Or the service bureau might be able to go directly to DV Streams.

You can find companies that handle these conversions in a number of ways. Ask around among your friends and you might find someone who has used such a service—or who does the work. Because you're likely to be converting heirloom images and videos, you want to be certain the company you deal with is reputable and won't disappear along with the sole remnants of your great aunt's arraignment for murder (charges subsequently dropped). This is an area that's attracted a certain number of dubious characters, so be careful.

If your needs are limited, you can do the conversion yourself. Good-quality scanners are now available for about $100. Frequently, these scanners are substantially less if you purchase them with other equipment. A scanner with a USB connector should work well with your Macintosh. Check the vendor's Web site or the packaging of the scanner to see if it's listed as working with the Macintosh.

NOTE

Before Mac OS X, scanners needed special drivers and software to work with operating systems. With Mac OS X, the special software isn't required in many cases, and drivers for many scanners are becoming more generic. During the transition to Mac OS X, you'll frequently find scanners that come with software that doesn't run on Mac OS X—only on Mac OS 9 and earlier. If this is the case, contact the vendor and ask this question: "Will the scanner work with the Image Capture application in Mac OS X"? Many times, it will, and you needn't worry about installing any special scanning software. For an acid test of scanners that work with Mac OS X, look at the products offered for sale at the Apple store (http://store.apple.com: they work with Mac OS X. You can buy them there or from a local vendor.)

Some scanners come with attachments that make scanning photo negatives and slides easy. If this is what you'll be doing, you should consider one of those.

In the case of video, you can often convert old videotapes to digital video using a digital camcorder. (The entry-level digital camcorders usually now have this feature.) Place the videotape in a VCR or camcorder. Attach the output connectors to the input on the digital camcorder (a special connector might exist for this.) When you play the VCR, the output will appear as input on the digital camcorder, and you can record it on DV tape.

Fixing It After the Fact

Your planning could be all well and good, but sometimes life has a way of throwing you curves. Here are some ways of recovering from problems that arise when some of your footage or images are unusable.

Substitute Footage

If someone walks through the middle of your shot and ruins it, all is not lost. In the case of video, split the clip into three: the good beginning and ending, and the bad middle. Now consider what you can substitute for the middle. Look through your clips in iMovie. Maybe something you discarded before will fit in.

More likely, you'll have to be more creative. Perhaps a reaction shot will do. A *reaction shot* is just that: the reaction of someone to something that's been said or done. Sometimes a reaction is no more than a nodding head or a "um-hmm" comment. If you have that footage—or if you can create it—you might be okay.

If the bad footage isn't long, another possibility is to split the clip as mentioned previously, and then to use a transition that obscures the problem.

If sound is in the clip, you can save it even while you manipulate the images. Detach the audio from the video track (as described in Chapter 15), and you can have the sound play uninterruptedly through a reaction shot or other interpolated scene.

In the case of still images, you can use iPhoto cropping and editing tools (or advanced tools in Photoshop) to manipulate the image.

Voiceovers

Remember, you can record audio on top of your video (or as separate tracks you pair with video in iMovie). A voiceover narration can cover a multitude of sins. In fact, if your project involves considerable live and unrehearsed footage, you might plan from the beginning to use voiceovers, so you're ready for problems.

Caution: The Difference Between Fact and Fiction

There's one important issue to remember. If you're creating a documentary or presenting information as fact, you're constrained in what you can do. (A distinguished television news program got into big trouble some years ago for interpolating the interviewer's reaction shot at the wrong place.)

Preparing Shots

Because you're going to have so many images and so much footage, it's important to identify the content. You have two sets of tools that can help you with this.

First, both iPhoto and iMovie import your media sequentially. This can help you to reconstruct a sequence of events (this is particularly useful when traveling or recording a live event). Before you rearrange clips and images, go through and change clip titles—at least here and there—to meaningful names. Add comments in iPhoto, as described in Chapter 11.

iPhoto records information about each image—including the date and time you took it. (This assumes your camera's settings are correct.) To see that information, choose Show Info from the File menu to open the window shown in Figure 16-1, and then click the Photo tab.

You can also see further details about exposure settings with the Exposure tab, as shown in Figure 16-2.

The second way of identifying images and video is to add identification directly to the image or video (or to the sequence). Take a photo of a street sign or a close-up of a meeting agenda. You might or might not use these images, but they'll serve to identify the images or video clips that follow.

You can also use your own version of a movie *clapper,* the board on which the date, time, scene, and take are written for movies. Each movie shot starts with a close-up of the clapper. You never see the clapper, but it helps the director and the editor keep track of the footage. You can do the same with your videos, or you can use your digital camcorder's built-in microphone to announce the scene. Try to avoid jokes, "Let's hope this is the final take," for example. "Take 1," "Take 2," and so forth can help you when it comes time to edit the movie. (The final take might not be the best one—particularly when you're matching it to other clips elsewhere in your movie.)

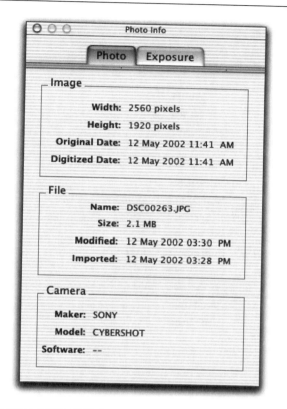

FIGURE 16-1   Check the date and time of the photo with Show Info.

Keeping Track of Things

Last, decide as early as possible in your project how you'll keep track of things. The first item to keep track of is the raw, digital media. Will you use that as your archive, or can you reuse it as soon as you copy the images and video to disk? Sometimes you want to save every last image and video clip (except perhaps those that are definitely out of focus or otherwise unusable). For many people, discarding unused images and video is easiest right after the fact. However you do it, decide what you'll do with the unused images and video clips before they take over your home.

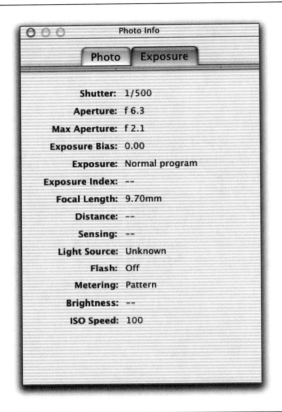

FIGURE 16-2 Exposure information is also available.

For the images and video you keep, you might want to keep track of them exactly as you keep track of anything else with your Macintosh. Do what seems right to you and what makes your project move easily. FileMaker and AppleWorks provide easy-to-use databases you can use to track your project. Some people use Excel as a project manager. As with media retention, decide at the beginning how you'll handle project management, and then do it.

Consider this one last issue with regard to keeping track of things. If you're doing a project for hire, clarify at the beginning who owns the unused media. You might find something that isn't needed for the current project, but that fits in well to a future one. The easiest time to deal with this is before the fact.

Summary

This chapter covered some of the basic project planning issues you need to consider when you work on a project. The powerful tools you have available let you create highly professional-looking projects as well as disastrous, boring, and plain bad projects. Considering what you want to do and how you want to do it can help you create the best projects possible. And when you create good projects, you get more out of your work (especially important if this is a hobby or if you're a volunteer).

Some of the topics covered in this chapter included how you can integrate legacy images, video, and movies with your new digital media. You've also seen some techniques on how to recover from problems in shooting new media. Finally, two sections helped you to organize and identify media as you shoot and import it. They also provided you with some ideas for Macintosh software to help you manage your projects.

The principles in this chapter apply to all projects. The next chapter is specific: it applies to projects that fall into the category of art. In those projects, your goal is to present your ideas and your point of view. This is in stark contrast to documentaries and other projects in which your goal is to present nothing but what has happened in a spontaneous and unrehearsed manner. The persuasive and interpretive techniques discussed in the following chapter apply as well to many other type of projects—in fact, they apply to nearly any project that doesn't represent itself as an unrehearsed documentary.

Summary

Chapter 17

Art and Artifice

In This Chapter...

- ■ Art Photography. This section examines the issues involved with still images.

- ■ Making Your Own (Dramatic) Movie. Here are the basics of making your own movie.

This chapter continues the journey toward making your projects look better and be more effective. In Chapter 15, you saw how to improve the look of photos and movies. In Chapter 16, you learned how to organize and plan your projects. Now it's time to look at the ongoing work you'll do on a project. This chapter hones in on the activities of the photographer, art director (for still images), writer, and director (of movies). By way of a preview, the next chapter goes deeper into some specific issues involved in shooting photos and movies. Chapter 19 looks at the role of models and actors. (Models and actors are jointly referred to as *talent* by many people. This term is sometimes used in a slightly derogatory way, as in, "The talent needs a cup of coffee.") Chapter 20 shows you how to move on to the next step in the world of the digital hub.

Remember, in the world of the digital hub, so much of the work is done or made easier by the technology that you might wear a whole millinery store's worth of hats. For now, put on your photographer, art director, writer, or director hat. (If you're determined not to play one of those roles—if your goal is to be a model or actor, for example—this chapter can still provide important background information.)

NOTE   *This chapter discusses making movies and creating photos that are, to a greater or lesser extent, works of interpretation and fiction. They might be framed prints you hang in an art gallery, or they could be movies that wind up at the next film festival. They can also be commercial projects for print advertising or commercials. They can have political or social messages, or they could be interpretations of events. In all cases, the objective is to bring both information and interpretation to the viewer. The interpretation can be such that someone can quite legitimately disagree with it. For the sake of simplicity, this chapter talks of art photography and fictional movies. The other types of work described here should also be considered as part of the discussion.*

Art Photography

If you want to create art photos, start by exploring the work that's already been done. Look at images—photos as well as paintings and drawings—with a critical eye. This means looking not only at the picture ("pretty mountains," "rough seas," or "distracted woman") but also at the composition of the image. Watch yourself watching the image: what do you see first? Then, what do you see only after studying the image for some time?

Look at great photos (these include photos in art galleries as well as many commercial photographs in advertisements). Ask the same questions. With commercial photos in particular, look at how your attention is drawn to the product.

If you live in a city with a good art museum, go there. You'll probably find gallery tours, guidebooks, and other instructional materials to help you develop your eye. A public library should have (or be able to get) good books about art and high-quality reproductions. And, of course, the Internet now provides a wonderful opportunity to explore fine art.

NOTE
*An excellent place to start browsing is Yahoo's list of museums and exhibits around the world—**http://dir.yahoo.com/Society_and_Culture/ Museums_and_Exhibits/**.*

As with all photos, two primary places exist to create an image. The first is when you compose the shot and take the photograph. The second is in the (traditional) darkroom or digital manipulation stage.

In composing shots, you can learn from the images you've seen in your research, as suggested previously. You might want to explore the following specific issues. Some of them apply when you take the photo, and others apply after the fact, when you're working with iPhoto, Photoshop, or other similar tools.

Focus and Attention

What are you photographing? What's the most important element in the image? For many people, the subject of the photo should be in the center of the image and that's the end of that.

But you can bring focus onto an object or scene in many other ways. If you use a shallow depth of field (that is, a large aperture or a small f-stop), you can literally focus on the object of attention, while leaving the rest of the image slightly (or largely) out of focus. (This technique works well with a telephoto lens.)

You can use similar types of techniques with tools such as Photoshop. For instance, you can blur parts of the image you don't care about, or you can use the magic wand to select the object(s) you care about, and then change the color of the rest of the image—often to black-and-white. This effect was striking when first used (one red rose in a black-and-white image, an orange glass of juice in a black-and-white image . . .). Now, many people find it overused. But don't forget the technique: after overuse comes disuse, and then rediscovery.

Two techniques discussed later in this chapter can also help you focus attention. You can frame the object you care about within the image's frame by surrounding it with space: a baby in the middle of a green lawn is more noticeable than a baby in a nursery full of babies. You also can direct reactions to the object of attention: photograph people (or animals) looking at it.

Size and Perspective

When photographing objects, sometimes it's impossible to tell how large they are. An image of a wristwatch on a white background suggests its size (the watch bracelet can only be of a certain size. An image of a wristwatch on a wrist gives an even clearer indication of its size. But what do you make of a photograph of the face of a clock? The face of Big Ben in London has been reproduced on many desktop clocks: a close-up of either one looks like the other.

To give people clues as to the size of objects, you can place objects of recognizable size in the image. A ruler, of course, is a classic and somewhat scientific way of presenting size. Other objects (such as the wrist in the previous example), can help. For a supporting object to help people understand the size of the primary object, the supporting object must be recognizable as to size.

One frequent size comparison involves people. Certain types of objects (trees, monumental buildings, and the like) can be of varying sizes. Placing people in front of them—either posed or walking by—can help identify the scale of an image.

You can use size comparisons to manipulate perception. Some short people prefer not to be photographed next to taller people unless they're seated. Other people who are somewhat shorter or taller than average prefer to be photographed only when sitting (this works if their height, or lack of it, is mostly in their legs). Advertisements have traditionally used size comparisons to their advantage: the vegetables in a bowl of soup look bigger if the bowl is smaller. When using these techniques, you must be careful not to step over the legal and ethical lines that apply to the work you're doing. Where the distinction between making something look good merges into distorting something is a tricky area (and beyond the scope of this book).

Another technique for manipulating size perception is the use of perspective. You can use this in two basic ways. Objects that are closer appear bigger than those that are distant. If you place smaller objects in the rear of a scene, the eye will often perceive them as being even further away than they are.

Framing

You can frame images and objects within images. This can be used to draw attention to certain areas of the image, as well as to make it more visually pleasing. Typical framing devices are objects found in the location where you're shooting—the branch of a tree in the foreground (but not obscuring the primary image), for example. As noted previously, you can frame objects with a lack of detail—blank space or relatively unoccupied space around them.

You can frame objects with tools such as Photoshop and iPhoto. iPhoto provides external framing for photos in albums and Web sites it creates. You can choose from a variety of frames as you create them. You can use parts of existing images you created by drawing or photographing them as frames for new images. This involves cutting a hole in the object to serve as a frame and placing the new image in that hole. A common example of this type of framing is the use of a recognizable building (such as a college library) as a frame around images or text in a presentation.

Directed Reaction

The last technique discussed here is directed reaction. In *directed reaction,* you direct the reaction of viewers by showing a reaction within the image itself. If the photo contains images of people laughing at an event that's shown, you can suggest the event is funny (or that it isn't funny and the onlookers are callous). Likewise, if people are shown crying at a visible event, you suggest they, at least, find it sad—and the viewer might also consider this response. When you have an opportunity to pose or compose images, consider this technique if the main event is ambiguous.

NOTE

The difference between posed and composed images is that posed images involve your placing people in position. Composed images, on the other hand, involve your choice of a location from which to shoot and the bounds of the image you shoot. All photographic images are composed, although some are composed to a greater extent than others (a point-and-shoot landscape view is only minimally composed).

Art Photography

This section provided only a brief overview of some of the techniques you can use to improve your photos. Experiment with these and other techniques, and be sure to look critically at as many photos, paintings, and drawings as you can to come up with other ideas.

Making Your Own (Dramatic) Movies

This section looks at some of the issues facing the writer and director in creating a movie. Although geared primarily to dramatic movies, the techniques also apply to many other types of movies. Remember these two primary points:

- Movies are a visual medium. You might be the world's best raconteur, but you need to adjust to a visual way of telling stories. As you'll see, DVDs pose an interesting further challenge.

- As with still images, the best way to learn many of these techniques is to watch movies critically. Great movies by great moviemakers are instructive, but so are failed movies. You can find books about movies, such as *Citizen Kane,* analyzing every step of the production process and how the movie is constructed. You might not find such books about bad movies, but you can learn to critique them yourself—and, in so doing, learn to critique your own movies.

Many books have been written on filmmaking, so this section provides an overview for you. If you're interested in beginning to learn about video- and filmmaking, here's a place to start. As you proceed, you can consult other resources. (The available books change as new ones are published and old ones go out of print. Browse the catalog of your public library and use an Internet search engine to find currently available books.)

The topics covered in this section are

- Telling the Story

- Creating a Shooting Script

- Making a Shooting Schedule

- Directing the Project

- Postproduction Issues

- Distributing and Promoting Your Movie

Telling the Story

Two aspects of telling the movie's story apply not only to movies, but also to verbal stories (including novels). Point of view and sequence are the issues common to all stories. An additional story-telling issue arises with the use of DVDs.

Point of View

Who is telling the story? Two basic approaches are here. One is that of narration: an individual recounts the story. You learn who this narrator is fairly early on. ("Call me Ishmael" is the famous sentence at the start of *Moby Dick*.) The narrator might be part of the story or an impartial observer. (See Agatha Christie's *Who Killed Roger Ackroyd?* for an interesting use of an involved narrator.) The narrator can be trustworthy or biased, but one theme is common: the viewer or reader sees nothing except through the eyes of the narrator.

In movies, the narrator can provide a voice-over narration. In other cases, the movie follows a narrator character and observes scenes through his or her eyes. Nothing happens that the narrator doesn't see.

Using a narrator is a common way to start making movies: after all, you yourself can add a voice-over narration and, as the writer/director, you are, indeed, telling the story.

You as writer/director can tell the story without the use of a character to narrate. You play omnificent creator to the story (which is true), and you tell it—display it, rather—as if nothing stands between the viewer and the events shown. Unlike the use of a narrator, such an "objective" telling doesn't constrain you to having a narrator in all shots or commenting on everything.

You can combine these two techniques, and you can also vary them. Perhaps the classic variation on the use of narrator is the great film, *Rashomon,* in which a story is told and retold by several people. Another variation is to pass the narration chore on from one character to another as the story progresses. (The television series *Law and Order* follows this sequential focus.)

No matter what technique you choose for the point of view of your movie, make certain it's consistent and logical. If you use a narrator's voice-over, use it throughout and in the same way. (The narrator might introduce scenes but never comment within them, for example. Or, the narrator might only comment on scenes.) Audiences are frequently confused when an inconsistency occurs in the telling of the story. An exception exists to the rule of being consistent: many movies start (or end) with a voice-over narration that's used nowhere else in the movie. Audiences accept this convention willingly.

So, before you begin your movie, answer the question: who is telling the story?

Sequence

Many stories are told in sequence from beginning to end, but several other sequence options are available to you. You can interrupt a sequential story with *flashbacks* or *flashforwards*—scenes that occur out of time sequence, but that are relevant to the current scenes. Some movies exist entirely as flashbacks or flashforwards.

Another possibility is to tell the story repeatedly from different points of view. In such a case, obviously, the sequence is sequential, but repeated.

If you aren't telling a story from beginning to end, make certain the sequencing is clear to the audience. Not being able to follow a story is one of the most common criticisms of movies—including some major releases. Every year, film critics muse in print about how jumbles of incoherent scenes get put together as a movie no one can follow.

DVD Issues

DVDs pose an opportunity and a challenge to moviemakers. Users can choose which scenes to play in which order. You can construct a DVD of independent scenes, which users can piece together as they see fit. If you do this, you should consider whether to structure all or part of the DVD.

For example, your movie might follow a character through an entire day. The first section could be called "Morning," and the viewer could choose from several scenes. Perhaps the character is interesting, so the viewer might choose to watch "Getting Up," "Going to Work," and "Taking a Break." Another viewer might choose to watch "Going to Work" and be done with "Morning." In "Afternoon," another set of scenes could be available, and so on through "Evening" and "Night."

This type of structure—easy to create on DVD—would have a high-level menu of

- Morning

- Afternoon

- Evening

- Night

The scenes would be placed within each option. This is a different structure from an undifferentiated one consisting of a high-level menu of

- Getting Up

- Going to Work

- Taking a Break

- Having Dinner

- Going to Bed

- Having Lunch

- . . . and so forth

Allowing the user to control the sequence and substance of a movie doesn't necessarily mean inviting chaos. This is an area many innovative filmmakers are exploring today.

Creating a Shooting Script

Before starting your movie, you need a script—in fact, you probably need several sets of written documents. If you're experimenting with your first movie, a page or two will probably be sufficient. The following is an overview of the documents you need. (The first document, a project proposal, was described in Chapter 16.)

Treatment

If you're working from existing material—adapting a novel or short story to the screen, for example—you usually start from a *treatment,* which is a relatively unformatted discussion of how the material will be presented as a movie. A treatment assumes a basic familiarity with the material, although you might summarize the story in the first paragraph of the treatment.

The treatment should discuss how the story will be told. This is where to discuss the point of view (something that frequently changes from the page to the screen). Transferring novels to the screen generally requires cuts. The treatment should focus on what's left in, not what's left out.

A treatment can be part of a formal approval for a project. For commercially made movies, some of the backers might read nothing but the treatment.

Storyboard

Storyboards are used extensively for short movies, particularly commercials and animated films. A *storyboard* consists of a sequence of images, with one or two sentences of description or pseudodialog beneath them. You can create a storyboard easily with a tool such as PowerPoint. The images can be sketches drawn by hand, or they can be images you create or modify digitally.

The sequence of images in the storyboard might be extremely detailed, with a single image for each shot or line of dialog (this is common in advertisements). For movies, the storyboard could have one image per scene.

The objective of a storyboard is to show how the movie will move. The treatment is a text-only document describing what will be in the movie. The storyboard shows—in a rough way—what the movie will look like.

Script

The actual script of the movie is more detailed than a treatment or storyboard. Movie scripts contain three elements:

- The dialog the characters speak (including a narrator, if any)

- Stage directions and instructions for the actors involving entrances and exits, "business"—such as picking up a knife, and the like. These directions also include events that take place, such as "the car explodes" or "the sun sets"

- Visual directions for the camera, such as a close-up on one character, or the camera following a character's line of sight to observe

A number formats are used for scripts, and each needs to distinguish among the three types of information in the script. If you're submitting a script for production, you need to use the format specified by the producer. If you're working on your own, use whatever format is easiest for you and the people you work with. Remember, actors will be scanning through the script looking for dialog—particularly their own lines. Camera people will be scanning through looking for the shots they need to set up. Designers will be looking for effects, events, and sets they need to create or manage. Thus, your script needs to be clear for each of these people. Of course, your script also needs to be coherent to the backer, producer, or director who reads it to get an overview of the project.

The script should be divided into scenes: a *scene* is generally a sequence of events that takes place in one place during a single period of time. (The place can be quite large—a galaxy in a sci-fi movie, for example, and the events could be complex—such as the battle of two animated space ships.)

Within a scene, individual shots might be specified in the script, or they could be added to it by the director and/or cameraman. All this information is needed in creating a detailed shooting breakdown as described in "Making a Shooting Schedule" later in this section.

NOTE

Chapter 19 delves into behavior on-camera but, for now, remember not only that movies are a visual medium, but also that things happen in movies. All movies are action movies—not just westerns and shoot-em-ups. Look for actions and events. Eschew contemplation. (If you want to study this issue, look at the various films made from Hamlet *and watch the "To be or not to be" soliloquy. Then read the text carefully. Can you find one film version that conveys the emotion of the words in all their meaning?)*

Improvisation

Some movies rely in whole or in part on improvisation for their dialog. You might think improvised dialog is more real but, in fact, it often is stilted and quite boring. If you're going to improvise scenes, construct your script as outlined in the previous section but, instead of dialog, specify what each character does (not says). Don't write, "Chris and Jean have lunch to discuss the movie." Instead, let the actors know what they're trying to do in the scene: "Over lunch, Chris asks Jean to invest $100 in an experimental movie. Jean refuses. Chris breaks off their friendship." With these guidelines, you'll probably get more usable footage.

If you're using improvisation, beware of its pitfalls. In particular, beware of actors setting things. Before the improvisation, they might decide on certain lines they'll use or actions they'll take, or, in the course of one take, something interesting might happen, which they then try to force into a subsequent take. The concentration of using these set pieces distracts from the improvisation, and you wind up with the worst parts of improvisation and scripting.

Making a Shooting Schedule

Movies are almost always shot out of sequence. To prepare a shooting schedule, you go through the script and for each scene you write the:

- Scene number

- Location

- Actors involved

- Props involved (*props* are things that are handled)

- Special needs (snow machine, for example)

- Time of day

Making Your Own (Dramatic) Movies

■ Time needed to shoot

■ Comments

■ Scheduled time

You can make this a list on a piece of paper, or you can use a database such as FileMaker, a spreadsheet such as Excel, or an all-in-one program such as AppleWorks. Whatever tool you use, make certain you can sort the data on any field.

When you go through the script, write down this information in order by scene, filling in the information from the script. When this is done, you need to come up with a shooting schedule. One common way of doing this is to sort the scenes based on location. It's usually easiest to shoot all the scenes in the dining room together, all the scenes by the highway together, and so forth.

Another way of organizing scenes is by the actors involved. In movies big and small, you sometimes need to work around an actor's availability. If you have a specific actor only for one or two days, you might need to shoot scenes in several locations all at once. (Or you might need to do some adjusting to the script to minimize that actor's presence in other scenes.)

Once you decide how to shoot the scenes, you can fill in the final information: the scheduled time. Pay attention to the time of day, especially for outdoor shots. If you have three shots taking place by the side of a highway at twilight, you might need to shoot them on three separate days if there isn't enough time to complete a scene during twilight.

The shooting schedule is your bible during the making of a film. Until you create one, everything is easy to follow: the treatment and script are both sequential and tell the story from beginning to end. Once you rearrange the scenes to accommodate production, you must rely on your shooting schedule. For actors, adjusting to shooting a movie out of sequence can be difficult—they might react to events that haven't yet occurred by shooting out of sequence. More important, sometimes an actor discovers something new in a part, but is unable to incorporate it because later scenes have already been filmed.

Directing the Movie

Once your shooting schedule is complete, it's simply a matter of shooting the movie. The following two chapters discuss some of the issues that arise during that process regarding locations and actors.

The tools a director has for telling a story with a movie have increased over the years and, certainly, the digital products such as iMovie (and the higher-end Final

Cut Pro) bring enormous power to anyone interested in movies. The basic elements of telling a story with a movie were set long ago, however. Among the most important pioneers was D. W. Griffith, director of many early movies, including *Way Down East* and *Birth of a Nation.* Lillian Gish, one of the stars with whom he worked, described the process of making those movies in detail in her memoir, *The Movies, Mr.Griffith, and Me* (Prentice-Hall, 1969). Reading about Mr. Griffith and Miss Gish is worthwhile to see how they and others developed the visual vocabulary we now take for granted. For example, in *Birth of a Nation,* a movie about the American Civil War, Griffith discovered early on that people had trouble following the battle sequences. He then filmed the movie so the opposing troops were always on the same sides of the screen.

As you work on a movie, keep your mind and eyes open. You might have a clear picture in your mind's eye of what the finished movie will look like, but if you're working with a group of people, you could well find that each contributes a slightly different point of view and the final movie might not look at all like what you planned. If you continually revise your vision, incorporating good ideas from others, the final movie will be much better than you planned. If, on the other hand, you preside over chaos, it will likely look much worse.

No clear-cut answer exists as to how you should approach this issue. Some directors were famous—notorious, even—for forcing actors to adhere slavishly to their predefined idea of what should happen in the movie. Some directors even have gone so far as to wish they didn't have to work with actors. Other directors allowed so much experimentation on their sets that their movies are never on time, are always over budget, and are satisfying only to the actors (but not to audiences, who are bewildered at what is happening).

Postproduction Issues

Once you finish shooting the movie, it's time to edit it and put it together. You'll probably have a number of clips for each of the scenes in your shooting schedule. Some can be discarded immediately for technical reasons. Others need to be viewed, considered, and edited together. The basic process for any movie is the same as the process described in creating movies with iMovie.

This is also the time in which you add sound effects and music to your movie. If you're using music as a soundtrack, you should be collecting or recording the music during the filming. (This is a task someone else can do while the filming is going on.)

Keep your shooting schedule updated with information from editing. If it's in a database, you can use it to track individual clips (or, more likely, editing sections of several clips). As you build the edited scenes of your movie, you can track what is where with your database.

Distributing and Promoting Your Movie

Unless you're making your movie purely as an experiment or class project, you want to distribute it so people can view it. You can consider several ways to do this. For short movies, you can post them to the Web so people can watch them online. (You can post small movies to your iDisk. And, if you're genuinely proud of movies you make, you can submit them to the iMovie gallery at **http://www.apple.com/imovie/gallery/**.)

You can burn QuickTime movies that aren't too long onto CDs and give them to your friends. Longer movies can be burned as QuickTime movies on DVDs for playing on a computer or imported via iDVD to DVDs for playing on a DVD player.

A market might exist for your movies and you could be able to sell your CDs or DVDs. One way in which many people have broken into filmmaking is with promotional movies. Perhaps a business will pay you to make a promotional movie, or such a business might support an entertainment movie in return for onscreen credit at the beginning or end.

Another possibility is to make a movie that's given away in exchange for a donation to an organization. Perhaps a local arts organization is interested in using your movie as a gift to donors. You might get some of the money to help defray your costs.

In the last few years, film festivals have become more and more important in the movie business. Online film festivals are in their infancy. If you're interested in specific topics or types of moviemaking, look for such online film festivals (or start one yourself!). They provide a forum both for moviemakers and for people interested in specific topics or types of movies to meet, discuss, and exchange movies.

Summary

This chapter covered some of the main issues involved in creating art photos and dramatic movies. In both cases, your concern isn't simply reporting what the camera sees, but in telling a story and providing a point of view and a commentary on it.

The first step for both still images and movies is to open your eyes and look at the many existing examples—good and bad—you can find in books, libraries, museums, and movie theatres. Don't simply look, but try to understand how the images were created and how the movies tell stories.

From there, you can proceed to understand the needs of these visual media. Whether a still image or a movie, you're telling a visual story with images. There's little room for words or commentary.

For movies, you have seen the basics of telling a story. Then you have seen how to move from a treatment to a storyboard and then to a script.

Once the script is created, you go back and reorganize it by scenes into a shooting schedule that enables you to schedule actors and locations effectively. After the movie is complete (there's more information on this in the following two chapters), it's time to move into postproduction and, finally, to distribute and promote your work.

Chapter 18

Photographing Places and People

In This Chapter...

- ■ Digital Etiquette. Here are some of the considerations you should take into account before using your camera. It's not just a matter of manners: some of these points have legal implications.

- ■ Directing the Shoot. You have the camera, and the scene unfolds before you. Before shouting "action," you'd better know what to expect and how to handle the unexpected.

- ■ Finding Talent. You can find people to help you, both as actors, and as technical support. Here are some places to look.

- ■ Scouting Locations. For most of you who are just starting out, it's easier to use real locations for your movies. Good locations don't fall out of the sky, though: you need to know what you're looking for.

- ■ Creating Locations. If you can't find a location, you need to construct one in a studio or other location. Here are some of the tips you can use to create a believable set.

This chapter continues exploring issues for the director of a movie (or a still photo shoot). Here, the focus is on what to do as you work with the people and locations you want to film—particularly when you don't control them directly. (The following chapter, which focuses on actors and models, deals with those issues.)

Remember, this is only an introduction to complex issues. While this is probably enough to get you started, as you proceed you might want to read some of the many books about movie making written by directors, actors, and critics. You should also watch every movie, video, and commercial you can get your hands on. Don't watch them for entertainment: watch them critically, note what works and what doesn't work, as well as how things are done.

NOTE *For the sake of simplicity, the chapter discusses the issues involved with movies. Similar issues (but fewer of them) also apply to still images, but except in the few cases where a distinction exists, still images are subsumed in the movie discussion.*

Digital Etiquette

Most people enjoy being photographed. Even more, most people like having their children, pets, cars, houses, and gardens photographed. Some people don't like to be photographed, while still others like to be photographed—sometimes. This section provides an overview of some of the issues you should consider before you remove your lens cap.

Getting Permission

You have a powerful tool in your hands: your digital camera or camcorder. With a click of a button, you can capture people's looks and behavior. You can preserve the image of a beautiful parade or of a run-down boarding house that should be closed by the building inspector. Use this tool carefully. More than one photographer has been attacked for taking photographs of people or places. Some have been arrested and even killed. Unless you're a journalist, you're unlikely to encounter such extreme reactions to your photography but, remember, in many cases, you're subject to rules and wishes of others.

What Journalists Can Photograph Without Permission

Rules and customs vary from country to country. However, this guidance from The Reporters Committee for Freedom of the Press can help at least in the United States. "Generally, what can be seen from public view can be photographed without legal repercussions. Photographs taken in private places require consent."

For more information, you can contact them or visit their Web site:

The Reporters Committee for Freedom of the Press
1815 N. Fort Myer Drive, Suite 900, Arlington, VA 22209
703-807-2100
http://www.rcfp.org/

Most important, if you're asked not to photograph something, don't. Some people believe for religious reasons that they or their loved ones must not be photographed. Others believe for personal reasons that they shouldn't be photographed. Whether it's based on vanity or religion, the wish should be respected. Your right to photograph a person, place, or object is normally subordinate to the right not to be photographed.

Certain places are off-limits to cameras. Some houses of worship don't permit cameras at all, or they might permit them only when a service isn't under way. Some museums and art galleries prohibit the photographing of their works of art. Military installations commonly cannot be photographed—and the definition of a military installation can be quite broad (civilian port facilities could come under this rule).

If you think you can outwit the rules, be prepared to be caught and punished— possibly severely. You might lose your camera, or your memory card could be confiscated or destroyed.

Most people not only don't mind being photographed, they enjoy it. In fact, as you see in the section "Directing the Shoot," you might wind up losing control of your camera to your subjects.

A special situation arises when you or your camera aren't visible. You can quickly find yourself subject to legal prosecution for spying if you place an unobtrusive camera where it can capture candid shots of people who haven't given permission.

Releases

For your own personal use, you generally don't need a formal release. You can ask permission or, if a language barrier or distracting noise exists, simply pointing to your camera while looking at your intended subject is usually sufficient.

NOTE *If you're taking photographs of people you don't know, consider getting their name and address (and email address). That way, not only can you identify them in your album, but you can also send them a copy of the photo. With email, this is simple and it's a nice thank-you gesture.*

If you're planning to use your photos or movies beyond your own use, you might need signed releases from the people you photograph. Different rules govern the use of photographs for news stories and for other uses. In fact, the same photograph or video might require a release for one use but not for another. For definitive information, consult an attorney. For more general information and for samples of releases, use a search engine such as **http://www.google.com** to search for "model release." You will find a number of sample releases, many of which you can reuse as is or customize for your own purpose.

Special Considerations

Even if you have permission to shoot—and even if you've been hired to record a wedding or other event—you can't (or shouldn't) shoot some things without explicit permission.

Eating is an activity that usually doesn't look good on camera. It might be fun to shoot, but most likely you won't keep the footage. It's hard to eat (or drink) on camera without looking bad.

Other activities that are frequently a waste of time to film include getting in and out of cars, as well as small activities (such as putting a key into a lock)—unless you have a zoom lens to focus on the activity.

Private moments—love, grief, or intimacy—require special sensitivity. As noted previously, photographs and videos used for news media are subject to different standards than those used for hobbyists or for sale to magazines, books, videos, or other purposes.

If you're working for news media, displaying a press pass from an accredited organization can help to distinguish you from others. And a press pass might gain you access to people and places that are useful to your work.

Directing the Shoot

In most cases, you're both camera person and director of your shoot. (With a tripod and remote control, you might also be on-screen talent! See Chapter 22 for more about that.) This section addresses the issues you face as a director of a shoot. Those issues are separate from those you face as a director of actors or models, which are covered in the next chapter.

You need to consider many of these issues. This chapter highlights some of the more common issues you should be able to handle with your own photography and movie making.

Planning Your Shoot

If you followed the procedures in the two previous chapters, you've planned your movie down to the individual scenes. You might even have planned for individual shots (professional directors do that). This applies not only to fictional movies but also to any movie scenario you can reasonably work out in advance. For instance, if you're hired (or you volunteer) to tape a wedding, you can sit down and list the major scenes you want to shoot. Ideally, you should work with the bride and groom on this, so there's no surprise as to scenes you did or didn't get. (Sometimes, the most problematic scene is the ceremony itself: bride, groom, officiator, and proprietor of the wedding location all might have opinions or demands with regard to filming the ceremony. Those opinions and demands should be worked out in advance.)

For any shoot you can reasonably anticipate, look at lighting and camera angles in advance. In the case of an event such as a wedding, visit the location at the same time of day as the event—and when it's set up for a similar event. Many catering halls and ballrooms have a variety of configurations in which they can be set, and your prime camera angle might be occupied by a bandstand when you arrive for the ceremony.

In all your planning, get familiar with what is where and how people are likely to move. Plan your shots and anticipate issues, such as where the sun will be. After you've done all this, put it all in the back of your mind if you're shooting a live event. You have to know when to let go of your preconceptions as events proceed. Your job, after all, is to film the event that takes place—not the event you have in your head or even the event that was planned. Having done your homework, you can concentrate on what's happening at the moment.

Rehearsing the Shoot

Rehearsing a scene with actors is different from rehearsing a shot. Rehearsing the shot is for your benefit, to make certain your camera angles are correct and you can get from one side of the hall to the other as, and if, needed. For this purpose, you can go so far as to have people stand in for the people involved while you test your shots. (You might get the bride and groom, but they could have other things to do.) Markers might exist that they—and you—can use to make sure they're in the right spot (and you're focused on the right spot). It might be the forward edge of the front pew or it could be a line marked unobtrusively on the floor with tape.

Such lines are called *marks*, and actors refer to *hitting their marks* when they get to the places they're supposed to be during a scene. Such marks are used by people other than actors. Michael Korda describes visiting former President Reagan in California and noticing marks on the floor that President Reagan—a former actor—hit when greeting Korda (at which time an assistant snapped an in-focus photo).

Setting People in Motion

If you're taping a wedding, the principles certainly know what to do. But if you're taping a less formal event (or even the wedding reception), the people at whom you aim your camera might not know what to do. Their reaction could be to freeze or to make funny faces. Two ways of getting good candid shots in informal settings are to ask people to ignore you and to behave or talk normally, or to suggest what they should do. "Lance, why don't you tell that story about the chenille bedspread?" or "Would you look at me and tell me how you met the bride?"

You might add that you'll be editing things later and ask people to continue going until you tell them to stop (or walk away to continue filming elsewhere). Try to avoid winding up with a soundtrack that consists mostly of your voice giving directions. It's difficult to eliminate your voice from the finished tape if it's interspersed with other people's comments that you want to keep.

Remind people, too, that not only should they continue, but that you'll also continue. If something bad happens, assure them you'll stop or fix it later. You don't want the soundtrack to consist of interesting comments from your subjects interspersed with their questions asking "Is this all right?" See if you can make a pact that neither you nor they will talk about the taping until the take is over.

NOTE   *Some people are embarrassed to use the words "Action" and "Cut"—it seems as if they're giving themselves DeMille-like airs. In fact, those are the easiest words to use to start and stop the action. If you want to make movies, make movies, and don't apologize for it.*

Stopping or Modifying the Action

If you do need to stop—and you're certain you need to do so—stop immediately. There's nothing worse than finishing a three-minute (or twenty-minute) take and learning you have to go all the way back to the beginning. Review the tips in the previous chapters for covering problems that could occur, and experiment with covering gaffes and mistakes. In this way, you can judge quickly whether you'll have to stop. In most cases, barring extreme conditions, you can continue shooting.

Finding Talent

If you're shooting events, the participants are provided. For your own movies, however, you might need to recruit people. You might need two sets of people: on camera models and actors (known as *talent*), and off screen helpers and assistants (known generally as *craft*).

In both cases, you can draw on several resources. Young actors are frequently willing to work for little or no money to get the experience—and the finished photos or video. If acting schools are in your area, contact them to see if they have a public notice board where you can post your needs.

When it comes to offscreen work, high-school students who are interested in movie making might be willing to work with you for the experience as well. If you're highly experienced, you have a lot to teach, and the work could be rewarding for students. If you're a novice (as are they), you can all work together to hone your crafts. If you're all learning together, be sensitive to this fact: although you might own the camera and be the director, you can't boss people around as if you were a Hollywood director. (Even Hollywood directors understand they usually get better results without the totalitarian stance. Being nice to the crafts is a cardinal rule for many directors.

In addition to acting schools, community theatres are good resources for acting talent. For off screen work, community colleges can be good resources for people interested in technology, construction, and the mechanics of movie making.

And don't forget the many people who are wonderful types and characters. Your life is usually made easier if you cast people who are used to performing in one way or another: teachers, members of public boards, politicians, and others who are used to public speaking or appearing in front of a group frequently work well in videos. One of the difficulties with untrained actors is they might have trouble repeating a scene over and over until it's right (often because of problems that have nothing to do with them). The woman who has presented a fire-safety class weekly for several years to volunteer fire fighters should know how to repeat something over and over.

Scouting Locations

For documentaries and videos that record events, your locations are given to you. For your own movies, you either need to find locations or to create them. *Scouting locations* refers to the search for locations you can use with little, if any, modification in your movie. Production companies for movies (and commercials) employ people to find such real-life venues, which can be used for filming.

To scout locations, you need to make two lists:

■ First, list the requirements for the location that are set in the script. Does the room need to accommodate two or twenty people? Does a working stove have to be there? Is there room for the horse to turn around?

■ Second, list the requirements you have as a director. In addition to the area to be photographed, there must be room for you and any assistants you're lucky enough to have. You might need power for lights or to augment/recharge your batteries. You could need space and facilities for people to relax between takes and to prepare for their scenes.

Depending on the needs of the project, you might want to indicate which requirements are negotiable.

To find locations, use every tool at your disposal. The first step is usually to consider if you have or know of a location that will do. Or, does one of your friends have the right spot? Proceed from there, casting a net wider and wider until you find what you need. (One interesting resource could be that bulletin board at an acting school. If they post notices for Actors Wanted, they might also post notices for Locations Wanted.)

When you find the right location, first ask permission to use it. Specify the purpose, as well as the date and time you need it. Be aware that some apparently public locations (sidewalks and streets, for example) might require permits for their use. In general, the more disruptive your filming, the more likely you are to require permits, or even payments, for the use of the space.

Once you find and book a location, go back over your shooting schedule to see what's needed to be added to the location. You might need to bring extra furniture or, more commonly, to remove some furniture temporarily from a room. You might need to bring specific clothes for actors or props to be used. Although your shooting schedule is your bible, go back to the script itself and reread the scene. Double-check that you have everything and, in the case of things that could be lost, stolen, or broken, that you have a backup ready.

Creating Locations

If you can't find a location, you can create a location in a studio. (Chapter 20 describes some of the equipment you can use to create a studio and provides some suggestions on where to create your studio.)

Location shooting is often easier for people who are just starting out with video because it's one less thing to worry about. If you're creating a set for a scene, you need to start from scratch to create the reality that will surround your actors. To begin with, watch some low-budget movies and look at what works—and what doesn't—in their sets.

You can borrow several tricks from film and television. One of the most important has to do with windows in a set. If you can see out a window, you need to provide a view from that window, which can be difficult. Cover windows with gauze curtains that allow lots of light (but no images) to shine through. (Soap operas do this all the time.)

If you're building a set, stairs are almost always a complication. Unless needed for the scene, consider a hallway or a staircase that rises visibly for two or three steps, and then turns to go up out of sight. In such a case, you need to build or borrow the two-step unit, but the rest of the staircase is hidden and can merely be a flat platform.

Limit the objects on your set. If you need to re-create the set, then you need to place every object exactly in the same place for every shot. Beware of objects that can change over time. Again, watch the soaps. You might see bouquets of flowers occasionally but, more often, you'll see decorations in the form of empty vases, decanters, small pieces of sculpture, and the like. The advantage these have over flowers is they don't change. You can mark a location for a small sculpture with tape on the top of a table, and then relocate it exactly whenever you need.

However, remember your set does need objects on it. Actors need objects to use (see the next chapter), and a barren set looks fake. (Even a prison cell has a multitude of objects in it.) As a test, find a location for your scene and write down every single object in it. (Even if you can't get permission to shoot in a location, you can probably get permission to make an inventory of its objects. Or you can make such a list from a painting or photograph.)

Summary

This chapter has looked at the director's issues in preparing and shooting scenes. It concentrated on the issues involved in photographing events and locations in real life, which you can't control or can only control minimally. You've also seen how to find talent and locations for your own movies.

Now comes the issue that's been absent from this and previous chapters: actors. The following chapter is directly primarily to actors, so you, as the director, should read it to see what's happening on the other side of the lens. And, if you're an actor (or you want to be one), that chapter will address your problems and the issues you face.

Chapter 19

Looking Good and Behaving Well on Camera

In This Chapter...

■ Learning to Have Your Picture Taken. This isn't an inbred skill. Have you ever noticed how many infants and toddlers bawl when they're placed on Santa's knee in front of a camera? Here's how to do your part to look good on camera.

■ Do, Do, Do... Whether you're acting in a movie or officiating as an announcer or a teacher in a special-purpose video, you need to remember a few basics about how to behave on camera.

■ What the Stars Know. Few people have as much on-camera experience as movie stars. Part of their job is giving interviews. And another part of their job is working with the many people who help to make movies. Here are some lessons the stars have learned.

■ What Max Factor Knew. Yes, a man named Max Factor really did exist. He knew how to help people look better on camera.

This chapter is geared to people who appear in front of the camera. This could be you, or it could be people you interview. It might be actors who appear in your video or anyone interviewed to describe or promote your project. Tips for each of these people and the role each person plays are provided here.

> **NOTE**
>
> *Photographing a mountain is easy: it stays still and changes slowly. True, the play of light and shadow varies as clouds pass and the angle of the sun changes but, basically, the mountain is simply there. Animals are more difficult to photograph, but our expectations are constrained. We expect them to be cute, ferocious, or asleep. Whatever message or information animals give is conveyed in their posture and position, as well as in the gesture and sound of those animals equipped to produce them. People, though, are different. They move. They communicate with their voices. And we expect everything to make sense—what the person says and does, as well as what you, the photographer, record. This chapter is about this most difficult issue in photography.*

Learning to Have Your Picture Taken

Some people look good on camera almost all the time. In a small fraction of cases, that's because those people instinctively know how to behave in front of that strange device that is a camera. In most cases, though, looking good on camera is a matter of study and practice.

You can wing it when you're called on to appear on camera but, chances are, the results will be disappointing to everyone. Another possibility is to learn what you need to know when the situation arises. The best option of all is to do your homework and practice in advance so you're prepared.

Do-It-Yourself with a Tripod and a Remote

One of the easiest ways to learn how to have your picture taken is to lock yourself in a room with a digital camcorder placed on a tripod. Turn on the camcorder, and then start. Most digital camcorders today have a viewfinder, as well as a small LCD, on which the picture is shown. You can rotate the LCD so the subject being photographed—you—can see it. For now, either don't rotate it or simply don't look at it. (You might have to turn the LCD away from yourself so it doesn't distract you.)

Set aside enough time in one or several sessions so you can try each of the following.

Talking to the Camera

Speak directly into the camera as you would when you're being interviewed. Describe what you did yesterday or tell a story about your dog, your children, or something you saw recently. The point of this session is to learn how to behave in front of the camera. As you review the tape, you'll probably see a number of things you could have to work on. Among them might be some of the following:

- Watch for "umms" and "uhs" as you pause or compose your thoughts in midstream.

- Watch your eyes. In real life, you often look up, down, or away from someone you're talking to as you engage in conversation. Looking up, down, or away from the camera is distracting. If you're going to talk to the camera, talk to it.

- Are you stumbling over words or not making sense as you tell your story? Many people do this. See "What the Stars Know" later in this chapter for some tips on speaking extemporaneously on camera.

- Are you fidgeting? This isn't a good trait to develop in real life but, on camera, it can be profoundly annoying.

- Are you moving excessively? You're working with a camera on a tripod that remains motionless. If you're being photographed, the videographer can follow your motion but, in most cases, it's better not to wander around (viewers can start to get seasick if you bob and weave, and the camera has to follow you). Before starting to speak, make certain you're comfortable—not stiff, but comfortable in a position you can reasonably hold for some time.

- If you're being photographed, the camera is most likely focused on your face. The face conveys a lot of information in addition to your words. Don't hide your face with your hands (this includes rubbing your eyes, scratching your ear, and so forth).

Repeat this exercise until you feel comfortable and until the resulting tape looks good. You should get to a point where you don't have to think about any of these issues: when you stand in front of a camera, they should all come naturally.

If you don't trust your own judgment, you can ask someone to help you review the tape. (You should certainly do this if your first reaction is you're perfect—or hopeless.)

Before you certify yourself as "camera-ready," try two more steps:

- If you did all this standing up, repeat it sitting down (and vice versa).

- Now that you've learned not to fidget, learn how to use your hands. Your digital camcorder should have a battery charger. If you're using the battery in the camcorder for your experiments, the battery charger isn't in use. Pick up the battery charger and describe how it works, where you put the battery, and how you plug it in. What you're looking for is the ability to look at this object you're holding in your hands, as well as at the camera, as you describe how to use it. Too much eye contact with the camera can make you look fake (and you might drop the battery charger because you're not looking at it). Too much attention to the battery charger could leave you with your head down, looking at it, and with the top of your head pointing toward the camera. This isn't easy but, fortunately, you can watch many product commercials on television and imitate to learn some of the basics.

The tips in this section can help you work well on camera. Professional actors and models study, practice, and take classes for years to hone their craft. If you want to move on, you should consider those types of training.

Reading on Camera

This is another difficult task, similar in some ways to handling the battery charger. Where do you look? Where *must* you look? First of all, you must see the text you're reading. If it's on a table in front of you (as is the case for a newscaster), you have to look down. If the text is on a large piece of paper next to the camera, you can make eye contact with the camera while reading the text. (On television, these large pieces of paper are sometimes called *idiot cards*.)

Depending on what you're doing, you might be able to combine both techniques. If you're teaching or otherwise talking to the camera for some time, you can have an outline next to the camera where you can see it. You can move your eyes from it to the text from which you're reading, and then back again.

Again, the point of this exercise is to get used to the task and to understand what you look like as you do it.

Talking to Someone on Camera

If you're talking to someone on camera—being interviewed or interviewing someone yourself, for example—you have some further issues to consider. The first is a simple one that requires a good deal of practice. If you talk to someone as the two of you are sitting at a desk or in adjoining chairs, the camera will observe the conversation—and you might never make eye contact with the lens (or the viewer). Many newscasts use a pair of anchors or announcers, and they hand off stories to one another. Watch them to see how it's done. The most common way is for one person to turn to the other, make eye contact, and ask a question or make a comment. The second person continues making eye contact for a moment, and then looks toward the camera. This is far less complicated than it sounds because, in real life, we make far less eye contact with one another than you might expect. (The widespread myth that an honest person "looks you in the eye" is simply that—a myth. In fact, having any kind of meaningful conversation is difficult if your eyes are locked onto another person's eyes. Try it and you'll see.)

You could find yourself in a more complicated situation: your on-camera partner might not be so experienced as you are. In this case, your job is to prevent that person from mumbling or talking directly to you (and, thus, looking away from the camera). You can try to do this by cheating toward the camera as you look at the other person. (*Cheating* in this sense means looking a little more toward the camera than toward the other person.) With luck, the person will catch on and follow your lead.

This experiment obviously requires you to work with a partner. You can critique one another (kindly and constructively, please) and mutually develop your on-camera skills.

Get Comfortable with Yourself

Many people don't like the way they look on camera. If this applies to you, treat it as a starting point. If you don't like your mannerisms and fidgets, reduce them. If you don't like your clothes, change them. And, if it's something you can't change, get used to it.

The ease with which people can take photos and movies means many people are being photographed more than ever before. As celebrities find out (much to their dismay), candid photos of them shopping or relaxing often wind up on the covers of supermarket tabloids. Periodically, the tabloids run exposés on off-duty stars, often with headlines such as "Who's the Grungiest?" You might not be tabloid fodder but, for better or worse, more and more people are in the situation in which the first step they take outside their door is liable to land them in someone's digital memory book.

One point to consider is most people don't have symmetrical bodies and faces: some people have a better side to their face. This could be because of a mole or a blemish, or it might be a bump on the tip of their nose (when viewed from one side or the other). If you're going to appear on the business end of a camera lens, part of your job is objectively discovering this sort of thing, and then—politely— asking to be photographed from the proper side. (This isn't much more complicated than the minor accommodation made for left-handed people at a crowded dinner table.) The photographer or director wants the images to look as good as possible, so, if you can provide this assistance, it's almost always welcomed.

NOTE   *Beware of overcompensating or causing new problems. Some people who fear they have more than one chin (or a "turkey-wattle" neck) compensate by holding their heads up to straighten out the problem. While this gets rid of the neck problem, they often appear haughty and aloof. As always, study your photos, critique yourself, and learn how to look your best.*

Do, Do, Do . . .

As the Gershwin brothers wrote in their famous song, "Do, do, do. . . . " This section is geared primarily to people appearing in front of the camera in dramatic roles, but many of the principles extend to other types of on-camera appearances.

> **NOTE** *To learn how to act in general or to learn how to act on camera, you should study and practice with a good teacher. Many good schools and classes exist. Also, many excellent books are available on acting. Among the most important are Uta Hagen's two books:* Respect for Acting *(with Haskel Frankel, John Wiley & Sons, 1973) and* A Challenge for the Actor *(Scribners, 1991). These books are used extensively in acting classes around the world and actors swear by them.*

Acting is doing. Feeling, thinking, and simply being a character are nothing if they don't lead to action the audience or viewer can see. Because movies are a visual medium, this ties right into the audience's need for visible action.

If you think you have the message that acting equals doing, don't go overboard with the wrong kind of visible actions. Don't illustrate your thoughts. Don't decorate your performance with distracting activities that keep your hands or body in motion, but don't forward the character's intentions (and, hence, the story that's being told). An action can usually be described in simple terms—to cajole, to convince, to refuse, to survive. Physical acts aren't necessarily actions in this sense. Many mediocre action movies are criticized because of gratuitous violence. Gratuitous violence usually consists of attacking someone for no good reason: killing someone in pursuit of an objective isn't gratuitous. It might be wrong and offensive, but it's not gratuitous. (When Othello strangles Desdemona, it's anything but gratuitous: inevitable and tragic, yes, but not gratuitous.)

Another issue that frequently arises for beginning actors is that of losing control. It might feel good to sob on camera or on stage but, for the most part, such sobbing doesn't work. It could embarrass the audience—and you might forget your lines. (The same is true for laughing hard.) Your job is to be in control of yourself. If you're just starting out as an actor or as a director, this trap could catch you.

One point to remember is this: unlike an actor, people in real life rarely want to cry or laugh. Most of the time, people do anything to prevent themselves from losing control. The greatest actors don't move you by crying. Instead, they move you by their efforts *not* to cry.

Anne Jackson Learns How to Cry

In her wonderful memoir, *Early Stages* (Little, Brown and Company, 1979), Anne Jackson describes how she learned this lesson. Studying with Herbert Berghof at the New School, she was cast in a part she felt she couldn't handle. As she describes it, "I read the stage directions with a sinking heart—my character had to 'break down and cry.'" She went up to Berghof after the class and explained that she couldn't play the part because she was a comedienne and didn't play "crying parts."

Berghof crossed out the stage direction, and then said to her, "You know, Annie, as in real life, nobody ever plans to cry." Jackson comments, "He'd opened the door a crack for me."

Still on the issue of losing control, here's another important point: actors should never hurt other actors. If you're a director, part of your job is to make sure everyone is safe. Remember this especially if you're starting out with digital video to explore what can be done. Horrible accidents (including deaths) occur periodically in even the most carefully prepared movies. If you want to convey a sense of danger, you can do this in many ways without putting yourself and others at risk. (Look at Alfred Hitchcock's movies to see how much danger and horror he can evince with a minimum of danger to the actors.)

Finally, if you're an actor in a movie—particularly if you're working with a director who is also new to the medium—remember this important point: don't wander around. If you examine movies and television shows carefully, you'll see the camera doesn't move much within a scene. Many shots might be within a scene and many camera angles could also exist, but the camera usually stays put. If you, as an actor, start to wander around, the camera might have to follow you. As the camera moves, it might encounter different lighting conditions. The sensors in a digital camcorder could take a moment to adjust to the new lighting and the transition might be unusable. If you're going to walk out of the shot and if you expect the camera to follow you, work with the director to make certain the effect is positive. (You don't want to walk out of the shot and hear a cheer from the crew who hope you'll never return!)

What the Stars Know

Part of the job of a movie star is being able to appear natural on camera—in movies, as well as in the interviews and publicity shots that go with movies and television today. Not only movie stars, but many other people—politicians and captains of industry, for example—take lessons and practice to hone their on-camera skills for these purposes.

The previous sections of this chapter have helped you learn to have your picture taken and how to behave on camera when you appear in front of it. This section wraps up a few additional tips you should learn and practice before you need them. These tips can be useful in interviews, which you can use to promote your digital hub projects. While these points might seem simple and self-evident, it's amazing how many people don't know them.

Where to Look

Before you start out on a given shoot, know where you're supposed to look. The director or interviewer should help you understand what's expected. If no information is given, ask or suggest. If people are around the camera, you might find looking at them, rather than the camera, natural. Unless you're looking at someone who is also on camera (an interviewer, for example), this is almost always a mistake.

Concentrate on what you're saying and what you're being asked. A lot could be going on behind the camera—the next interview might be setting up or the weather map could be upside-down. That's not your business.

The ability to concentrate and compose your thoughts under the stress of a live interview can help you to be invited back again. If you're the director, try to make the situation easier for the people you're working with by minimizing disruptions.

The Tally Light

The *tally light* is a light (usually red) that's on when the camera is recording. On a digital camcorder, the tally light is visible both to the operator and to the person being photographed. In a studio with multiple cameras, the tally light might switch from one camera to another as the control room staff chooses one shot over another.

When the tally light is off, the camera isn't recording. You might as well stop what you're doing because it won't be seen. On the other hand, if the tally light is on, keep going. The director will stop a shoot that has gone fatally wrong. If the tally light stays on, the director believes that whatever catastrophe you might think is happening can be fixed later. Don't direct or observe yourself: do your job and trust the people you work with.

What the Stars Know

NOTE

Obviously, this trust can be misplaced sometimes. Remember, many of the biggest stars wind up doing interviews in less than ideal circumstances, and they manage to survive. Being asked back often depends on your ability to rise above the circumstances. And being asked back might, in turn, mean publicity and promotion for your projects.

What to Say

If you're an actor working from a script, you needn't worry about what to say. If you're speaking without a script (in an interview, for instance), you do have to worry about what to say. Relying on the interviewer to take care of everything is often a mistake. You should be totally prepared yourself. (If you're the interviewer, you can apply these rules yourself.)

First, have your *talking points* ready. What do you want to say? If you're promoting a dog show, have the date, place, time, and contact information available. For a media interview, provide that information to the interviewer, so it can be repeated or used as a graphic on the screen.

In addition to talking points, think of questions you could be asked (and share them with the interviewer). An interviewer might try out questions on you in advance of the interview: feel free to make suggestions for rewording or alternative questions. Except in the case of aggressive exposé interviews, the case is usually that everyone wants the interview to be interesting to viewers and to cover the major points. Summarizing the questions in advance isn't wrong. (However, rehearsing the interview in detail can rob it of spontaneity.)

You might think of a few phrases you can use in the interview. Use them only if they make sense—there's nothing worse than wasting most of an interview trying to work in your sound bite. But having some phrases that sound good, make sense, and are comfortable for you to say could give you a reputation for being a good interview.

What Not to Say

In addition to preparing talking points and sound bites, make certain you don't use information that shouldn't be revealed. Even if you're off microphone before or after the interview, don't provide off-the-record information in a casual setting. The interviewer could easily forget what's on and what's off the record. A journalist taking notes should be able to keep track of this but, even in that case, you run the risk that something could slip out of your mouth (or the journalist's mouth or typewriter) that shouldn't have been said. The simplest way to keep a secret is the oldest way: don't tell anyone.

Also, if you're doing interviews to promote your work, think carefully (and in advance) before making negative comments about other people and projects. You're revealing the kind of person you are (or think you are) in an interview, and you're frequently using yourself and your ideas to help persuade people to look at your work.

What Max Factor Knew

Yes, Max Factor did exist. Mr. Factor was a makeup artist who worked in the early days of movies. Max Factor's major achievements centered around his understanding of the special needs of movies for makeup. In fact, he won an Oscar in 1929 for his work in this field.

Makeup and lighting are closely allied. Theatrical lighting is often colorful, with a variety of strong colors blending on stage to create a natural effect. Video lighting is often less colorful: its major objective is illumination, not coloring. (Remember the repeated admonitions in earlier chapters about having enough light.)

As a result, the lighting used in video often washes out color and makes people's faces pale. Max Factor was one of the pioneers who understood that movie lighting and movie close-ups require actors to appear natural (but with substantial help from the makeup artist).

Three reasons exist for using makeup in video.

- Because the bright lights could wash out detail or natural color, you might want to use makeup to counteract this effect.

- You might need to correct a minor blemish on the skin.

- In dramatic situations, you could need to change a person's appearance.

The first two reasons are encountered most frequently in the videos you'll make. People who normally wear makeup can usually adapt their standard makeup for video. As with so many issues, the suggestion here is the same: try it and see what it looks like. Put on the makeup you normally use and see what it looks like under the lighting conditions you'll be using for your video. You might need to modify it—for some people that means reducing the amount of makeup.

Summary

This chapter addressed some of the trickiest issues in photography: taking photos and movies of people, as well as looking good and behaving well on camera if you're the person being photographed. You might be photographed for a variety of purposes. You could be making a video or posing for photographs, or you might be appearing on video (perhaps television) to promote your work. Each situation requires different considerations.

But all of these have certain common features:

- First, before the fact, get comfortable with yourself and the camera. Practice, practice, practice being photographed. Critique yourself as you review the photos and videos. The point is not self-congratulation or self-flagellation but, rather, to make appearing in front of a camera second nature to you.

- As an actor, remember actions (not activities) are what tell your story. (The same is true for a speaker.) Make certain you can identify your actions, objectives, and intentions with regard to the people you're talking to in a dramatic scene. If you're talking to the viewer, consider the same points.

- Next, consider what you need to know to speak in an interview and to behave well on camera. Maybe you're promoting a movie—or your candidacy for office. Being well-prepared can help you look good, get your message across, and be invited back.

- Finally, remember Max Factor's Oscar. Makeup for the movies—and, today, for video—is essential. It's not the same heavy greasepaint used in nineteenth century theatrical extravaganzas. Often, natural beauty does, indeed, come from a tube.

Movies are a little more than a century old. Movies with sound, as well as movies with color, are much younger than that. You're starting from technology that's more advanced than that available to actors such as Charlie Chaplin, the Gish sisters, and many of the Hollywood stars from the '30s and '40s. (Color wasn't commonplace until after World War II.) Many of the people involved in shaping the movies have written memoirs. If you want to understand the medium you have at your fingertips, watch the movies and devour the memoirs. You can skip over the gossipy bits: what you're looking for are the asides that show you how people have confronted and faced the same problems you face today.

Chapter 20

Creating a Digital Studio

In This Chapter...

■ Finding a Studio. When a corner of the kitchen table is no longer satisfactory, you need to find your own workspace. Here are some suggestions.

■ Equipping a Studio. Now that you have the space, what do you put in it? These are some of the essentials for studio work.

■ Advanced Imaging. High-end cameras and digital camcorders have some common features you don't find in the consumer and prosumer models. They're described here (and their prices are shown).

■ Advanced Audio. The audio tracks in your digital movies can accommodate higher-quality sound than you can record with the built-in microphones. You can use the suggestions in this section to improve your audio.

■ Advanced Lighting. Light has been a mantra throughout this book. Here are some relatively low-cost solutions for providing the kind of lighting you need for good photos and movies.

■ Moving to Pro. Apple has advanced software tools that move beyond iMovie and iDVD. This section provides a brief overview of Final Cut Pro, DVD Studio Pro, and Cinema Tools for Final Cut Pro. This section also shows how these advanced software tools differ from the basic tools you can get free from Apple.

This chapter—the last in this part of the book—provides a roadmap for you to move on to more advanced and sophisticated techniques and facilities. You might want to do this simply to improve your skills and resources, or you might decide to move into a more professional mode. Remember, the tools you have with prosumer cameras and camcorders and the basic Apple digital hub applications are more sophisticated than many of the tools available even to professionals only a few decades ago. Adding more sophisticated software, more powerful hardware, and more complex facilities won't, in and of themselves, make your work better. However, they will enable you to improve your skills and move on to new adventures.

This chapter provides an overview of some of the resources available. You can use it as a shopping list, or you can pick and choose from the suggestions here to improve your working environment gradually.

Finding a Studio

The first thing you need to do in finding your workspace is to determine what you'll be doing there. Will you shoot still images? Will you shoot video? Will you use it to edit video you shoot elsewhere? Will you use it for meetings with clients? Maybe what you want in a workspace is a quiet area where you can use your editing tools and store your files and cameras.

If you're photographing people in your studio, you need facilities for them. You can do advertising shots of products that you leave stacked in a closet, but for people, you need better accommodations. You need a dressing area, chairs, and secure space for them to store their possessions.

If you're using your studio as a business, you might need to adhere to building and zoning, as well as health and safety codes. Some of the material you work with (particularly the electronic equipment and hot lights) can be a fire hazard under some circumstances. You might be using draperies as backdrops that are required to be flame-proofed.

If you want a studio in which you'll shoot photos and videos, you need space—and that includes, if possible, a high ceiling. If you want to shoot anything except head-on shots, you need to be able to shoot up or down, which requires height.

You need power for your cameras and recharging batteries. If you use lighting, you need power for the lights. Your power demands probably won't be enormous unless you get into powerful lighting, but you will need many locations into which you can connect equipment. If you're building or renovating a space, don't skimp on power outlets.

If you're using your studio to shoot photos or videos, you need a way to get the images out of the studio. A high-speed Internet link is vital to many people. However, you can also transfer your work on removable disks as well as on the memory cards and DV cassettes you use in your cameras and camcorders.

If you're sharing space, you need to secure your equipment. You might be in a shared studio where certain equipment is shared, but, even in that case, you probably want a closet or cupboard into which you can put your own cameras and data.

NOTE   *If you're considering a shared space, ask around to see if other people are in the same situation. You might be able to join with them. Also, you could be able to use studio space in a local school or college during off times. A fee might be involved, but you could possibly work it off by teaching, mentoring, or assisting at the school.*

Equipping a Studio

The equipment you need in your studio is dictated by the work you'll do. If you're doing studio portraits of people, animals, or babies, you want a selection of props, chairs, tables, and backdrops you can use. If you're not sure what to get, study the types of photos and videos you intend to make and see what other people use. The range of props and backdrops isn't large.

If you'll be photographing objects (for advertising, perhaps), you have special requirements. Light boxes let you photograph relatively small objects on neutral backgrounds. These are used typically for the product shots that appear in magazines, newspapers, catalogues, and online Web sites.

If your studio is your home base for shoots that take you out and about, you could use it to store a collection of props and other equipment you'll take on location. For this purpose, your studio might resemble a warehouse more than a photo studio.

Advanced Photography

Most of this book has dealt with consumer and prosumer cameras and camcorders. You can use the prosumer still cameras for professional purposes—many professional photographers do so.

Two advanced features apply both to still and video cameras. If you haven't already obtained a tripod, now's the time. Small tripods sell for a little over $25, and prices go up from there. Look for a tripod that's sturdy (the major criterion). The ease with which it folds and unfolds, its weight, and the presence of leveling devices are other matters that are subsidiary to its sturdiness.

Also, now's the time to consider a remote control for your digital camera or camcorder. High-end still cameras often have shutter-release cables you can attach to them. This enables you to activate the shutter from a distance (a few inches) without touching the camera, so you don't jiggle it or change its focus.

In many cases, wireless remote controls are available for digital cameras and camcorders (they are included with some digital camcorders and do not have to be ordered separately). They enable you to control the shutter, as well as focus, zoom, and other controls. When used together with a tripod and the camera's LCD display, you can be some distance away and still manage it successfully.

Still Cameras

The higher-end still digital cameras generally are distinguished from the consumer and prosumer models by their removable lenses. (On a prosumer camera, you can add filters to a lens, but the lens itself is firmly attached to the camera.)

The advantage of having a replaceable lens is you can choose your camera body for the features you want (ruggedness and weight, for example), and you can then choose your lens independently. Most lenses today are 35mm lenses, and you can mix and match camera body and lens from two different vendors.

If you have a significant investment in 35mm lenses and filters, buying a digital camera body without the lens can provide you with a cost-saving alternative. (The digital camera bodies are expensive, so being able to reuse a single lens probably won't be cost-effective.)

Camcorders

In the case of digital video, the professional cameras provide significantly better quality than do the prosumer models. The highest-quality digital video camcorders can cost over $100,000 (the Sony HDW-F900, an experimental camera used to shoot *Episode II—Attack of the Clones,* a movie in the *Star Wars* sequence).

The major difference in digital camcorders is the number of image sensors—charge-coupled devices (CCDs)—and their resolution. Most consumer and prosumer digital camcorders have a single CCD to register the image. Its resolution varies, but you normally wind up with something along the lines of 250,000 to 350,000 effective pixels to construct the image. These cameras typically cost up to about $1,500.

Above that price—starting at about $2,500—you'll find three CCDs, one for each of the three basic colors. This immediately provides three times the color information. Furthermore, the CCDs may be of higher quality than those in the lower-priced camcorders. (For comparison, the Sony HDW-F900 previously mentioned has more than a megapixel of resolution in each of its three CCDs.)

Moving up to a camera with three CCDs will likely provide you with substantially better quality that you can see. The cost isn't prohibitive for many people.

But before you make any changes, consider the purposes to which you'll put the camera. If you're shooting video that's going to be streamed in small windows over the Web, the quality of a medium-priced digital camcorder could be sufficient. The three CCD cameras are bigger, as well as more expensive.

Consider, too, what you'll do with your video in the future. If you're streaming it over the Web today, but want to develop an archive of video for future use, you probably should be thinking about a higher-quality camera because the display technologies of the future will probably be better than those of today.

Running the World's First TV Station's Web Site from a PowerBook

Chris Neher is Webmaster for WRGB-TV, the world's first television station. (Its history is online at **http://www.wrgb.com/tv6info/history/history.asp**.) Based in Schenectady, New York, it serves New York's Capital Region and is an affiliate of CBS. WRGB Online is located at **http://www.wrgb.com**. Chris has been designing for the web since 1994 and has been a Mac user since 1984.

Like many Webmasters, Chris creates and manages the site on a Mac. He uses Apple's professional tools—the ones you might consider as you move beyond iPhoto, iMovie, and iDVD in creating your digital studio. I asked him to describe the process. Chris said, "As Webmaster, I use an Apple PowerBook G4 Titanium running Mac OS X and also run various flavors of Windows via Virtual PC on it in order to check page layout in various browsers and operating systems. The PowerBook has 768MB of RAM installed. It outputs to an additional monitor running at 1600 x 1200 resolution, so that I have a wide, dual-monitor desktop for a large workspace.

"One of the interesting parts of our Web site is CyberChef. The CyberChef's video recipes are either shot on Mini DV format tape or recorded from live remote broadcasts directly to DVD-RAM. These sources are then captured via FireWire and edited with Apple's Final Cut Pro digital nonlinear editing software on the same PowerBook. All of the various multimedia featured on WRGB Online are created using the same process. High and low bandwidth versions are then compressed for the web using Discreet's Cleaner 5. We chose QuickTime delivery for WRGB Online because it offers the highest quality for progressive downloads. These Progressive QuickTime movies start playing as soon as they begin downloading and don't require the user to wait for the whole file to download. QuickTime is also cross-platform and supports the widest variety of file formats—currently over 200."

Advanced Audio

The audio channels on digital video can support much higher quality than is normally provided by the built-in microphones. The following are some of your choices for recording audio. You can purchase each of these microphones for a reasonable amount (from $25 dollars, in most cases).

Onboard Boom Microphones

You can buy a directional microphone to attach to your digital camcorder and plug into its microphone connection. (In some cases, you'll need to attach an adaptor or dock to the camcorder to add the microphone jack.)

A directional microphone is exactly what its name says: it picks up sound from the direction in which it's pointed. If you're taping individuals who are talking in front of the camera, a directional microphone might provide better sound than the omnidirectional microphone that's built in. That microphone will pick up sound from in front of the camera as well as the ambient sound in the vicinity—including your voice (if you talk while taping) and even your breathing.

Lavaliere Microphones

The directional boom microphone lets you aim the camera and microphone together at the scene you want to record with video and audio. Even more precise is a *lavaliere microphone* that clips to someone's shirt, blouse, cravat, or tie. It picks up sound from that individual only and is more precise than the boom.

A lavaliere microphone is an excellent choice, particularly when the distance between the camera and the subject is great, or when ambient noise is around the subject. The lavaliere is sensitive, so do be careful that clothing doesn't rub against the microphone and cause sound that's recorded. (Most small lavaliere microphones come with foam covers that protect against wind and a certain amount of clothing-induced sound.)

With a lavaliere microphone, you can tape someone at quite some distance talking to the camera using a zoom lens. If you start with a close-up of the speaker's face, you can gradually zoom out to reveal the entire scene—all the while continuing to pick up the voice from the lavaliere microphone.

Wireless Microphones

Even better than the wired lavaliere microphone is a wireless microphone. You can purchase wireless microphone sets for a little more than $100 (prices go up substantially for the highest-quality sets).

A wireless microphone consists of two parts. The microphone itself clips to clothing, as does a wired lavaliere microphone. Instead of a cord running to the microphone jack of the digital camcorder, however, a cord runs to a transmitter that's usually the size of a deck of cards. That transmitter can be clipped to the back of a belt or hidden under clothing (or even in wigs—a common location for a Broadway musical's transmitters). The transmitter uses either VHF or UHF radio bands and is set to the same frequency as a receiver. (Several preset frequencies commonly exist. You need to be able to switch frequencies to make certain your transmission doesn't interfere with someone else's.)

The receiver has an antenna that picks up the transmission. It, too, is often the size of a deck of cards. It has a cable you plug into the microphone jack on your camcorder.

Wireless microphones are subject to interference, and their range isn't enormous. For many purposes, though, they're perfect.

Boom Microphones

Lavaliere microphones (wired or otherwise) generally are visible on camera. If you want to hide the microphone, you can use a boom microphone. Unlike the onboard boom microphone that attaches to your camcorder, a free-standing *boom microphone* hovers over the scene. It might be operated dynamically to point in turn to various speakers. Boom microphones are used commonly in film and television dramas.

Handheld Microphones

Finally, you can use a microphone held by the speaker. This is the most visually intrusive of all the microphones, but it gives the speaker a great deal of control. Handheld microphones are commonly used by singers who want this control. Handheld microphones can be wired or wireless.

Advanced Lighting

You can add more advanced lighting to your photography in several ways. Two of the simplest ways are described here.

Adding an Onboard Lamp

Your digital camera or camcorder almost certainly will come with a built-in flash. This is satisfactory for filling in light at short ranges (3–4 meters/9–12 feet). You can add an onboard lamp that provides substantial additional lighting and attaches to the camera itself. Unlike a flash, you turn it on, and it stays on until you turn it off.

These are frequently rechargeable. They provide a significant amount of light, and they minimize the red-eye effect that's caused by the sudden flash of light. The disadvantage of rechargeable onboard lamps is they can be fairly heavy because of the weight of their batteries.

Lighting Setups for Studio Work

You can buy studio equipment for lighting both still and video photography. If you plan to do much work under artificial light, you might want to invest in such equipment. You can assemble your own equipment, or you can buy combinations of equipment, sometimes in a carrying case.

Basic lighting often consists of three light sources: one from each side to provide basic illumination and a third source focused on the center of the scene (often a person's face). This isn't a collection of floor and table lamps: professional lighting equipment uses bulbs that provide intense and pure light. (Standard incandescent lighting such as that found in a home or office imparts a yellow cast; fluorescent lighting imparts a greenish cast. You can use the white balance setting in your digital camera or camcorder to mitigate these problems, but avoiding them by using professional lighting equipment is far better.) For home use, bulbs are prized for their longevity. That feature isn't at the top of the list of professional lighting equipment.

A studio lighting setup can run into thousands of dollars, but you should be able to put together (or buy) a three-light configuration with bulbs and stands for a little over $100.

Advanced Lighting

NOTE   *What you call a "bulb" is a lamp. Lamps go into lights or fixtures.*

Moving to Pro

Apple (and other vendors) have products that take up where iPhoto, iMovie, and iDVD leave off. Here are brief descriptions of the pro products and how they differ from the products you've been using so far.

Final Cut Pro

Final Cut Pro is Apple's professional-strength video-editing tool. Its basic functionality takes off where iMovie ends. Among the features you'll find in Final Cut Pro are more audio tracks (iMovie is limited to two tracks), more effects (and more sophisticated effects), advanced logging and identification of clips, and other tools professionals need.

One of the recently added features of Final Cut Pro is its support for Offline RT. With *Offline RT,* you can import your video into Final Cut Pro in a compressed format. You edit on your computer (even on a PowerBook) and, when you finish editing, you can synchronize the original footage with your edits, so they're applied to the full video.

Final Cut Pro costs about $1,000 when purchased by itself from Apple. (Special deals including hardware or other professional products are often available.)

DVD Studio Pro

As the professional companion to iDVD, *DVD Studio Pro* provides more features for your DVDs than iDVD. Among these features are more complex menus. In addition, you can export your finished DVD data not only to a DVD-R disc, but also to DVD-RAM or DLT tape to be sent to a replicator for pressing DVDs.

DVD Studio Pro, too, costs $1,000 from Apple. Like Final Cut Pro (with which it's tightly integrated), it frequently is part of promotional bundles.

Cinema Tools for Final Cut Pro

Finally, *Cinema Tools for Final Cut Pro* completes Apple's set of professional tools. You can use it to edit Offline RT, DV, SD and HD formats, as well as 35mm and 16mm film. With this product, Apple is aiming at users in the professional production area.

Summary

This chapter provided some ideas for expanding your resources. Depending on your goals, you can set up your own digital photography studio, you can move on to advanced cameras with replaceable 35mm lenses and multiple CCDs, you can improve your audio capture, and you can invest in lighting equipment. With the exception of the high-end digital cameras and camcorders, these investments are relatively modest—particularly when weighed against the improved work you can do.

Finally, the chapter briefly introduced you to Apple's professional editing tools: Final Cut Pro, DVD Studio Pro, and Cinema Tools for Final Cut Pro.

This chapter ends this part of the book. The final part is a set of case studies. In each case study, you'll find specific guidelines and suggestions. Furthermore, each of the case studies illustrates basic principles you can use in a variety of situations.

Part 4

Case Studies

Chapter 21

Kids and Scrapbooks

In This Chapter...

■ Digital or Paper? What Do You Need? Each format has its advantages and disadvantages. You can use either or both.

■ Planning Your Scrapbook. As always, start by deciding what it is you want to do. Then you can figure out how best to achieve your goals.

■ Helping Kids with Scrapbooks. Scrapbooks are great for kids. This section shows you how to work with them so that they get the most out of their scrapbooks and learn while they're at it.

■ Ideas for Scrapbooks. Finally, here are some specific suggestions for scrapbooks you might do yourself.

This part of the book provides ideas and suggestions for using the tools of the digital hub in a variety of ways. After all, for most people, it's what you can do with those tools that's exciting. Using them for their own sake quickly palls. You'll find chapters in this part of the book on creating scrapbooks (this one) and portfolios (Chapter 23). You'll find chapters focused on teaching (Chapter 22) and on advertising (Chapter 24). And, in the last chapter of the book, you'll find information on archiving—which is a lot more than just backing up data.

One distinction that's important to make is between scrapbooks and portfolios. A certain degree of overlap exists but, for the purpose of this book, a *scrapbook* is considered a book of memories designed mostly for yourself or for friends, and a *portfolio* is a collection of material planned for other people, and is somewhat more formal and structured than a scrapbook. The physical process of creating a scrapbook could be similar to that of creating a portfolio.

NOTE   *Scrapbooks can be more than just a collection of memories. They can be learning experiences (there's a section on kids and scrapbooks later in this chapter). In addition, scrapbooks can be important diagnostic and therapeutic tools for people confronting serious problems in their lives. The scrapbook techniques outlined here can be useful in that area, but the specifics of using scrapbooks in the fields of mental health or of social work are far beyond the scope of this book.*

Digital or Paper? What Do You Need?

Your scrapbook can wind up on the Web, on a CD-ROM or a DVD, or in a traditional paper-based binder or album. This is a choice you need to make at the beginning because, with a paper-based scrapbook, you need the physical album or binder before you can do much work. If you're assembling material for a digital scrapbook, you can postpone decisions about placement and organization until far along in the process.

Neither choice is better than the other, and each has its advantages. And each works equally well with the tools of the digital hub, with one exception: video. Video doesn't work on paper. But you can still incorporate it into a paper-based scrapbook. If you burn a DVD or CD-ROM, you can buy an envelope that can be pasted into a scrapbook into which you can place the disc. In that way, output from iMovie can live in the paper world as happily as output from iPhoto.

Consider the purpose of your scrapbook and the resources you have available. If the scrapbook is to be distributed to doting relatives, the nondigital version (perhaps with an enclosed disc) could be just what they need to wave under friends' noses when they're dummy at bridge. On the other hand, a digital version might lend itself much better to distribution to many doting relatives who are scattered around the world.

Paper Scrapbook Supplies

Many tools and supplies are available to help you, no matter which format you choose. If you're working with a paper-based scrapbook, you'll find blank albums and books of all sorts in office and art supply stores. Blank books with nice bindings and fine paper are also sold in gift shops and museums.

And, there's still more to use to help you get started. Use a Web search engine to search for the type of scrapbook you're interested in—a baby scrapbook, for example. You'll find companies selling blank scrapbooks as well as digital images you can use for your own. One common use of the digital files is to create pages with relevant graphics (ribbons or balloons, for example), onto which you then paste standard photos you've already printed.

If you're going to create a paper-based scrapbook, you need at least these supplies:

- The scrapbook itself
- Pages for it (unless they come bound into the scrapbook)

- Materials for putting items into the scrapbook. These could be glue sticks or clear envelopes that adhere to the pages. Your scrapbook might come with pages that already have slots for you to insert items.

- Scissors for cutting materials, and markers, crayons, or pencils to write in the album.

Before putting items into a scrapbook, decide if you can destroy them or not. Pasting a newspaper clipping into a scrapbook effectively destroys it for any other purpose. Putting the clipping into a plastic envelope in the scrapbook lets you remove it for other purposes. If your scrapbook contents come from iPhoto, you can keep the digital form on your computer's disk (or on a removable CD-ROM), so you needn't worry about having destroyed the print.

When you use iPhoto to print photos for your scrapbook, you can crop them to any size you want. You also can choose to use the standard sizes provided in iPhoto. Remember, using standard sizes lets you use standard-size envelopes and album pages.

Digital Scrapbook Supplies

On the digital side, you'll find templates for scrapbooks in many places. In iPhoto, you have templates for books and for HomePage Web sites. In iDVD, you have templates for a variety of DVD formats and themes. HomePage itself (accessed on the Web via your .Mac account) has still more formats. And, if these aren't enough, all Web authoring tools have templates, and most of them have idea sites on the Web you can explore.

Planning Your Scrapbook

Each of the chapters in this section (as well as many other chapters in this book) starts with the admonition to plan ahead. This one is no different. Take a few moments to consider the purpose and structure of your scrapbook, when you'll create it, and how you'll keep and distribute it. Making these choices before you start can make your scrapbook better and will ultimately save you time, aggravation, and even money wasted on unneeded supplies.

Purpose

Start by considering the purpose of your scrapbook. In the section "Ideas for Scrapbooks" later in this chapter, you'll see some suggestions for specific types of scrapbooks. The purpose of the scrapbook is something else. Do you only want to keep track of memorabilia? Is this a learning exercise—for you, for your kids, for a class? Do you want to experiment with new tools or ideas? Is this a test run from a scrapbook that you must get right the first time? (Better to make a mess of "Our Picnic In the Park" than of "Our Baby's First Year.")

One of the great attractions of scrapbooks is they can serve many purposes at once. Working with your children on scrapbooks during summer vacation not only produces a scrapbook they can show their kids 20 years from now, it can also provide an opportunity for teaching and for developing stronger family ties.

When to Do Your Scrapbook

In the past, a scrapbook containing photos could only be constructed after—sometimes long after—the photos were taken. Today, of course, with digital hub tools such as iPhoto, the time lapse can be almost insignificant.

Keeping up with the content means your scrapbook grows from day to day as you travel, learn, or otherwise go about your business. This approach tends to provide a relatively unedited scrapbook. If you want to use an order that isn't chronological or if you want to be highly selective, you might want to do your scrapbook in batches or at the end of a project.

You know yourself and your work habits: whatever you do, make sure you get the scrapbook done. If saving material for the end means you never have anything more than a paper bag of clippings and photos (or, worse yet, a bunch of files on disk with no rhyme or reason to their order), maybe you should attend to your scrapbook on a daily basis.

NOTE *Many people find it easier to discard material sooner rather than later. If you take 50 photos of a woodchuck eating a geranium, you might easily be able to pick the cutest one within minutes of the woodchuck's meal. For many people, reviewing the photos days or weeks later might encourage them to keep five, ten, or even all fifty. Remember this advice: take lots of footage, but toss it as soon as possible if you know you aren't going to use it.*

Keeping Your Scrapbooks

What will you do with your scrapbooks? Answering this question is important because it can affect the format of your scrapbook. If your goal is to produce a single copy that you (or your child) will keep, paper and digital are equally possible: in fact, some advantages exist to paper because you can paste brochures, menus, photos, crayon drawings, and other materials into it.

On the other hand, if you're planning to distribute your scrapbook to grandparents, friends, or others, you might choose a digital scrapbook, so you can make and send multiple copies easily. In that case, the menus, brochures, and crayon drawings need to be scanned before they're added. In a pinch, you can photograph such materials, but the quality almost always will be superior if you use a scanner. The exception to this is if you have odd-sized materials that are too large for your scanner. A map that's too big to fit on a scanner can be photographed—either on a table or held up by one or two people. Its details might not be clear, but it could serve the purpose (for instance, introducing your trip to Crater Lake—it's the thought, not the details of the roads, that matters for the introduction).

NOTE   *Some important issues are involved with keeping digital scrapbooks for long periods of time. See Chapter 25, in which archiving is discussed, for more on this topic.*

Helping Kids with Scrapbooks

As noted previously, many purposes are involved in creating scrapbooks. One common purpose is to help kids learn the various skills involved in creating a scrapbook—organizing, writing, laying out materials, telling a story, and so forth. Many parents or grandparents plan scrapbook projects with kids during vacations. This also is the type of project older children sometimes undertake. People in volunteer organizations also frequently help kids with scrapbooks.

Getting Started

If you haven't done this before, it might be tough to get started. Don't worry: it's not. If you want more information than you find in this chapter, ask friends, neighbors, or teachers in your child's school for ideas and tips.

The first steps have already been outlined: decide on the type of scrapbook you want to create (digital or paper), assemble your supplies, define its purpose, and set up a schedule for when to work on the scrapbook.

Depending on the child and the child's age, some of these decisions might be the child's, others could be joint, and still others might be yours. For example, deciding to keep a scrapbook about a vacation trip might be your suggestion. A teacher might suggest students keep scrapbooks during vacation about what they have done—this could even be required.

Nancy Brousseau, Teacher and Scrapbook Expert

Nancy Brousseau, a good friend and neighbor of mine in Philmont, is a distinguished teacher and sheepbreeder. (Her sheep are shown in *Mac OS X: The Complete Reference,* in the section "Image Capture.") A Massachusetts native, she lived in New Hampshire before moving to Columbia County in rural mid-state New York in the late 1960s. An educator for over 30 years, primarily in the field of reading, Nancy is still involved in the local school district although she and her husband Al are officially retired. They also raise Southdown and Dorset sheep, as well as Angora goats. Nancy holds a B.A. from the University of Massachusetts at Amherst and an M.A. and advanced accreditation from the State University of New York. She is a member of the Association of University Women and past president of the Alpha Nu chapter of Delta Kappa Gamma International.

As a storyteller and a poet, Nancy has presented author workshops in classrooms, and she's the author of such stories as "The Dump Bike" and "The Fish Tank Mysteries," among many others, as well as *The Book of Common and Uncommon Fairies.*

I spent some time talking about kids and scrapbooks with Nancy. Some of her comments appear throughout this section, but one of her recurring themes is this. When I asked her about a parent's (or other adult's) role in helping a child with a scrapbook, Nancy said, "It's essential. The child is making the scrapbook and you're helping, but part of the help consists of organizing the work. If you're doing this in evenings, on weekends, or on vacation, remember that there's lots of competition for time. Set a schedule that you and the child can adhere to. Think short, short, short—long isn't fun. Five minutes a day will do it—even five minutes a day, three days a week. But make it a specific three days. Both you and the child need to be able to find the time, and five minutes is usually available. It's amazing what you can do in five minutes if you take that time several times a week. Remember, it's better to want to spend more time on the project than be dreading how you'll finish out the half hour you've allocated."

You can assemble the supplies yourself, maybe as a gift to the child. Or, you can make an excursion to shop for the perfect scrapbook or the perfect paper. For most children, learning to shop isn't a major educational goal, so you might want to minimize that preparation. But, for other children, the excitement of shopping with an aunt or other adult just for the child's own scrapbook can be an incentive to get started.

During this part of the project, set your schedule. Make it regular and make the sessions brief. If you decide on "three times a week," you might find yourself at the end of the week with three sessions to schedule—and the next week looming.

Dividing the Work

How you divide the work depends to a great extent on the child and the age of the child. For a younger child, you might want to suggest the topic for a day's entry. "Why don't you draw a picture of what you saw when we bought stamps at the post office?" can move a child off square one. An older child might need no such guidance. Still other children in other circumstances could welcome a discussion about what to do.

For a scrapbook on what the child has done over the summer, feel free to insert *brief* items in the scrapbook. Maybe the child does one (or two or three) math problems each session: you can write $2 + 17 =$ in the scrapbook and the child can do the rest. (Teachers can provide you with some materials to help you here.)

Something more personal and more rewarding for the child is involved in doing these exercises in a scrapbook, rather than in a preprinted workbook from school. (Of course, if the workbook is required, you have no choice.) Integrating the math and the language exercises with the trip to the sewer plant and the picnic in the park can help create a scrapbook that, in 30 years, helps the now-adult kid to understand who that long-distant child was.

A special case of dividing the work arises when several kids work on a scrapbook together. This is frequently done in classrooms today (it's called *collaborative learning*). Your role is the same when working with a group of children as it is when working with one child: make sure things get done, answer questions, and get out of the way.

With a group of children, though, you have an additional set of roles. You should keep any eye out so the tasks are shared reasonably. (This doesn't necessarily mean evenly—with children of different skills and ages, different expectations might exist.) You also might need to assume a role of referee, which, of course, doesn't exist, when a single child is working on the project.

What do you do if you're working on a scrapbook and the child knows more about the Mac than you do? It's not hard to use iPhoto—any child can do so, and you might have a child who's a whiz at iPhoto and who you're trying to help create a scrapbook. I asked Nancy Brousseau what you should do in this situation and she said simply, "You're the adult." The kid might be a computer whiz, but beyond the mouse clicks and Internet connections are all the issues of organization, taste (in selection of contents as well as their presentation), and the myriad skills that come with experience. You don't have to know everything—in fact, it's pretty certain that even the youngest and least experienced child will know more about some things than you do.

Making Sure It Gets Done

An abandoned scrapbook—particularly if it's the first one for the child (or for you) can have a disproportionate impact on future scrapbooks. For that reason alone, it's important to make sure the scrapbook gets done.

Some of the tips have already been mentioned, such as setting regular, brief work periods. In addition, look at the entire project from your own point of view and decide whether it's reasonable. You or the child might have overly ambitious goals. Take them down a peg or split the scrapbook into two projects. You can always do a second scrapbook if time permits. And, what could be better than having a successful scrapbook created during one vacation and winding up with the idea and enthusiasm for the next scrapbook for the next vacation?

Handling Problems

Scrapbooks for kids are a learning process, and part of that learning process is recognizing and dealing with problems. The problems could be relatively minor— too few pages in a prebound paper scrapbook or dead batteries in a digital camera. They can also be more serious—the scrapbook documenting the birth and growth of a puppy can be interrupted by its illness or worse.

More commonly, the serious problem is one the child can't resolve, but you can. If this is the case, do so, but not surreptitiously. If the pages in the scrapbook accidentally become glued together, elves aren't going to come at midnight and cut them apart. Help the child see the problem, explain how it can be fixed, and, if it's something you (and not the child) can fix, either volunteer or simply explain that you'll do it. The goal is to keep going and to keep it fun. (It should go without saying that any discussion of such problems and their possible solution should wait until after any tears have stopped flowing.)

According to Nancy Brousseau, "You can always fix a kid's scrapbook. It's a record of what happened, so if there's a problem, it's a legitimate part of the scrapbook. It may not be the scrapbook you thought you'd be creating, but it's a scrapbook all the same. And this record of adventures and misadventures might just be the scrapbook that the grandchildren clamor to see again and again at the holidays. Did Mommy do *that*?"

Setting the Value of a Scrapbook for Kids

If you're expecting a child, you can begin what could be a lifelong interest in scrapbooks with a little preparation of your own. Make your own scrapbook—perhaps "Our Trip to the Zoo." (It might be the last chance you have for a quiet excursion like this for several decades!) It doesn't have to be a big scrapbook. Use it to brush up on your scrapbook skills (which might have atrophied since your youth).

Close-ups of zoo animals' faces are fascinating to children and adults alike. Even general shots of the zoo and its visitors can be fascinating because when you're done, you'll turn this scrapbook over to your child. It's reasonably certain that, 20 years from now, you and your kids will laugh at the outrageous clothes that people wore in the old days (that is, today).

This scrapbook is special because you make it special. If it's a treat for the child to be able to look through his own scrapbook, you're on the road to allowing the kid the treat of making his own scrapbook.

One of the great advantages of digital images is you can reproduce them at will. You might treat this scrapbook carefully, but if it becomes the valued possession (first possession!) of your child, its pages and photos could need replenishment over time.

Ideas for Scrapbooks

You can create scrapbooks on any topic. Generally, scrapbooks fall into three categories: events, journals, and issues.

Event Scrapbooks

Events such as births, weddings, graduations, and even funerals cry out for scrapbooks in some peoples' minds. Remember, scrapbooks (as referred to in this book) are collections of personal memories: these are your remembrances of what happened. If you're creating a record of the event for others, read Chapter 23.

Scrapbooks of events often are paper-based for the simple reason that they might include many items that can't be digitized. The menu from the wedding dinner, baby's first lock of hair, or the tickets to an important game could have prized places in the scrapbook.

If you're creating an event scrapbook, you can, of course, use iPhoto to create and crop your photos. You can use iMovie and iDVD to create CD-ROMs or DVDs to place in the scrapbook, too. But still other opportunities exist.

In iPhoto, for example, you can create an album containing the photos you want to print for your event scrapbook. You can then publish that album on the Web (or create a book from it). With almost no additional effort, you have your paper-based scrapbook, as well as a digital scrapbook you can share with distant friends and relatives.

As noted previously, you can buy specific event-related scrapbooks. You can also find templates for printing pages with appropriate graphics (or, of course, you can make your own).

Journal Scrapbooks

Journal scrapbooks document a journey, a period of time (such as a vacation), or even a life. Many people over the centuries have kept such scrapbooks, and they're invaluable aids to biographers and scholars, as well as to friends, relatives, and descendants.

If you go to a library or museum, you'll find many of these scrapbooks replete with sketches and drawings—of mountains, flowers, people . . . nearly anything the author wanted to remember. You have no better tool than your Mac for creating such a scrapbook. If you're creating a scrapbook of memories for yourself, you don't need the organization tools of iDVD or even the advanced editing features of iMovie. What you want are the words of your recollections and observations, along with the relatively unedited snapshots from iPhoto and maybe some clips or even stills from iMovie.

To assemble a journal scrapbook, you can use any word-processing application that lets you insert graphics. TextEdit comes with Mac OS X. Microsoft Office and AppleWorks also are widely used tools that accommodate both text and graphics.

If your journal is primarily visual, you can use iPhoto as your journaling tool. As described in Chapter 11 and shown here in Figure 21-1, in iPhoto Preferences, select Comments for Assign/Search uses, and you can type in a description for each photo in your album. (Having a separate album for each journal makes sense.)

Then, simply type your comments for each photo at the bottom of the iPhoto window when you're in Organize mode, as shown in Figure 21-2.

The disadvantage of this approach is it's totally picture-based. (That is, you can't have an entry with no picture.) For most people, a text-based application

Ideas for Scrapbooks

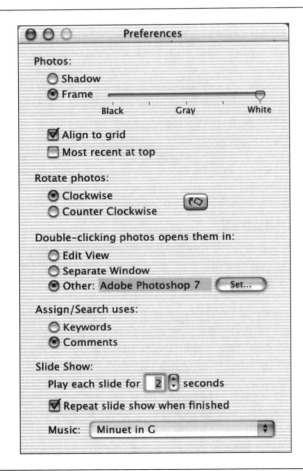

FIGURE 21-1   Set iPhoto preferences to use comments for photos.

such as TextEdit, Microsoft Office, or AppleWorks will be the tool of choice because many entries will have no photos associated with them.

Portfolios documenting a process of development or understanding are related to journal scrapbooks. These portfolios—widely used by both teachers and students—are designed for others to read (and often to evaluate). Journal scrapbooks are normally private. In many cases, journal scrapbooks are sealed or hidden until after the author's death. (Portfolios are discussed in Chapter 23.)

FIGURE 21-2   Comments for a photo

Issue Scrapbooks

Finally, there are issue scrapbooks. If you're assembling materials to convince others about a cause or issue, you're in the area of portfolios described in Chapter 23. For many people, though, keeping a private scrapbook about a subject or issue is rewarding and useful. The issue might be weighty or not—teenagers' scrapbooks about their favorite movie star often seem less weighty with time.

Summary

This chapter examined some of the issues related to scrapbooks and suggested some specific ways in which you can use the tools of the digital hub in creating scrapbooks. Scrapbooks can be paper-based or digital. In either case, the digital hub tools can help you create them.

Scrapbooks often have multiple purposes, and one common set of purposes revolves around scrapbooks kids do with the help of parents, teachers, or other older people. Excellent learning tools, scrapbooks also serve as laboratories for good work habits and provide a window for the adult to look back on the young child from which he or she grew.

The key to scrapbooks—and what differentiates them from the other types of projects discussed in this section—is they usually are collections of memorabilia designed for the author to keep and refer to at a later time. They aren't usually designed for other people to read (that function—in this book's terminology—is provided by portfolios, discussed in Chapter 23).

When you start to explore the projects you can create for others—that is, projects other than scrapbooks—one common use of digital hub tools immediately springs to mind. They're excellent at helping people create instructional or teaching projects, which is the topic of the next chapter.

Chapter 22

Instructional Materials

In This Chapter...

■ Why Use Digital Media for Teaching? Specific reasons exist to go digital. They're described here.

■ Types of Instructional Materials. Each form of teaching materials has its own advantages and disadvantages. They're described in this section.

■ Preparing to Create Instructional Materials. Before you turn on the camera or microphone, make sure you're ready to use your time and materials wisely. Some concrete steps make the process faster.

■ Taping Live Events. Some benefits exist in recording an event live as it happens. For one, everyone—teacher and students—can be heightened in their responsiveness. But you need to prepare and understand the possibilities and pitfalls.

■ Capturing Screen Shots and Interactive Behavior. Screen shots and movies are commonly used to illustrate computer training materials. You need to know about some specific issues.

This chapter turns to many of the issues involved in creating teaching materials. These could be done for profit on a large scale, or you might be creating a video— or a one-page flyer—for a class of a dozen ten-year-olds. This chapter refers to instructional materials in the broadest sense to avoid itemizing the specific formats you might use. Some of the ideas and suggestions might pique your interest and set you off on your own adventures.

As noted previously, many of these hints are applicable to other areas. The hints appearing in other chapters in this part of the book can also help you in preparing teaching materials.

Why Use Digital Media for Teaching?

Film, video, and all sorts of sound recording technologies have been used for years for educational purposes. Make sure you know why you're using digital media, so you can make your instructional materials as good as possible. Your project could be a for-profit teaching venture that takes its place alongside the video and audio courseware familiar today. This could be an educational institution's internal project, or it might be the most common form of training and education: instructional materials for in-house use or designed as adjuncts to products, services, or technologies.

Sharing Scarce Resources

One of the advantages of any type of recorded instruction is that scarce resources can go further. A single teacher can be available day and night via QuickTime on the Web or through CDs and DVDs. Elaborate demonstrations can be shown and reshown at a student's request.

Whether video, audio, CD, DVD, or Web, digital media used for this purpose should clearly promote what the scarce resource is. For instance, this isn't simply a course in algebra—it's a course in algebra taught by someone special. In that case, maybe a "get to know the teacher" segment is appropriate.

Replication and Standardization of Teaching

Particularly in the corporate world, recorded training is valued for its standardization. If you're providing training for employees to understand a corporate vacation plan or if you're providing the instructional materials for a customized software product, you can quickly update the materials for all users.

In this case, consider using streaming video or placing your materials (slides, photos, or movies) on a Web site, such as a .Mac site. In this way, you can update the standardized training for everyone at the same time. If you distribute CDs or DVDs, you need to redistribute new ones. Even in a relatively small and controlled environment, this can be a problem.

Individual Teachers

The digital hub tools make it possible for individuals to do it all themselves. This is one of the most exciting aspects of the tools. Just as writers found they could write and publish their own material with word processing and page layout software, so teachers can teach, provide illustrations and demonstrations, and produce their own Web sites and DVDs.

If this is your goal, consider these points.

First, excellent documentation exists of significant productivity improvements in one-person projects over projects with groups of people. That's the good part. The potential downside is you can do something that makes sense to you—and only to you. You can avoid this by doing reality checks periodically—letting people see your work and finding out how they receive it. If you're experienced at teaching your subject, you can get input in the finer points of digital media. If you know digital media, but you aren't experienced in teaching, you'll need tips from teachers and students.

Approach the project as if it were done by a cast of thousands. You might do everything yourself, but try to separate your roles. If you're directing or editing while you're teaching, your mind isn't focused on the material.

Who Are the Students?

Make sure you know who your audience is and how many people are in it. The most critical choice to make is whether you're preparing materials for individual use or for use in classes. Some training materials are geared to both audiences but, in most cases, you'll produce better materials by making a choice.

If you're focusing on individual students, you can assume a much greater degree of interactivity than if a classroom full of people will be watching a video. This interactivity can mean stopping and starting. It also can mean setting up DVD menus that let people choose summaries or even skip entire topics. In addition, in a classroom setting, a teacher or moderator generally leads discussions and answers more detailed questions. Teachers also provide assignments and test students on their understanding of the subject matter presented: in an individual student setting, you must do this in your instructional materials. (This isn't always an either/or choice because you can provide tests and suggested assignments for teachers.)

Types of Instructional Materials

Using tools such as iMovie, iPhoto, iTunes, and iDVD to prepare instructional materials seems an obvious and simple use of them. It is, but, as always, a little planning goes a long way. A wide range of instructional materials and types of instruction exist. Clarifying what you want to do and how you want to do it can help you produce the most effective instructional materials. Here's an outline of some of the major types of instructional materials you can produce with the digital hub suite of tools.

In practice, you often combine these different types of materials, using each for its own special virtues. What you should gather from this section is, first, you need to think about the different types of materials, and, second, you should look at the issues from the point of view of the people who will be viewing and using your materials, not only from your own (or the teacher's) point of view.

One terrific advantage of digital media (discussed in the first chapter) is that it's so easily convertible from one format to another. Increasingly, people are developing multipurpose materials. Once the digital media is recorded and digitized, you can use it in print form, on a DVD, as a poster—and more. Thus, in thinking about the types of instructional materials you can create, think not only in the old-fashioned way of a single purpose, but also in a new way in which you might be producing a multitude of products from a single production process.

Books and Other Printed Materials

iTunes, iDVD, and iMovie won't be much help to you if you're creating printed materials, but iPhoto can be a perfect companion. For many purposes, its tools provide everything you need. After all, cropping is the extent of most adjustments made to images, and changing the palette from color to grayscale (for printing) can be done either in iPhoto or automatically as you print (Mac OS X takes care of that for you).

You might want to use three additional types of software, which the following sections describe. Other products are also available for other purposes, and many people swear by them, but the products listed are the indispensable ones that played a role in creating this book.

Text Editing and Page Layout Tools

Two types of tools exist for creating text. The first type, exemplified by Microsoft Word and AppleWorks text documents, lets you type what you want, insert images, format paragraphs, insert page breaks and page numbers, and do all the other word processing things you're used to doing. The application takes care of the actual formatting of each page. These are *text editing* programs. You have a certain degree of control, but it takes your general requirements—page break here, two columns there—and carries them out. Minute adjustments to the page layout are its concern, not yours.

Page layout software, such as Quark XPress and InDesign, lets you make those minute adjustments. Less sophisticated, but still powerful, the AppleWorks Draw documents also let you lay out pages. For lengthy documents (such as books) that require automatically generated indexes, tables of contents, glossaries, and the like, InDesign or FrameMaker are generally the tools of choice. (InDesign and FrameMaker are both from Adobe, **http://www.adobe.com**. *FrameMaker* is the original large document application, and it isn't available on Mac OS X, although it runs in Classic. *InDesign* provides most of the FrameMaker features, with the exception of some SGML tools.)

Advanced Image Editing

For advanced image editing, most people rely on Photoshop from Adobe. Consumer and educator editions are available with subsets of the full application. For more information, contact Adobe or—if you're an educator or other specialized user—your channel supplier.

NOTE *The consumer version of Photoshop is Photoshop Elements. Another version of Photoshop, Photoshop Limited Edition (Photoshop LE) has been distributed in the past with scanners and other image-manipulation software. It has been supplanted by Photoshop Elements.*

Utilities

Finally, several utilities can come in handy. For file conversion, *Graphic Converter* (bundled with many desktop Macintosh computers, available as shareware from **http://www.lemkesoft.com**) is a handy and reliable utility. For screen shots, Snapz Pro X (from **http://www.ambrosiasw.com**, also bundled with desktop Macintosh computers) is indispensable.

If You're Getting Started . . .

The tools of the Macintosh and of the digital hub enable people who never thought of creating media projects to do so. This is powerful and empowering, but it can also leave people stymied in trying to understand how to do things. For books (as well as all the other types of materials described in this section), your library or local bookstore can provide many general guides to writing, editing, producing, directing, and authoring materials.

In addition to the software products listed in this section, four indispensable reference books can help you, not only with printed materials, but also with other types of products:

- Use a dictionary as a reference, especially for words with alternate spellings and hyphenations. Whether in printed materials, slides, or menus on DVDs, inconsistencies are annoying and unprofessional. If you want to, keep track of the spelling and style choices you've made (such as "screen shot" or "screenshot").

- Likewise, use a desktop encyclopedia to check dates, names, and other incidental information. If a lecturer makes a casual aside about the treaty ending the War of 1812, referring to it as the Treaty of Bruges (not Ghent), it can be disappointing.

NOTE *Dictionaries, encyclopedias, and other reference materials are available online through Sherlock, part of Mac OS X.*

- For structuring of books, *The Chicago Manual of Style* is the primary reference in the United States. Yes, common standards exist for which goes first—table of contents, preface, or introduction. You don't have to reinvent the wheel, and you can make your materials look more professional by adhering to standards. Note, book formats and layouts are one area of diversity in an increasingly heterogeneous world.

■ Finally, *The Elements of Style* by Strunk and White provides the best guidance on how to write and structure your material clearly. Fewer than 100 pages long, this book has never been surpassed.

Lectures

The simplest and most basic form of instruction is lecturing. You can create a movie, DVD, or even MP3 lecture. Students can then view or listen to your lecture at their convenience.

You can include graphics and sound in a lecture (demonstrations are covered in the following section of this chapter). As teachers and students know, relevant graphics and sound can enhance a lecture and keep students' attention. In preparing recorded lectures, though, remember that some of the issues involving attention don't apply. If a student is bored, the Off button is only a click away. The lecture can be resumed at another time. Thus, keeping a student's attention during a lecture can be less critical than in a stuffy classroom. (Of course, the student who totally loses interest can walk out digitally much more easily than walking out of a classroom.) Furthermore, a student can replay a section that isn't clear.

Lectures on video can be taped in places where a class could never go. The most obvious choice often is for the teacher to be in a neutral or educational setting: a classroom, a library, in front of a muted drapery, or the like. However, consider moving the teacher and lecture to a more interesting (but relevant) location. Television documentaries and educational programs do this well: geologists lecture in front of dinosaur skeletons, art historians speak from museums, and entomologists lecture from mudholes.

As in a classroom or auditorium, a lecture that consists merely of someone reading from a book or from notes is tedium itself. Lectures often work best in the circumstances described here.

Introducing Material

Use relatively brief lectures to introduce topics and provide a roadmap to a larger piece of material. A "talking head" lecture is a good way of introducing a teacher who has prepared training materials that use a variety of other techniques. The disembodied voice heard while you look at slides and demonstrations is associated with a person in an introductory lecture.

Types of Instructional Materials

Audio-Only Lectures (Lectures on Tape, CD, or MP3)

Audio-only lectures are well suited for people who listen to them in cars, on public transportation, or while engaging in other activities. If you're preparing such a lecture, remember your listeners are, by definition, already engaged in at least one other activity. Structure is more important than ever. Breaking lectures up into focused, same-length units can be a good idea.

Emphasis

Use lectures for *emphasis* within the context of other materials. "I think this is important . . ." can gain added weight when an individual addresses the camera. (Done poorly, this can look like a late-night, low-budget television commercial, so be careful.)

Beware of long lectures with no visual interest (if you're using video). For audio, beware of long, undifferentiated (that is, unstructured) lectures that don't let the user know what's happening.

Demonstrations

Demonstrations are one of the most potent forms of instructional materials, and they're well suited to the tools you have in the digital hub. The demonstration could be as simple as a basic chemistry experiment or changing the toner cartridge in a photocopier. It might be as complex as a time-lapse series of photos or videos illustrating the growth of a plant or animal.

Demonstrations work well in conjunction with other types of materials. Don't use them to liven up lectures, though: "livening up" generally proves a distraction. Use demonstrations to illustrate, teach, or demonstrate: they should be relevant to the material at hand.

Here are some specific tips for preparing demonstrations.

Use Frames of Reference

If you're filming objects rather than people, make certain frames of reference exist regarding size. To show how to use a piece of equipment, consider zooming in from the entire device to the area you're demonstrating: don't start with a close-up of the toner-cartridge release lever (wherever that might be!).

Provide Calibration Tips

If the demonstration can be distorted in playback (if color or sound, for example, can be modified by the viewer), make certain you provide it with calibration mechanisms or a discussion of what should be seen. (This can be subtle. If the demonstrator says, "This orange flowerpot . . ." then a viewer who sees a green flowerpot should know something's wrong somewhere with the color.)

Identify Everything

If it's touched, shown, or mentioned in the demonstration, it probably should be identified. Working with demonstrations often pushes you to identify objects you use and can describe but can't identify. (The most common example is the *size box*—the rectangle in the lower-right corner of windows that lets you resize and reshape the window. Those few people who've considered what that object is called often call it a *resize* box.)

Describe What's Happening

Pictures might be worth a thousand words, but they don't replace them. Make certain you explain what you're doing, so viewers can follow along. As you review a video of a demonstration, you might focus on what you know to be important: the viewer might focus on an extraneous aspect unless attention is drawn to the frying pan, easel, or other primary focus.

Exclude Irrelevant Material

In demonstrating processes and procedures, make certain the demonstration is ready to work and that you can exclude irrelevant aspects. Taped or live, nothing is more disconcerting than someone demonstrating a computer program who says, "Now just ignore what I'm doing for a moment, I'll tell you when it matters."

Do One Thing at a Time

If you're demonstrating alternate ways of doing something or two different aspects of the same subject, demonstrating them separately usually makes sense. Or you can prepare a common introduction, and then use two diverging paths, one at a time. Avoid the confusion of switching back and forth in a single demonstration.

Special Tips for Computer Demos

If you're demonstrating the use of a computer and you want to show the image of a display, you have special challenges. If possible, use the largest screen image size (that is, a low resolution of something such as 800×600 or even 640×480 rather than $1,024 \times 768$). Adjust System Preferences to use large icon sizes and use large text (18 point) for text you're typing.

You might want to clean up your screen before including it in a video. Certainly, clean up your desktop and use as neutral a desktop picture as you can. You want people to see what you're demonstrating, not how you've configured your computer.

Videotaping a computer display isn't the easiest thing to do. If you can, you might want to combine a lecture (with or without a computer display in the picture) with a close-up of the display. The close-up can be a still image of the display (see the following section, "Slide Shows") or it can be a QuickTime movie that captures specific actions on the display (see the section "Capturing Screen Shots and Interactive Behavior"). Each of those provides a clearer and more distinct view of the display.

Make Your Demos Easy to Find

If you're creating a movie or a DVD, make your demos separate clips so they're easy for users to find. On a DVD, consider using duplicate menus so the demos are listed on one menu as a group and then listed on other menus in the context of the topics to which they relate. On movies, allow plenty of lead-in time—or even a pause for a title—so people scanning the movie can easily find the beginning of the demo.

Make It Visual

Although this should go without saying, remember to make demonstrations visually interesting. If there's nothing to see, don't demonstrate it.

Slide Shows

Slide shows can consist of presentations such as those you create in AppleWorks or PowerPoint, graphics from any source, or a mixture of the two. They can contain movies, and they can be saved as movies with automatic advancing from one slide to the next.

Slide shows are terrific for free-standing noninteractive kiosks: you can set them up to run themselves, hide the computer mouse and keyboard, and let people watch without worrying about interference with your computer. Slide shows can be used for many projects and are discussed further in Chapter 25.

Recorded Interaction

The previous sections have focused on the teacher and the presentation of material. In many classrooms, the interaction between teacher and students is an integral part of the learning experience. You might choose to capture that as part of the materials.

Taping a Master Class

Uta Hagen's Acting Class (**http://www.utahagenvideo.com**) is a two-video set of master classes conducted by the legendary actress who has won three Tony awards over a 50-year career in the theatre, television, and movies. I asked Pennie duPont and Karen Ludwig, who produced and directed the project, about the process of filming the classes:

Said Pennie, "Our first choice was a no-brainer: taping a masterclass. Because Uta Hagen already had two best-selling acting books, *Respect for Acting* and A *Challenge for the Actor,* our goal was clear: to capture this brilliant teacher in action, so the viewer would feel as if he or she were taking the class."

Karen pointed out the high shoot-to-print ratio (described previously in this book in the context of other projects). As Karen told me, "The students were already in place—from Toronto, Chicago, L.A., and New York—all professional actors who performed scenes from plays and/or her famous Object Exercises, and would then rework them based on Uta's critiques.

"One of the most critical aspects of this process is that we had to shoot over 200 hours of tape to wind up with the final 3 hours. Due to the nature of a class, where it's unpredictable, you have to make sure you cover it as it happens. The actors aren't being 'directed.' It's all in the moment. So, if you haven't shot it, you can't restage it the way it unfolded—at that moment.

"In addition to having a fascinating teacher and great students, good sound is crucial and more than enough footage so you can make the points you want in the editing room."

The advantage of taping the entire class is that the discussion and questions can reinforce the lesson, provide variety, and get viewers thinking. The disadvantage is this: just as poor teachers exist, so do poor students. And, just as there are teachers who don't work well on video, the same applies to some students. With an experienced teacher, you might well be able to videotape a lecture and use it with little cutting. With student discussions, you'll probably need to plan on fairly high shoot-to-print ratios.

Reenacting Discussions

One way of approaching this is to prepare the student discussion and questions. Beware: this can look corny and canned unless people are skilled at acting. Even asking students and a teacher to repeat a lively discussion they had in the cafeteria in front of the video camcorder an hour later can be treacherous. But persevere. Remember the tips from the first chapter and keep shooting. Maybe the cafeteria discussion will fall flat in its reenactment, but there might be further spontaneous discussion you can use.

Intercutting Discussions and Questions

Yet another approach to interaction on tape is to intercut questions and discussions. Here, you tape students' comments before, during, or even after the class. With iMovie, it's a cinch to splice these cuts into a lecture or other taped material.

You can even create an apparent discussion with these intercut questions. If you find yourself with a rather lengthy and visually uninteresting lecture, one way to break it up is to insert questions or comments in this way.

NOTE   *This technique is appropriate for instructional materials. It emphatically isn't considered ethical for news or for nonfiction video that purports to be factual. Inserting questions, answers, or comments that weren't part of the event is poor journalism, unethical, and, in some extreme cases, illegal.*

Arguments, Laughter, and High Jinks

Discussions can become heated, funny, or plain silly. If you're in the room, you have a variety of cues as to what's going on. On tape, most of those cues are gone. The emotion might be lost (humor often is). Worse, some types of emotion (anger, for example) can be magnified. There's no reason instructional materials should be dull or boring, but neither should they be offensive or off-putting. Review these moments of interaction with particular care.

Live Interaction

As noted in the previous section, questions and discussions can clarify points and enhance the presentation of material. This is an argument for including the classroom discussion in the recorded material.

You can plan to incorporate live interaction into your instructional materials. The traditional way in which this is done is to pause at certain points (such as the end of a lesson) and allow a classroom instructor or moderator to take over. Teachers' notes can suggest topics for discussion, or the prepared materials can include such jumping-off points.

Note, instructional materials that incorporate live interaction by their very nature assume a group of people will be participating. They might watch videos separately, but they need to come together for the discussion. If participants aren't physically in the same place, they can use *distance-bridging tools* (a fancy term for telephones and instant messaging).

One of the most interesting advances in discussions is exemplified in Apple's iChat instant messaging software. Its Aqua interface is elegant and powerful. It enables you to chat with designated people from the America Online network, from **mac.com**, or from your local area network (LAN).

NOTE   *You can read more on iChat in Chapter 24.*

You can combine live and recorded interaction by taping discussions. For example, an individual school can prepare recorded discussions and commentaries on widely available instructional materials to create a customized and unified new experience. (Remember, of course, in combining your own material with previously recorded material, you must be aware of copyright restrictions. In general, if you produce your own discussion and don't include copyrighted material within it, you should be fine. Be careful about inserting clips from copyrighted material into the discussion.)

Student Work

Demonstrations work well in instructional materials—when done by both teachers and students. The tools of the digital hub make it possible for everyone to take photos and make movies. This opens two interesting possibilities for student work.

Homework

You can assign specific tasks to students and review their performances via photos and video. This is scarcely different from asking a student to write a report on paper. (See Chapter 21 for more on this subject.)

Structure the assignment as much as you want. If you (or an assistant or a teacher you don't even know) will be reviewing 30, 300, or 3,000 assignments, you don't want boredom to set in, but you also want some degree of comparability if you need to rate or grade them. If the assignments are integrated into the course materials, test the students first to make certain the assignments are clear. Testing involves not only making certain people understand the assignments, but also that the assignments they produce are what you expect. People might think they understand assignments, and then do the wrong thing.

Types of Instructional Materials

Class Add-Ons and Extensions

The Web inspires a degree of interaction and collaboration never before seen in the world. In addition to recording classroom discussions and planning for live discussions among the viewers of your instructional materials, you can incorporate donated discussions, demonstrations, and questions into the instructional materials.

Consider making the entire project interactive by adding a Web site to the materials. This Web site needn't be fancy: your .Mac HomePage site will be fine. You can put some of your video up there, along with photos and samples of your slides. Students can email you questions, suggestions, photos, and their own videos. You can then add them to your Web site or incorporate them into your class.

Preparing to Create Instructional Materials

Now that you know why you're using digital media and you've chosen the types of materials you'll produce, it's time to get started. But there's one further set of steps before you turn on the camera and microphone.

Special Equipment

Equipment that's optional in other environments is mandatory (or at least highly recommended) for instructional materials.

Tripod

Creating a project such as this without a tripod is almost inconceivable. You don't need a fancy one—$50 buys a good tripod, and a satisfactory one can be had for half that.

A *tripod* not only steadies the camera, it also lets you reposition the camera in the same spot repeatedly. Unless you're miraculously able to shoot everything in one take, you'll probably need to set up the environment several times. Spike two legs of the tripod with tape on the floor. (*Spiking* refers to marking positions with small pieces of tape, chalk, or other devices.) If the top of the tripod is adjustable, either leave it alone or mark its positions with more tape. You can indicate several different heights for your tripod for several different setups.

Camera and Camcorder Remote Control

Especially if you're taping yourself, choose digital cameras and camcorders with wireless remote control, so you're not constantly jumping up and down to focus. In the case of digital camcorders, the LCD display generally pivots, which means it can be seen by the person being photographed. If that's going to be you, twist the LCD around, so you can check the focus and zoom when you're standing or sitting.

Power Adapter

Another tool that comes in handy is a power adapter. Many digital camcorders come with a cable that lets you connect the camcorder to a power adapter or to a battery-like interface, instead of running off a battery. If you'll be taping fairly long sessions with the camera in one place, don't worry about battery power.

Microphones

If you're recording voice-over narration, get a USB microphone for your Mac. If you're taping lectures or demonstrations with live sound, invest in a lavaliere microphone (cordless or corded). The sound is vastly superior to the built-in microphones on camcorders, and the price is modest.

Do It for Real

Before preparing the digital version, try to teach (or have the teacher teach) the material to real students. See what works and what doesn't, what's clear and what's confusing. Fix it before you start taping.

Of course, digital media are different from traditional classroom teaching. What you can't demonstrate in front of a class you can demonstrate in a close-up photo or video. As you teach (or watch someone teach), look specifically for those aspects that will be particularly amenable to the features of video. Simply taping a lecture usually isn't a good idea.

Test Assignments

Test assignments that will be given as part of the course. Particularly if you aren't experienced at teaching, you might discover that preparing tests and assignments is the hardest part of the class. When teachers think about tests, they often discover the course material needs to be changed.

When people prepare the assignments, look for misunderstandings. If everyone misses a certain question, either it's unclear or the topic is not presented properly.

Test Results

If possible, test the results. People can complete a course and pass every test, but are unable to apply the knowledge they've learned. Is your method of presentation working? Do people understand?

Particularly in the corporate world, many students are asked to evaluate courses they take. By all means, look at these questionnaires if you can. If you have access to questionnaires, look at ratings of similar courses. Look for topic areas that are consistently highly rated or marked as confusing. You obviously can't steal someone else's material, but nothing is wrong with looking for issues that are hard (or easy) to understand in a given subject area.

Taping Live Events

This book has emphasized the capability to use iMovie, iPhoto, and iDVD as postproduction tools to edit digital media. Indeed, this is the way most media is created today.

But another way exists. You can tape a class live, not stopping for anything. Whether it's a class or a performance, certain heightened energy often occurs when the teacher or artist knows no postproduction is available to fix things.

In some cases, the live and unedited nature of the class contributes to the educational experience. In *The French Chef Cookbook,* by Julia Child (Knopf, 1968), she describes the beginnings of her classic television show, which was taped in live, unedited segments. As Child writes, "I would far prefer to have things happen as they naturally do. . . . One of the secrets of cooking is to learn to correct something if you can, and bear with it if you cannot."

If you're taping a live event, your first decision is whether to have students and/or an audience (they might not be the same). Sometimes a live audience spurs the teacher on and, other times, it's a distraction.

Because taping a live class is usually done because of the extra immediacy and focus of the teacher, make certain you don't counterbalance this by being a distraction. Remember, live doesn't mean unrehearsed (in fact, it probably should never mean unrehearsed). The teacher should know what you plan to do—and you should know what the teacher is going to do.

Capturing Screen Shots and Interactive Behavior

You usually need to capture screen images from your computer for video and slides. On Mac OS X, *Grab* is a utility that comes with the operating system, and it lets you capture all or part of the screen: the parts of the screen you can select are individual windows, as well as areas you select with the mouse. Grab has a timer option that lets you start the clock running, and then it gives you ten seconds to pull down a menu, move the cursor, or otherwise set up the screen shot you want. (You can read more about Grab in *Mac OS X: The Complete Reference.*)

Snapz Pro X, a Mac OS X shareware utility available from **http://www.ambrosiasw.com**, is also included with many Macintosh desktop models. Snapz Pro X is more ambitious than Grab and enables you to capture the full screen, objects on the screen (such as windows), areas you select with the mouse—and even QuickTime movies showing your mouse movements. Snapz Pro X is bundled by Apple with some Macintosh computers (the desktop models, in many cases). The version that's bundled isn't fully featured, but it enables you to create many types of screen shots. If you want to release the full power of Snapz Pro X, you can visit its Web site and upgrade for a modest fee.

Note, capturing such interface actions as a QuickTime movie with Snapz Pro X or a similar tool always yields better results than videotaping someone using the computer.

With few exceptions, Snapz Pro X has been used to create the screen shots in this book. Some of the settings used might be helpful to you in similar cases:

- ■ **TIFF files**   Snapz Pro X enables you to select the type of image file that's created. You can use other shareware tools, such as Graphic Converter (**http://www.lemkesoft.com**), to change files from one type to another. Commercial products such as Photoshop, as well as general-purpose products such as Word and AppleWorks, can also do this. However, it's easiest to start out with the type of file you'll need. In the case of this book and many other printed materials, this is a TIFF file, and that's the option chosen in Snapz Pro X.

- ■ **Grayscale**   Just as you can change file types, you can change the resolution and color palettes using utilities. Again, it's easy to start with the right settings. For this book, the grayscale palette is selected, so color is removed right at the start. Note, this setting is appropriate for images you're using in a book or other printed material that doesn't use color. If you want to use images for both black-and-white printing and for other purposes (perhaps a Web site), don't remove the color information!

- ■ **Borders**   The convention used in this book is that windows are depicted with the Aqua drop shadow. You can accomplish this in two ways. First, you can shoot the window with its Aqua shadow against a white background (such as a blank text or drawing document). Second, you can use the Snapz Pro X option to add the Aqua shadow to the image. This setting is applied to images that contain an entire window. Images containing more than one window or parts of windows have no borders.

Summary

This chapter explored issues and possibilities related to instructional materials that you create with the digital hub tools. The excitement you feel when you first see what you can do with the digital hub tools needs to be channeled, so you create the best possible products.

First, decide what you're trying to accomplish. Then, consider the types of materials you can create—separately or as complex hybrids. The chapter covered the preparation steps you need to take (such as teaching classes before taping them, if possible). And you've seen some of the special tools you can use and the challenges facing you if you record live events.

Chapter 23

Creating Portfolios

In This Chapter...

- **What Is a Portfolio?** Starting from the idea of a collection of various-sized papers, portfolios have grown to have many meanings, some of which are quite specific and well understood in various circles. The basics are described here.

- **What Goes in a Portfolio?** Portfolios can have a variety of purposes, which are discussed in this section.

- **Creating Portfolios for Specific Purposes.** Teachers, artists, and many other people have needs for portfolios. Some of the formats are presented here.

- **Putting Your Portfolio Together.** Finally, this section looks at some of the hints you can use in preparing your portfolio's content and putting it together.

Portfolios are perhaps the most general type of project you can create with the digital hub tools. A portfolio can consist of a paper bag into which you jam a ragged assortment of clippings and scraps, but it also can be a well-organized collection of important documents and an introduction to yourself or to an organization.

This chapter explores the variety of portfolios and some of the organizational and production tips you can use to make the most of digital hub tools in creating your own portfolios.

> **NOTE** *Some overlap exists among the concepts of scrapbooks, portfolios, and advertising. In this book, distinctions are made among the three. Scrapbooks are collections of things assembled—often by kids—as souvenirs and remembrances. Portfolios are records of work or of work processes. And advertising is generally a highly structured and controlled, yet usually simple, message. This distinction is made simply for convenience in writing the book. Feel free to use portfolios as scrapbooks and either as advertising.*

What Is a Portfolio?

Portfolios originated as large cases or binders in which to place pieces of paper. At the time (some three hundred years ago), no standard paper sizes existed, so portfolios tended to be large to accommodate a variety of sizes. From the beginning, portfolios were used for art work, maps, and souvenirs, as well as more mundane objects.

The capability to collect a variety of documents together is an important part of the concept of portfolio. A secondary point to note is portfolios often represent an unordered collection: different types of objects arose to keep the ordered collections of files, volumes of books, and the like.

Today, the word "portfolio" continues to be used for the object containing documents (as in "fine leather portfolio") as well as for the contents of a portfolio. In fact, portfolio is frequently used to refer to a collection of documents or of work that hasn't physically been assembled. (Portfolio also is used in diplomatic and investment circles with somewhat similar meanings.)

Your Mac and the digital hub tools can help you create a portfolio in either of these two senses. You can use it to create documents (on paper or on disc) to place in your portfolio alongside traditional documents. Or, you can use it to assemble, store, and then view your portfolio. The result might be a DVD or CD-ROM, or the result could be a folder on your disk (or even the entire disk!). It also could be a Web site.

Portfolios often collect together materials created for other purposes. Thus, you can find portfolios of artists' work (or that of architects and other designers), portfolios of students' projects over the course of a semester, and so on. When you decide you want to assemble a portfolio from your (or someone else's) work, it's much, much easier if you've done some initial planning when the work was first created.

If you're doing work for hire (as consultants and professionals often do), think about whether you might want to use your work in a portfolio or other promotional medium. If you might want to do this, arrange at the beginning to have that right. Asking a client at the start of a project if you can use photos, diagrams, descriptions, and other parts of the work in a portfolio is easy. Asking that question two years later could be tougher—the client might well have moved.

If you're creating work that's later sold (as artists and photographers do), your sale of the work could include reproduction rights. While you could be able to use the work or photographs of it in your own personal portfolio, you might be unable to reproduce it without the permission of the new owner.

Also, if your portfolio documents a process—say, your business advice to a company that is formulating a marketing strategy—you might be unable to use any of your work. In such cases, the company could well want the final strategy to emerge—miraculously—with no clue as to how it was developed (or even that a business consultant was involved). Don't feel bad if you're one of the hidden people who must work in this way. What you must do, however, is find a way to collect and publicize the public information that can be displayed.

Portfolios based on paper generally have an inherent order to them, although CD-ROMs and DVDs might provide wildly varying ways of proceeding once you

A Yearbook Made of Sports Cards

Sports cards are sometimes called trading cards or baseball cards. They contain photos of players along with statistics and other information. Collectors trade these cards and keep them—often in clear plastic sleeves that fit into binders and allow you to put up to nine cards on a page. (Other sizes exist.) Because the sleeves are clear, you can see the front and back of the cards without removing them.

Students at Pratt Institute's School of Art & Design created an innovative yearbook in 2002 using the these materials along with the Mac, Photoshop, and Quark XPress. Each student's photo and information appeared on the front of a card. When the cards are arranged alphabetically in the clear plastic sleeves, the backs of the cards on each page form a single mosaic-like image.

get them in a portfolio. Various types of order depend on the type of portfolio: chronological order predominates in process and performance portfolios (described in the following section). Organization based on categories, subjects, or even the alphabet can be appropriate. If you're creating a purely digital portfolio, the issue could be moot: whatever order the user wants can be created.

What Goes in a Portfolio?

Nearly anything can go into a portfolio—that, after all, was the point of creating these devices. If you're working with a traditional, paper-based portfolio, you can slip paper, photos, or discs (CD-ROMs or DVDs) into the portfolio.

If you're creating a totally digital portfolio, anything that can be digitized can go into it. (And, of course, anything that can be digitized can go onto the CD-ROM or DVD, which then can be placed in a paper-based portfolio.)

Five basic types of materials generally go into portfolios.

- Products
- Process and performance
- Perception

- Fiction
- Administrative materials

Products

A portfolio can contain *products*—work, or representations of work, which are examples of your work. Normally, a product-based portfolio contains either your best work or all of your work. In some cases, it might contain a logically selected portion of your work—a year's work, work related to a political cause, or work done for a certain client or type of client.

Process and Performance

Portfolios also can contain materials that illustrate *process* or *performance*. Frequently used in the education world, these portfolios demonstrate how an individual or group of people comes to learn or understand something. The materials along the way document the learning process. Each could be less than a perfect product but, together, they re-create the process.

Perception

Portfolios can be used to assemble a range of materials intended to sway perceptions about a cause, event, company, or other issue. In this way, portfolios are similar to the advertising messages discussed in Chapter 24. The difference is this: advertising usually consists of individual messages (often a wide variety—print ads, videos, and even media such as skywriting), while portfolios assemble all of these together.

Fiction

Up to this point, the assumption has been that the materials in a portfolio are real, even if they are reproductions of works of art. However, there is a long tradition of fictional works that masquerade as portfolios. Perhaps the classic examples of these are the epistolary novels—novels that purport to be letters among their principal characters. In a pure epistolary novel, the fictional letters are allowed to stand on their own: no narrator interprets or links them together. (What is generally considered the first novel in English, *Pamela*, was published in 1740 and written by Samuel Richardson. Previous proto-novels by authors such as Defoe and Swift themselves masqueraded as history books.)

Since the invention of the printing press, authors have yearned to break free of the tyranny of the book's physical format. Digital portfolios provide the most significant opportunity for this to happen.

Administrative Material

Portfolios typically contain a certain amount of administrative material ranging from title pages to instructions on how to use, and then return, the portfolio. Even though this might consist only of a single page, don't forget it. As you smile to yourself, remember that unintentionally anonymous portfolios need to be thrown out every day in galleries and offices because their creators have left this important information out.

Creating Portfolios for Specific Purposes

Portfolios are used in a number of specific areas. Some of the most common are discussed in this section, with their individual requirements and characteristics described. The types of portfolios described here are those created for:

- Products
- Artists, artisans, and craftspeople
- Education
- Publications
- Professional work
- Personal journals

Products

Perhaps the most common form of portfolio is the portfolio created for a product or set of products. These product portfolios can be descriptive and informative, they can be sales materials, or they can be any other communication tool for conveying information about a product.

You can assemble such portfolios in a remarkably sophisticated manner by using the supplies you find in your local office products store. Preprinted and scored folders with pockets for paper and brochures abound in office supply stores. You can use your computer to produce documents that fit precisely into these forms and folders. A number of companies produce these forms: among them are Avery, Rank Xerox, and MACO/Wilson Jones. Each form is numbered by the vendor, and you can access prepared formats in common applications.

Many of these special-purpose forms evolved from mailing labels. That is why today you use commands with the word "label" in them to format labels, brochures, and a host of other special-purpose products that aren't labels.

For example, in Microsoft Word, choose Labels from the Tools menu to bring up the general labels formatting window. Then click Options, as shown in Figure 23-1, to select the individual product you want to format.

In AppleWorks, you find the label formatting commands in the database section. Create a database, and then choose New Label Layout from the Layout menu. You'll be walked through the process of selecting and formatting your data for specific forms, as shown in Figure 23-2.

All the portfolio tools and media discussed in this chapter can be used to produce product portfolios. Often these portfolios are among the most varied in their formats and styles. This is because, in many cases, the portfolio itself needs to attract the attention of the purchaser. Thus, you'll find strange shapes and sizes, garish colors, all sorts of motion DVD menus, and any other attention-grabber in product portfolios.

In this way, product portfolios are quite different from the next set of portfolios—those created by artists, artisans, and craftspeople.

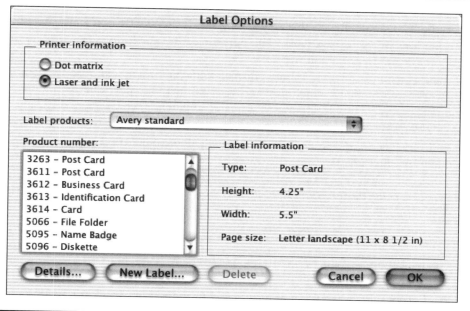

FIGURE 23-1   Formatting labels with Microsoft Word

Creating Portfolios for Specific Purposes

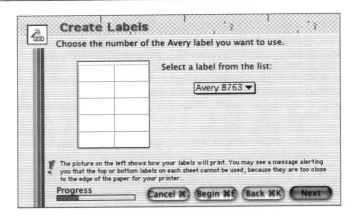

FIGURE 23-2   Formatting labels with AppleWorks

Artists, Artisans, and Craftspeople

These people use portfolios in two different ways. In the first, an artist creates a portfolio to provide an introduction to a gallery owner or representative. The portfolio is commonly a single object (that is, it isn't copied), frequently containing expensive reproductions of the artist's work. The purpose of the portfolio is to facilitate the introduction and to pique interest.

These portfolios follow a common format: you change it at your risk. Remember, your work is your creative medium, and your job with the portfolio is to represent it and yourself as clearly as possible to someone with whom you want to do business. The gallery owner or artist's representative could be unamused (or totally uninterested) in a portfolio that doesn't fit in a file cabinet with all the others or that makes demands not made by other artists.

> **NOTE**   *This is the most traditionally structured of all the types of portfolios discussed in this chapter. You might want to use the structure in a modified form for other types of portfolios.*

The basic components of an artist's portfolio are listed here:

■ **Letter**   It starts with a brief letter of introduction explaining its purpose. Are you looking for representation? A show? Who are you and how can you be contacted?

■ **Resume**   This is the resume that introduces you professionally. It should contain relevant material only—education, awards, shows, publications, and pertinent jobs. It should be structured as formally as any resume. Note, two resume styles exist. In the business world, resumes are normally one page long, but in the educational world, bulk is good. If you're starting out, your resume might be small. You can find guidance for young artists at the Web sites listed at the end of this section.

■ **Artist's Statement**   Artists' statements have become an important part of any artist's portfolio of work. An *artist's statement* is a relatively brief first-person statement of what you're trying to do with your art, what difference you want to make in the world, or any other major issue that applies to all your work (not a single piece). At first glance, this might appear a great place to explore digital media—iPhoto, iMovie, and iDVD can be used to create wonderful artists' statements. But beware: a text-based statement could serve you best. This is because it can be copied out and pasted into press releases, newspaper articles, brochures, and the like. Perhaps the more expansive media-rich artist's statement should become a piece of art instead.

■ **Biography**   Often (but not always) written in the first person, a *biography* is a brief history of your life. While your resume should include relevant jobs, education, and the like, this is where you describe the kind of person you are. (If you haven't prepared a resume and biography before, you might find it easy to work on them together—you'll realize that some material belongs in one rather than the other, and you can sort it out quickly on your Mac.)

■ **Materials (visual)**   Here is the bulk of your portfolio. In the case of most artists, artisans, and craftspeople, this consists of photos and movies of your work. If your work itself is created on DVDs or CD-ROMs, this can be the work itself. And, if your work is designed to be reproduced (if, for example, your work is mass-produced postcards), it can be the work itself. The ordering of this work is as important as the hanging of paintings in a gallery. And don't think that if you present your work on a CD-ROM or DVD, no ordering exists: Multiple orderings might exist, but there are definitely orderings to your work.

■ **Materials List**   Following the materials should be a list of what they are, possibly with prices, dates created, or other supporting information. To pursue the gallery analogy, this is the catalog to the paintings on the walls.

■ **Press Clippings**   Copies of reviews, interviews, or other material that has appeared about your work.

■ **Return Postage or Instructions**   If your portfolio is designed to be kept, make that clear in your cover letter. If your portfolio is the traditional kind— a binder with many fairly expensive reproductions representing a lot of assembly time, you probably want it back. Let people know how to return it.

The second type of portfolio is designed to be distributed along with the artist's work. Whether this is a several-thousand-dollar painting or a small carving that costs little, buyers of work by living artists and craftspeople generally like to know more about the person behind the work. Thus, a portfolio that can be reproduced relatively inexpensively might accompany such work. In addition to being an intrinsic part of the sale of the artwork, it could also aid in further sales, of course.

One of the attractions of creating an artist's portfolio using digital hub tools is that the question of the cost of reproduction can be eliminated. If the portfolio is entirely digital, no difference exists in the cost between the portfolio you leave with a gallery owner and the portfolio you can afford to give away with the sale of your lowest-priced work.

NOTE   *Many resources are available on the Web for artists, artisans, and craftspeople. A number of organizations provide significant assistance for the business and professional side of these activities. Among the sites you might find useful are Arts Resource Network, a project of the Seattle Arts Commission (**http://www.artsresourcenetwork.org/professional_growth/**) and New York Foundation for the Arts (**http://www.nyfa.org/**).*

Education

Portfolios have achieved a great deal of prominence in the education world over the last few years. They are used by both teachers and students. In both cases, portfolios are used to present products—samples of work as well as processes and performance.

Teachers

Teachers frequently use portfolios to document the processes by which they evolve their performance and hone their professional skills. The portfolio can serve as a detailed description of their techniques, and can be used both in looking for a job and in furthering professional development.

NOTE   *The National Board for Professional Teaching Standards offers National Board Certification based on a two-step process, one step of which is a portfolio. (For more information see **http://www.nea.org/issues/certification/02nbptsfacts.html**.) Another excellent resource about teachers' portfolios is "Designing Teacher Portfolios"—A Joint Project of The College of Education and Psychology, North Carolina State University and Public Schools of North Carolina (**http://www2.ncsu.edu/unity/lockers/project/portfolios/portfoliointro.html**).*

A teacher's portfolio contains materials similar to those found in an artist's portfolio, but some additional items are normally included. These largely reflect the fact that an artist is at least a semipublic person (and, therefore, might well garner press notices), whereas a teacher's activities are normally far more private. You might add some of these items to a teacher's portfolio:

- **References**   Names and addresses of people who can be contacted to provide further information. You might add a few words indicating your relationship ("studied with . . .", "worked for . . . ").

- **Educational transcripts**   These provide substantially more information than the information on your resume.

- **Letters of recommendation**   Rather than including the contact information, you might have letters attesting to your qualities. These should be included.

- **Goals, teaching philosophy, and educational theories**   These replace the artist's statement.

- **Lesson plans, photos, assignments, and student work**   These obviously replace the artist's work.

Students

Student portfolios are widely used in many schools as a way of evaluating progress and understanding of material. Part of their attraction is they provide a way of looking at a student's work that's as far removed from the perspective of a standardized test as possible.

Student portfolios are far less structured than artists' or teachers' portfolios, in large part because their purpose is so different. They should start with identifying information and a statement of purpose. Thereafter their structure depends on student, teacher, and subject matter. (Refer to Chapter 21 for more information about kids and scrapbooks. Most of those ideas apply also to students' portfolios.)

Publications

Portfolios can be used to publish information. Publication portfolios differ from those described previously because they *are* the subject (the portfolios discussed previously were *about* products or people).

Publications are much like product portfolios in that their formats and features are totally customizable. The issues raised in the portfolios mentioned here might apply to publication portfolios, and you should consider them if they fit into your plans.

Professional Work

Professional work portfolios are the general cases of the second type of portfolios discussed in the section "Artists, Artisans, and Craftspeople," as well as the education portfolios for teachers. You can use the outlines in those sections as a way to get started.

Stonemasons and the Digital Hub

Timothy Smith and his wife Laura Smith run a stonemasonry business in Columbia County, New York. They've been in business for over 20 years. They build stone walls, paths, and steps, among other things. They employ a five-person crew, and can be reached via email at **tltsmith@mhonline.net**. I asked Laura how digital hub technology has changed the way they do business and particularly what effect it's had on their portfolio.

Laura told me, "We bought a digital camera at the beginning of the year for our stonemasonry business. I knew it would be helpful, but I had no idea that it would completely change the way we do business. We do work for a lot of folks with weekend homes. Most of our clients have email, which has been great for sending proposals, bills, and information. The camera has allowed us to take pictures of our work daily, if necessary, and send it to the client. We don't have to wait for clients to see the work to get paid.

"It's so easy to take many pictures of our work, new and old, that we have much better pictures for our portfolio than we have in the past. We even take pictures of stones at quarries for approval."

For some professionals, these portfolios of their work are a basic marketing tool helping them get new jobs. This is particularly the case for designers of objects (such as houses) that aren't easy to lug around to potential clients.

You can use a portfolio of professional work as your own resume. If you do so, follow the general outlines in the earlier sections on artists and teachers. Depending on your particular career and your goals, you might make your professional portfolio more or less extensive. Remember, the point is to introduce yourself, what you do, how and why you do it, and how well you do it.

Many professional portfolios are grouped together on search engines and portals such as Yahoo! You might find them under "portfolio" or under the common category "personal exhibits." Professional portfolios are typically grouped by profession or business.

NOTE | *Many colleges, universities, and trade schools provide assistance to students and graduates as they assemble portfolios of their student and professional work. Among them is the University of Wisconsin—River Falls (**http://www.uwrf.edu/ccs/portfoli.htm**).*

Journals

The last type of portfolio consists of a journal of a person, group, or event. Its organization is generally chronological, although other organizations are possible. These are the generic form of the process portfolios described previously.

Putting Your Portfolio Together

You've defined your portfolio, decided what goes into it, and laid out its structure. Now all that remains is to do the work. The techniques for using digital hub tools have already been described in this book, but you might want to consider a few more points. These are grouped into several categories:

- Content hints

- Producing your portfolio

- Updating your portfolio

Content Hints

Here are some hints for formatting content for a portfolio. They apply to all cases in which you're distributing digital files.

■ Don't forget, almost every application that supports printing lets you create PDF files (see Chapter 6). PDF files can be read by Acrobat Reader on almost any computer platform. If your portfolio contains word processing documents or proprietary-format graphics documents (such as Photoshop documents), consider saving them in PDF format.

■ If your portfolio is to be viewed from other computers and on other operating systems, make certain your file naming will work. In particular, make certain you use standard three-character file extensions. On operating systems such as Windows, a JPEG file that doesn't have the .jpg extension won't open properly.

■ This same tip applies to files placed on a Web site.

Producing Your Portfolio

These are a few suggestions for producing your portfolio with digital hub tools (rather than simply producing its contents with digital hub tools).

■ Use the HomePage publishing or Album printing features of iPhoto to create a Web site or hardcover album of your portfolio.

■ If you use iMovie to create your portfolio, you can include still images, slides, and graphics. You can then export it as a QuickTime movie and burn it onto a CD-ROM. This enables you to distribute your portfolio quickly and in a reasonably inexpensive way.

■ iDVD is, of course, the most sophisticated of the digital hub tools for creating a portfolio. It enables the user more control over how the material is viewed. iDVD puts a correspondingly larger burden on you to make what's on the DVD clear.

■ You can create a Web-based portfolio in a variety of ways. You can create one from iPhoto using HomePage. You can also export selected photos from iPhoto to a Web site that's created on your disk. You can then modify the various HTML files produced. And, of course, you can use a Web site development tool, such as Dreamweaver or GoLive, to do the work.

■ Use the DVD-ROM section on a DVD to distribute files along with your movies. Click the Theme button and the Status tab, then use the pop-up menu to select DVD-ROM Contents and just drag them in.

Updating Your Portfolio

This is the sort of issue that appears at first glance to require no thought or consideration—but that's rather complex. In addition to all the other decisions you've made about your portfolio, you have another one to make: what time frame does it cover? Does the time frame represent your work and your goals as of a certain time, or are you committing to update it periodically, so it's always new? (If you think this is a minor issue, read the vehement arguments about "modern art." Is "modern art" the art of today or the art of the period that followed the impressionists and more or less ended after the abstract expressionists?)

Make certain you understand the choices you make and that you follow through. The Web is littered with sites that say, "I will keep this updated with my philosophy of life as it evolves" and that don't deliver on the promise (threat?). If you or your organization plan annual updates to your portfolio, make sure you can do it. If not, plan three- or five-year updates.

Finally, what happens to a portfolio that's obsolete? That general topic is covered in Chapter 25.

Summary

This chapter has examined the broad area of portfolios and shown you how to create and organize your own portfolios with digital hub tools. A portfolio is a collection of materials in various media that are put together for a purpose. That purpose may be to describe a person or product, it may be to document a process or performance of a person or organization, it may be to create or change perceptions, or it can even be used as a tool of fiction. Knowing what you're doing helps you to do it better.

For teachers, artists, professionals, and other people, specific portfolio structures, formats, and organizations can help you create portfolios that are particularly effective. The layouts of these have been described here.

Finally, you saw some content-preparation and portfolio-production tips that can speed up and improve your work.

Portfolios generally consist of a lot of information, and they present rather complex information ("this is who I am, what I think about teaching, and how I do it"). On the other hand, advertising generally consists of fairly limited information (sometimes even a single word or phrase or a ten-second video), and the message is usually quite targeted and specific. Advertising is the subject of the next chapter.

Chapter 24

Creating and Advertising Promotional Materials

In This Chapter...

- ■ Planning Your Advertising. The chapter starts with a brief overview of advertising and how it works.

- ■ Choosing the Message and the Look. The digital hub tools help you produce unified advertising using themes you can customize. This section looks at the concepts and the specific steps you can take to implement them.

- ■ Multipurposing Content. Because the Macintosh makes sharing files and data among applications so easy, you can zoom among the tools of the digital hub, your word processor and page layout software, and even databases.

- ■ New Digital Adventures in Advertising. Customization and participation are only two aspects of advertising made much easier with the digital hub. They're discussed in this section.

The tools of the digital hub make it possible for anyone to create advertising and promotional materials. You, too, can create a world-class advertising campaign for your business and, using the phenomenal power and inexpensive cost of Internet publishing, you can reach millions of people with your advertising message. Nothing prevents you from doing so—or from sending an unclear, unattractive, uncoordinated, and generally repulsive advertising message to one and all. The results might not be what you expect.

As with the other projects described in this part of the book, the digital hub technologies bring new possibilities to individuals and organizations. What you do with them—and how well you pull off your projects—is your business. Because these are new possibilities for so many people, you need to think about what you'll do and how you'll do it.

Advertising Attributes

This chapter addresses advertising issues. Advertising is used here to refer to communications that combine most of these attributes:

- ■ *Advertising is public.* It might use mass media, such as broadcast or print, or it could use individually targeted and addressed media, such as direct mail. However, advertising generally doesn't refer to individual communications. (*Marketing* is the term generally used for sales calls.)

- ■ *Advertising messages are generally well honed and relatively simple.* They might promote businesses, products, services, or ideas. More complex messages fall into other categories, such as instructional materials.

- ■ *Advertising is often repeated.*

- ■ *Advertising is often customized to different markets.*

- ■ *Advertising is generally time-sensitive.* The products, services, and ideas advertising promotes change over time. Also, different aspects of the products, services, and ideas become more or less important over time.

- ■ *Advertising is generally competitive.* Each message must struggle with other messages for attention and credibility.

- ■ *Advertising might be aimed at getting people to act—to buy or to vote, for example.*

- ■ *Advertising could also be aimed at ratifying decisions that have already been made.* (Apple's advertisements are among the best in the advertising industry and often are followed more intently by Apple computer owners than by anyone else.)

- ■ *Advertising as we know it today took shape with the invention of the printing press.* That technological revolution made it feasible to communicate to large groups of people without bringing them together.

While you might disagree with some of these characterizations of advertising, these are the aspects addressed in this chapter. Remember, the purpose of this chapter is to help you understand some of the principles behind advertising, so you can use it effectively with the tools of the digital hub. For more information, consult any of the excellent textbooks and articles on the subject of advertising.

Try to think of advertising in the broadest possible way: everything from Coca-Cola to the flyers distributed by a candidate for the local library board. The techniques are the same. And, with the digital hub tools, the local library board candidate could well be using the same tools as the advertising manager for Coca-Cola. Not similar tools: the same tools. The advertising industry is a veritable hot-bed of Macintosh computers.

Also, be aware that an understanding of advertising doesn't mean you'll do it yourself. If you have no intention of doing advertising for yourself or anyone else, this chapter will let you see how other people approach the subject. If you hire professionals to handle your advertising needs, knowing what they're doing can help you produce the best possible advertising.

Advertising Attributes

Planning Your Advertising

This chapter is no different from the others in this part of the book: it starts with an admonition to plan what you're doing. Set objectives—measurable, if possible— for your advertising and consider how you'll determine if your advertising is working.

How Advertising Works (Maybe)

Advertising messages are often repeated. The theory goes that it takes several repetitions of a message for it to sink in. In the world of media clutter, messages often aren't even noticed in many cases. Thus, advertisers try to make certain their messages are noticed. This can be done with special effects, humor, shocking images, and a host of other techniques. Often, those effects (such as humor) themselves rely on repetition. When you're watching television and you say to a friend, "Watch this commercial—it's funny," you've already seen it before and responded to the humor with attention. Advertisers like this.

In placing advertisements, advertisers often talk about reach and frequency. *Reach* refers to the percent of a target market that sees the commercial at all. *Frequency* refers to the number of times an individual sees the commercial. Some media are, by their very nature, more focused on reach or on frequency. The commercial Apple used to introduce the Macintosh in 1984 is (in addition to being considered one of the best commercials of all time) is an excellent example of a commercial that ignored considerations of frequency. It was shown nationally only once—during the 1984 Super Bowl football game. This TV show attracts one of the largest audiences in the world, so the commercial's reach was enormous.

This commercial also illustrates another aspect of advertising that savvy advertisers use. The commercial itself became news. In fact, although Apple only paid to broadcast the commercial once nationwide, it was rebroadcast over and over on news shows, and it was written about in the press. (This can also be dangerous. Many examples of commercials accidentally become news.)

| NOTE | *One of the best sources of information is the Advertising Research Foundation, which can be reached on the Web at **http://www.arfsite.org/**. This foundation publishes a respected magazine, the* Journal of Advertising Research, *which contains a great deal of useful information. Because advertising information is so often treated as highly secret, competitive information, public sources of information about advertising and the research conducted on it can be hard to come by.* |

Advertising that relies on repetition requires not only a degree of memory on the part of the reader or viewer, but it also requires it to be recognizable, so the memory is sparked. This is one of the reasons many advertisements use distinctive layouts and typefaces. As you see in an upcoming section, "Choosing the Message and the Look," you can use the options in the digital hub tools to create memorable advertising easily.

Setting Objectives

The purpose of your advertising can change over time. And, at any given time, you could have several objectives in mind. What's important is for you to know what your objectives are. What's amazing is how many people never get to this crucial step in planning.

If your advertising is keyed to an event—a fund-raising picnic, for example—its purpose is clear. Likewise, if it's designed to promote a product, that objective is known. Another broad category of advertising, known as *image advertising,* is where you promote the kind of company you are and the kinds of things you do. Many companies run both types of advertising, often at the same time.

The media you use sometimes determine the objectives of your advertising. If you run a small business and are approached to buy an advertisement in the annual business directory for your community, generalized image advertising might be your only option. You certainly can't consider promoting a time-dependent event in an ad that will be available for an entire year. You might be able to promote individual products or services.

Make your objectives specific. Advertisers speak of campaigns, and each *campaign* usually has its own objective. And each campaign has its own message. You should be able to express that message succinctly. If you can't do so now, you won't be able to create effective advertising.

Quantifying Results

If you've set your objective, you still aren't ready to implement your advertising campaign. Make sure you can measure its results. For a large corporation, these measurements can be complex and expensive, often involving market research, analysis of sales data, and even coverage of the company and its advertising in the press. For a small organization, the measurement could be much simpler: does the phone ring (or email arrive) more often? Are sales higher?

If you can't quantify the results you expect, it might be that your objective isn't quite clear enough yet. Quantifying your results could involve a variety of tools on your Macintosh. You might decide to track calls, emails, or sales in a way you haven't done before. Set up your database or spreadsheet now so it'll be ready when you need it. As you prepare to collect your results, you could discover additional data you want to collect—and you also might very well discover nuances or changes to make in your advertising.

. . . And Then Change

Prepare and release your advertising—and then get ready to change. Remember, the tools you're dealing with make it possible for any organization (even a part-time, self-employed person) to move quickly. If your results are below your expectations, think about what you can do (or decrease your expectations). Also remember, projections and plans are designed to help you: they aren't the goals themselves.

Choosing the Message and the Look

Your advertising has a variety of tasks to be performed: it must get attention, be recognizable (so repeated exposures are noticed and counted as reinforcement, not just additional unrelated messages), and communicate its message. The tools you have on your Macintosh and in the digital hub help you do this—and do it repeatedly. Although a brilliant idea could come in a flash, more often advertising is refined and adjusted repeatedly. (In fact, advertising for major advertisers might be the most heavily revised of all materials.)

NOTE

Anything can make your advertising memorable and distinctive. The trick is to find something noticeable (and memorable) that reinforces your message without distracting from it. Examples of such features are distinctive typefaces, a recurring image or spokesperson, a certain style of design or illustration, and an editorial style. Each of these has been used successfully, each has been copied and overused, and then fallen out of fashion. For example, at one time, ads with dense copy were all the rage. Then, print ads with few words—or no words—became popular. Out-of-focus photos or images cropped so they were off-center have also had their moments in the sun. Teaser ads—ads omitting a product name—have had some success, but they require rather high media budgets. This is because when the tease is revealed, you need to make certain your potential audience has seen and remembered the initial unidentified ads.

The first step in choosing the implementation of your advertising (that is, selecting the exact wording of the message and the look of the advertising) is converting your planned objectives into words and images. The second step is to make certain this implementation is feasible. To do that, check to make certain all the media you might use will accommodate your message and its look. Here are the steps to take in iPhoto, iMovie, and iDVD.

Creating the Look in iPhoto

iPhoto can help you in advertising in three ways. The first is simply to use its organization and editing facilities to keep track of your photos and to export them for use in other software. In addition, using the Share button, you can create Web pages with HomePage or with the Web page export option; and you can create books. When you create HomePage Web pages and books, you can make a variety of choices. If you use the Export command to create Web pages with your photos, you can subsequently go into the HTML that's been generated and make any changes you want.

In creating a book, you have the choices described previously in Chapter 11 and shown here in Figure 24-1.

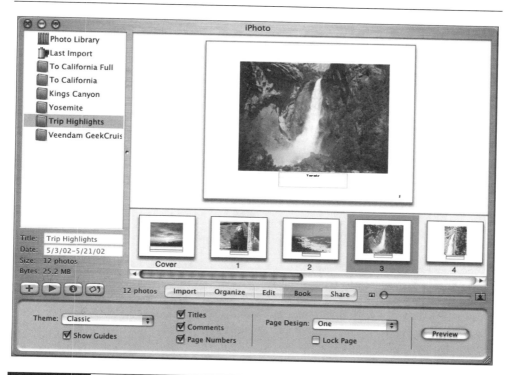

FIGURE 24-1   Format a book with iPhoto.

You can't control the actual fonts used in preparing the book, but you do have a variety of choices regarding the theme of the book and its page design. (Page design includes not only the layout but also the number of photos per page.)

Your choices can vary according to the page and the photos on it. But you can also use these choices to help construct a visual identity for your advertising. (You can experiment with looks even if you don't plan to create books with iPhoto.) Explore the choices to help choose page layouts for print ads.

In HomePage, you have limited control over the layout of your Web pages. As shown in Figure 24-2, your choices are limited to the frames (if any) around the images and to the text at the top of the page.

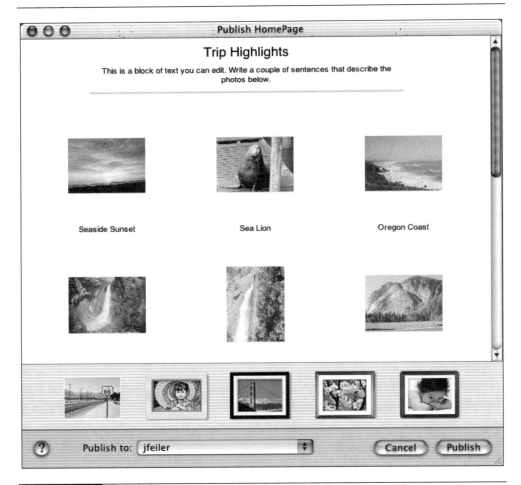

FIGURE 24-2   HomePage layout settings

Even with these limited settings, you can implement your own distinctive look. If you use a certain type of frame, combine it with images that have a "look" to them and then top it off with text that has a distinctive tone: you'll have your own style.

Because iPhoto provides the most limited ways of customizing books and Web pages, if you're using it for your advertising, you might want to start with it because you can implement these features in other tools, but you generally can't get iPhoto to be as flexible as iMovie or iDVD.

Creating the Look in iMovie

Several customizable features of iMovie can help you to hone a distinctive look for your advertising. One of the most potent is the Titles option, as shown in Figure 24-3.

In addition to the actual wording of the titles, you can set their location, duration, style, and color. Any or all of these attributes can combine to create the look of

FIGURE 24-3   Title settings in iMovie

your advertising. You can use your title settings to carry over into other media formats. For example, although iPhoto doesn't support titling of images in this way, you can use a tool such as Photoshop (or AppleWorks) to superimpose text over photos. If you use the same fonts and styles as you do in iMovie, you'll make your graphics consistent.

Creating the Look in iDVD

The theme customization commands in iDVD are perhaps the most sophisticated of any of the digital hub tools. You can use them in iDVD itself and, as with iMovie, you can use the effects you create in other types of media by using editing tools, such as Photoshop, iMovie, or Final Cut Pro.

Figure 24-4 shows how you can customize a theme in iDVD.

You can set a background image or video, set the title font, location, and color, and even add audio tracks (to both video and still images). You can apply a theme to an entire project or only to sections of it.

Themes help people navigate through your DVD. You can use elements of the theme (such as a distinctive typeface, an image, or a logo) in your other media

FIGURE 24-4   Customize themes in iDVD.

and, as you experiment with themes in iDVD, you can use their salient elements in other aspects of your advertising.

Figure 24-4 helps to illustrate an issue that frequently arises when you're trying to implement a look in a variety of media. The background image shown in the previous figure is beautiful, but it contains a variety of levels of brightness. The foreground (the beach) is dark, and it's suitable as a background for light-colored letters. The sky has many gradations, and text placed against it might be hard to read.

You can take advantage of these features. For example, because the bottom of the image cries out for light-colored text, this can help you distinguish that text from the other text you might use. Or you can go to iPhoto or iMovie (or Final Cut Pro or Photoshop) and adjust the image or movie that forms the background of the menu theme in iDVD. By increasing or decreasing the brightness and contrast of the image, you not only can make it brighter or darker, you can also make it more uniform.

iDVD lets you save themes as favorites. When you click the Save in Favorites button at the bottom of the Customize tab, you're prompted for a name, as shown in Figure 24-5.

FIGURE 24-5   Share themes by saving them as Favorites.

Choosing the Message and the Look

If several people are working on a project, you'll probably want to share the themes as Figure 24-5 shows. Otherwise, leave the themes private for your own user ID alone.

Creating Looks with Other Tools

In the preceding sections, you've seen how some of the customization features of iPhoto, iMovie, and iDVD can help you create consistent images that will make your advertising more recognizable. You can use other tools in this way. Photoshop is perhaps the most frequently used tool in this field. As shown in Figure 24-6, you can warp text in a variety of ways.

You select the text to warp, and then choose Warp from the Text submenu in the Layer menu. This brings up the dialog box shown in Figure 24-6, in which you can choose the type of warp you want.

The combination of a specific type of warping with a certain font can create a unique look to your text. If you do investigate warping, be careful in its use: standard

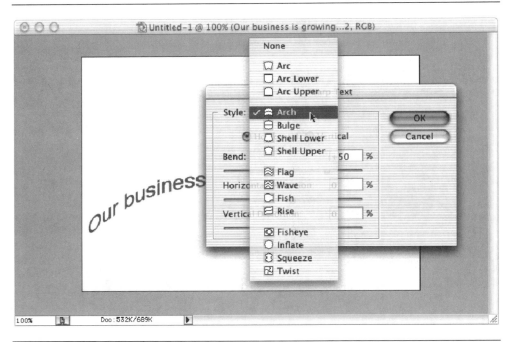

FIGURE 24-6   Warping text in Photoshop

text is designed for easy reading, while warped text is designed to draw attention to itself and can be hard to read.

Multipurposing Content

Bounce back and forth among the tools in the digital hub (and with all the tools on your Macintosh). Because so many of the graphic effects are ultimately implemented by the operating system (specifically the Quartz imaging engine) and because you can copy-and-paste images among many different applications, you can easily create consistent looks to your advertising in a variety of media.

More than any other computer platform, the Macintosh is designed for this type of data sharing. Take advantage of it—and prepare for it. Preparation for this data sharing usually takes the form of experimentation. If you're choosing a font and style for DVD menus, using that same font and style in your movie titles as well as in your word processing documents is reasonable. Experiment with all of them, paying particular attention to whether common phrases (such as your company's name) will fit in the various media using the given font.

NOTE *If you aren't used to working with fonts, you might be surprised to discover that fonts of the same size are different sizes. You can prove this for yourself with any word processing application. Type a word of medium length (eight to ten letters will do). Change its font—not its font size—between Helvetica and Times. Observe how the word's dimensions change both horizontally and vertically.*

The degree to which you reuse your material is up to you. You can reuse still images from movies as graphics for printing, or you can reuse the actors or objects you photograph by photographing them both on video and with a digital camera. The reuse of the actual image will result in poorer quality of the still image (because stills from video aren't as good as digital camera images). Nevertheless, both these techniques are multipurposing of content at one level or another.

New Digital Adventures in Advertising

The widespread availability of digital media as well as the rise of the Internet have made a number of new advertising techniques possible. You can explore them as well as the next person. In fact, an individual might have more options available than a large multinational corporation. You, after all, are likely to approve your own ideas, rather than having to go through channels to have them modified and approved . . . sometime.

Customization

Technology makes customizing advertising messages possible to a degree never before imagined. For decades, mail merge programs have allowed customization of direct mail. Today, more extensive databases and a wider variety of customizable tools have made this technology even more attractive to advertisers.

You can customize your messages in a variety of ways. If you communicate directly with people (as in mail or email), you can use the information you know about them to automatically tailor the communication. If your customers communicate with you (perhaps by logging on to your Web site), you can also do the same type of customization. Either technique can make the exchange much more useful. Here are two of many issues you should consider, however:

- Make certain the information you obtain is obtained legally. In general, people need to know the types of information you collect on them. Certain information (such as accounting data) can be assumed. Other information—such as that obtained from a Web site without explicitly asking an individual—needs to be identified. For more information on standards and guidance in the general area of privacy, see **http://www.truste.org**.

- Make certain the information is correct. This means not only that the data is correct in and of itself, but that the person you're dealing with is who you think it is. (In other words, if someone borrows a friend's password to log on to your Web site, the information you "know" is wrong because the person isn't who you think it is.)

Furthermore, if you're going to customize your communication, think about the ways you can do so before you develop your advertising (and before you collect the data you'll use for customization). For example, such planning might lead you to require a login ID for your Web site so at some point in the future your visitors can receive customized information. The tools of the digital hub can serve as a basis for customization of messages. Their implementation will probably involve other tools and skills—perhaps relational databases and application servers (such as Apple's WebObjects).

Participation

Another feature of advertising in the digital age is the heightened degree to which people can participate in advertising. Just as the digital hub tools make creating movies and forging your own DVDs much easier than ever before, those tools make it easier for your customers and potential customers to do so.

Many companies now solicit testimonials on digital media. If you do so, make sure you get a legal release to use the information submitted. It's important to follow up with that piece of detail as quickly as possible. If you don't, you might lose track of the individual (addresses—both email and postal—change quickly and frequently).

You can also encourage people to use your information and advertising for themselves. In the first days of the Web, this was done by encouraging people to link to your Web site. Today, advertisers offer a wide variety of features people can use in building their own Web sites and creating their own digital media.

The area of cooperative advertising flourishes anew with the Web. *Cooperative advertising* refers to the practice of large companies preparing advertising, which is then customized to a greater or lesser extent by local companies. Prepare your Web site with an eye toward a localized copy of it being updated by your customers.

For more sophisticated users, you can create an iMovie project with space for people to add their own clips—you can provide the basic information and set up titles and transitions so they only have to insert a single clip. Or, you can do something similar with an iDVD project. If you use iDVD, remember the media to be used in the DVD needs to be kept together with the DVD project itself if you plan to transfer it from one machine to another. In the case of DVDs, you're likely to have better results if you solicit video and images from your customers and you create individualized DVDs for them.

Direct Communication

Along with various forms of mail and telephone calls, instant messaging has become an important communication tool. With Mac OS X 10.2, Apple has provided its own instant messaging software—iChat. You can use *iChat* to communicate with clients, vendors, and others. iChat is far more than a messaging system. For example, you can easily use it to share files, including images. Just drag the file or image into the iChat message window and you can send it.

iChat interacts with the America Online Instant Messaging System (AIM). It also supports the concept of a local network of chatters—the people who are on the network with you. You can use it for internal chats and messages in this way.

New Digital Adventures in Advertising

Summary

This chapter has examined some of the techniques of advertising and some of the ways you can use the digital hub tools to develop your own advertising.

As with each of the types of projects discussed in this part of the book, you start by planning your advertising. Setting its objectives, planning how to quantify its results, and preparing to change things as your advertising proceeds are the basics you need for a successful advertising campaign.

The look of your advertising helps it communicate and helps people recognize your ads. Recognition is important because it's the rare advertisement that fulfills its mission with a single exposure. You can use features of the digital hub tools to customize your advertising and to make it consistent across various media.

Finally, some of the possibilities with customization and participation have been discussed. In all the aspects of this chapter, you've seen how you can use digital hub technologies, along with the Internet, to improve the highly focused and directed communication that forms the heart of advertising.

With this chapter, nearly every aspect of the digital hub has been addressed in this book. There's only one more issue to deal with: using these tools to archive your information so you can store your information and then go back to it as you want. And related to that are the issues involved in displaying your work and using the digital hub to assist in exhibitions.

Chapter 25

Creating Archives and Exhibitions

In This Chapter...

■ Presenting Exhibits with the Digital Hub. You can create your own museum-quality exhibits with the tools of the digital hub. Here are some tips to use and some examples of what you can do.

■ Archiving Your Work. You're not done with a project until you clean up and put away your tools—and your digital data. This section helps you decide what to save and how to do so.

■ Summing Up: Making the Digital Hub Disappear. Finally, remember that the point of it all is not the digital hub itself but what you can do with it.

This, the final chapter of the book, looks at issues of presentation and preservation with the digital hub and its tools. The section on presentation brings together a number of different tools and technologies discussed in this book. As you've seen in this part of the book, you can use the tools for scrapbooks of personal mementos, for portfolios to present your ideas to others, and for specific types of communications, such as teaching and advertising. You can also use these tools to present—or to aid in the presentation of—the kind of information and materials you would find in a museum. This last type of project differs from all the preceding ones in this part of the book because it's intrinsically bound to nondigital objects, like those in a museum or library. (It can also be bound to digital objects, but they normally aren't under your control the way your own photos and movies are. The chapter makes this distinction clear.)

Preservation, as used here, refers to those issues concerned with preserving both your digital-hub final products and the support and work files you've used along the way. You might be preserving them as a record of your work or in case you need to repeat or revise your work. Either way, you have to deal with these issues.

The final part of this chapter gives you some tips for moving on. At the end of Part 3, you saw how you could move on beyond the digital hub tools to your own digital studio. Here, you see how you can move in another direction—not to more sophisticated digital hub tools, but rather back into your own work and play with the skills and knowledge that you've learned from the digital hub.

Presenting Exhibits with the Digital Hub

Up to this point, the digital hub tools and the movies, photos, CD-ROMs, and DVDs you make with them have been the center of attention. In this section, you will find some ideas and suggestions for using the digital hub tools to support exhibits of (usually) nondigital artifacts, images, art, history, and the like.

Think about your last trip to a museum and, if you can, remember what museums were like a few decades ago. Years ago, museums were repositories of artifacts. Paintings were hung on walls, sculptures were placed on plinths, and glass cases in arrayed rows displayed minerals, tools, and other small objects. Small cards announced a bare minimum of information about each item.

Today's museums and exhibitions are far more involving. Rather than simply being warehouses for relics, museums attempt to place the materials in context and to involve the visitor. This applies across all exhibition types—from large national museums, to booths at trade shows, and to small displays in schools, libraries, and community centers. The tools of the digital hub provide you with what you need to turn that collection of dusty objects into an exciting learning (or marketing) experience.

Supporting Traditional Exhibits

The first thing to consider in supporting traditional exhibits is that you are, indeed, supporting them. Your movies, photos, graphics, CD-ROMs, and DVDs augment, enhance, and illustrate the stars of the show.

To get an idea of what you can do with the digital hub tools to support an exhibition, walk through any museum or trade show and look around. What, other than the paint on the walls and the exhibits themselves, can you *not* do with your Mac? Here are some suggestions.

Printing Exhibition Materials

You can do two types of print jobs to support an exhibition. The first is the production of pamphlets, brochures, advertising, and catalogues to support the exhibition. This a standard word processing or page layout work. You can easily incorporate graphics from iPhoto or other image organizing and edition programs. You can do the printing yourself but, as discussed in Chapter 6, you might find preparing the material on your Mac, and then having it printed in a print shop much more cost-effective. Remember, you can save the output from most word processing or page layout programs as PDF files, and then you can send them electronically to a print shop.

The second type of printing consists of *one-off* (single copy) jobs for labels, descriptions, and other materials to be placed in the exhibit. If you plan to do a lot of these, you might want to investigate the purchase of an ink jet printer that will let you produce output larger than a single piece of paper. In today's market, three groups of ink jet printers are available.

- The most common (and cheapest) ink jet printers print on envelopes and standard size paper. You can get these printers for less than $100 (sometimes they're free with the purchase of a computer). Prices rise up through $300, depending on features.

- At the high end, plotters and large-format printers print on rolls of paper. The paper can be 24, 36, 42, or 60 inches wide (depending on the printer model) and the image can be as long as the paper is. If your image is taller than wide, you can rotate it before printing using the options in the Print dialog box. These printers start in the $2,000 area and go up to $5,000 and $6,000. (They go even higher for commercial printers that are usually purchased by professional printers.) Depending on the manufacturer, these are called *wide format* or *large format* printers, and they're often listed with or as *plotters*.

- In the middle, you can find ink jet printers that print on paper up to 13" × 19". These can be found for $400–$500. You can use these printers to print wall signs for exhibits; using small paper (or combining several jobs on one page and then cutting it apart), you can also use these to produce labels.

If you aren't in the exhibit business, you might find the third group of printers worth exploring. If you routinely need larger output, check around for a print shop that can do large format jobs for you.

NOTE   *If you need a large number of posters or flyers, the cost will almost always be less to have them printed professionally rather than on your own printer. Also, if you're printing exhibit labels, check out the transparent labels available in office supply stores from vendors such as Avery. These labels are designed primarily for people to use in addressing envelopes, but they also work well (particularly the larger ones) in creating labels to be affixed to walls or display cases. They're much less expensive than hand lettering. The labels can be prepared with a program like AppleWorks or even Photoshop, and they can incorporate whatever graphics you choose.*

Creating Explanatory Images

The tools of the digital hub are ideal for creating images and video, as well as text that places the exhibition materials in context. In some cases, this can be done easily as the exhibition is arranged: a price list, after all, is one example of this type of material.

In other cases, knowing you have these tools available can affect the exhibit far in advance. If you're showing materials that were created or unearthed, photos and videos of those processes can help place them in context. In still other cases, photos and videos of the exhibition's construction or assemblage can also add to what people see in the gallery or display space.

Creating Interactive Kiosks

One of the most interesting and involving things you can do is to create an interactive kiosk for people to use, either in the exhibit itself or in a nearby area. You can take two common approaches.

In the first approach, you can use the digital hub tools to create a DVD. You can then place a DVD player and a video terminal in the exhibit and let people navigate through the information for themselves. In public areas, you need to secure everything, but the demands of a DVD player and a display terminal regarding security are quite simple.

Your biggest concern might be preventing a remote control from "walking," but that's not an insurmountable problem. One approach is to buy a generic remote control, and then glue it firmly to the display case. Make certain you allow for the replacement of batteries or even the entire remote control, if necessary.

The second approach to creating an interactive kiosk is to place a Macintosh in the exhibit. You can build a space into a display cabinet in which to put the computer. All you need beyond that is a display and (usually) a mouse, and (sometimes) a keyboard.

One of the challenges of a public kiosk is preventing and solving problems. Sometimes people love to experiment a little too much—and sometimes people like the "challenge" of messing up a display. With Mac OS X, the task of creating a public kiosk is quite simple. You can take several approaches. The first two are described briefly here, and more information is available in *Mac OS X: The Complete Reference,* as well as on the sites listed.

The first approach involves the use of Apple Remote Desktop. If the computer is networked, you can log on to it from another computer and monitor its status, adjust its settings, and otherwise repair possible problems. More information is at **http://www.apple.com/remotedesktop**.

The second approach is to use Mac OS X Server and NetInfo to boot the computer from a remote computer's disk. This also requires the kiosk computer to be networked. But this means if you set things up properly, no one can destroy the underlying desktop files, which are on your computer, or a file that's far removed from the exhibit. More information is on Mac OS X Server at **http://www.apple.com/macosx/server**.

The third approach doesn't require a networked computer. You simply safeguard your kiosk computer. Here are the steps you take.

1. Create a new user for the computer. In System Preferences, choose Accounts or Users (depending on your version of Mac OS X). Create the new user, and don't let the user administer the computer.

2. Choose Set Auto Login and supply the password for that user. The user will then be automatically logged in.

3. In that same preference (Accounts or Users), select the Login Options tab. Select the option to disable Shut Down and Restart buttons. (Optional.)

4. Also under Login Options, you can choose whether to present the login screen as a list of users or simply with space for the user name and password. Under normal circumstances, this screen won't be seen, but you should consciously choose which display you want. If revealing user names will inadvertently reveal their passwords, you should opt for the user name and password. (Inadvertently revealing passwords can occur if one of the users is known and always uses the same password. This is bad, but it does happen.)

5. In the Login Items preference, add whatever applications you want to launch or documents you want to open. If, for example, you created a QuickTime movie you want to play, add the movie to this list, and it will be launched automatically.

When the computer is started or restarted, this user will be automatically logged in, and the designated item(s) will be opened. As long as the user can't administer the computer, no user of the computer can cause serious harm. Files can be added—but only under that user's directory.

If someone chooses Log Out from the Apple menu, that person will be returned to the login window in whatever display you chose in Step 4. If, in Step 3, you chose to disable Restart and Shut Down, the computer will be out of commission until someone logs in (or presses the Restart button on the computer—if it isn't locked away in a kiosk cabinet). It's important that you can log out in this way,

Josef Albers's "Interaction of Color" on Tour

Joseph Roberts and I developed the CD-ROM version of Josef Albers's seminal work, *Interaction of Color*, which is published by Yale University Press and has been part of a number of exhibits of Albers's work. In a touring show, it was presented in an elegantly designed kiosk with a locked door inside where the Macintosh was kept. Observing what happened was interesting.

In one museum, the guards were instructed that if anything looked peculiar, they were to call someone from the museum's technology department who would arrive (at some point), open the locked door, and then diagnose the problem. The kiosk sported an "Out of Service" sign on many occasions.

At another site (Smith College), the guards were given a key to the kiosk and told simply to push the Restart button if anything looked amiss. The computer was set up in a similar way to that described here, so restarting it automatically launched *Interaction of Color*. At Smith, the kiosk was almost always in use (successfully). As many help desk people know, it's often easier simply to restart the computer than to diagnose the problem. (Of course, if the problem recurs frequently, you'll have to diagnose it.) The steps outlined here should provide you with a stable environment that, if it becomes destabilized, needs only a touch of the Restart button on the processor.

and then log in again as another user, because this is the way you, as a user with administrative privileges, can regain control of the computer.

Archiving Your Work

This part of the book started with scrapbooks—projects you undertake primarily to keep materials and memories for yourself—and it moved on through a variety of other projects designed to present information to others. Now, archiving needs to be addressed. *Archiving* is that set of processes and activities you undertake to preserve whatever you've done. Archiving isn't a communication process—those have already been described. Archiving means preserving a record of what you've done. This can be a record of every step of the process, of critical steps, or of a final step. You might be archiving the end results or the raw materials (video footage, for example). Chapter 9 dealt with routine issues of storage and backups. This section looks at the heavy-duty issues of permanent archiving rather than those daily issues.

Archiving Your Work

NOTE   *Before getting started, there's one overarching decision you need to make, and that's whether to archive things at all. This depends on the materials, as well as on your personality. The guest book that was signed by members of a wedding party certainly seems like a prime candidate for archiving, while the grocery list from yesterday doesn't. Yet some people toss the guest book and keep the grocery list. Reading this section might help you to clarify some of the archiving issues and, thereby, reach your own conclusions.*

Preservation Decisions to Make

Start, as always, by deciding what you want to do.

What Are You Preserving?

Are you preserving the project at every step of the way, at completion, or at specific points? Are you preserving the various raw materials (video, photos, and so forth) or only their edited version? Each of these decisions impacts your archiving practices. You can't answer these questions fully until you answer the next one.

Who Are You Preserving the Project For?

Are you documenting how you did a project? Or are you keeping the project so you can pick it up again and resume work on it? Will scholars be interested in what you've done, or is this simply a matter of good housekeeping? These decisions help you determine what to preserve.

How Long Will You Preserve the Project?

This is one of the biggest issues. Do you want to keep the project for a revision next year or for someone to study 20 years from now?

Preservation Choices to Consider

Once you answer the questions in the previous section, you can make the choices in the various categories listed here.

Media Issues

Your choice of media is influenced primarily by the amount of data to be archived. Secondarily, your choice is influenced by the length of time for which it will be archived. Today, CD-ROMs can comfortably store 600–700MB of data. DVD-R discs (in data mode) can store just under 5GB of data. If your needs are in those ranges, your choice should be obvious.

If you need to store more data, consider the various tape options. If this is a one-time archiving project, you can borrow a tape cartridge device, or you can send your data on its hard disk to a company to store it on tape.

However you stored your data, consider making a duplicate right at the start. Not only will it be cheaper right then, but you'll also know where it's located.

Thereafter, make certain the data can be read. This means storing the media carefully, and it normally means making certain you can read the data at least once every year or two.

For long-term storage, you should recognize you'll probably have to convert the archived data to another format. Diskettes are rarely seen now. Zip and Syquest cartridges are far from as common as they used to be. Even today's CD-ROMs and DVDs might be supplanted by other formats.

Furthermore, although CD-ROMs and DVDs use relatively stable technology, reports have occurred of the degradation of optical discs severe enough to compromise the data. This degradation is more pronounced with the CDs and DVDs you burn yourself than with commercially prepared discs. No substitute exists for a duplicate of the archive and for reading it on a periodic basis. And, of course, remember, offsite secure storage in climate-controlled conditions is a vital component of long-term preservation.

OS and Software Issues

Reading your archives—either on a periodic test basis or when you decide to unarchive the data—brings up its own sets of issues. The first is that of the operating system. If you have a shoebox full of diskettes with data from five or ten years ago, they might be in fine shape, but you probably won't be able to read them. You need not only the disk drive but also the software to read them.

Keep track of the operating system(s) in use when you used the data, as well as when you archived it. For example, someone running Mac OS X 10.1 could well archive a multiyear project in which early parts were developed under Mac OS 9. To be certain you can fully access the data, you should archive Mac OS X 10.1, as well as Mac OS 9.

Also, make certain you have the proper versions of the applications. File formats change over time. You probably should archive the applications along with the operating system.

And, for good measure, make certain the hardware to run all of this is still available. Many people have disposed of an ancient computer only to discover they have inadvertently made their backups and archives unusable.

Archiving Your Work

If you're tempted to convert files to later versions of the operating system or applications, make certain you keep copies and test everything. There are many sad stories of a final conversion of files—untested—that managed to leave a project in an unusable condition.

Legal Issues

Finally, remember legal issues exist regarding the ownership of the archive and of its embedded intellectual property. In particular, if you're planning for a long-term archive, make certain you have whatever permissions you need to reuse everything you have so carefully saved.

On the other hand, remember this careful planning to save things can come back to haunt you. Many corporations have strict standards for record retention, so what should be saved is kept, and what isn't needed is discarded in appropriate manners. Libraries, for example, routinely discard lists of users of public access computers, as well as the names of borrowers of materials once they're returned. Periodically, law enforcement and other agencies would like to get such records but, in most cases, they don't exist once they're no longer needed for library functions.

Summing Up: Making the Digital Hub Disappear

This book started by introducing you to the digital hub—to its concepts, its hardware, and its software. In Part 2, you learned how to use the digital hub tools (iMovie, iPhoto, iTunes, and iDVD) to create your own movies, photos, music, and DVDs. In Part 3, you saw how to make the movies, photos, music, and DVDs even better. And, in this part of the book, you learned how to combine the tools into various types of projects.

You certainly can stop here: you have tools and projects to keep you busy for a long time. Of course, you can also move on to the next step, integrating all these tools and ideas into your daily routines. In addition to the basic tools of the digital hub, Apple provides professional-grade tools to do more sophisticated versions of these tasks. Final Cut Pro and its companion product, Cinema Tools, let you move far beyond iMovie. Likewise, DVD Studio Pro lets you create much more sophisticated DVDs than you can with iDVD. And, of course, tools such as Photoshop and Illustrator let you take your digital photos (or other images) and transform them in a variety of ways.

But this isn't a necessary progression. The tools of Apple's digital hub provide a level of sophistication and power that's right for many people. If your job is film editing or DVD creation, yes, you should seriously consider eventually moving on to Final Cut Pro and to DVD Studio Pro. But if you're a teacher, a parent, a student, a building contractor, a diarist, or anyone other than a professional media author or editor, you'll probably find the digital hub tools right for you. Your focus, after all, is on getting your work (and play) done.

In Chapter 1, some of the features of Mac OS X that make the digital hub possible and easy to use were described. There's one more. In Mac OS X, it's easy to keep a number of applications running at the same time: *virtual memory* means applications that are running by, but you aren't using, just sit there. For instance, you can keep iPhoto running so you can move photos into and out of albums, and from those albums into your other documents—both from applications such as iMovie as well as from AppleWorks, Microsoft Office, FileMaker, and others.

If using the digital hub means finding the camera, recharging the batteries, and then searching for where you put iPhoto software, it will never become a tool you use as easily as a pencil or telephone. And it should become such a tool. Apple has done its part to streamline the interface and make all these products as intuitive as possible to use.

Chapter 1 suggested you be prepared, and it provided some tips on how to do so. Here are two additional tips. First, in addition to batteries, make sure you have enough disk space. Particularly when you're dealing with video, you need a lot of disk space. Don't clean it off when you need it—clean it off when you're done with it. Remove the barriers to using the digital hub tools before they arise.

> NOTE
>
> *The issue of disk space can't be overemphasized. This is one of the most common frustrations among computer users. Software doesn't work well under extreme constraints of disk space or memory. In Mac OS X, the memory constraints are much eased with virtual memory. If you don't have sufficient disk space for the operating system to function, however, it can misbehave severely and even crash (which is rare for Mac OS X). Having enough disk space doesn't mean buying a new disk: it means having enough free disk space on your startup disk to work with and having (if necessary) sufficient disk space on removable media (such as CD-ROMs and DVDs, as well as tapes) to store unused files. Make sure you do that backup and storage before you need to.*

Last, don't let your digital hub muscles atrophy. If you use these tools once a year, you'll forget not only where the cameras and batteries are but also how to use them. Sure, the basics are simple, but the tricks you develop, your habits for storing files—all of these require some use. Periodically, take out your cameras, and take photos and videos. If all else fails, several times a year, you'll have to

Summing Up: Making the
Digital Hub Disappear

give (or go to) parties where you can take photos. As you grit your teeth and put out another tray of hors d'oeuvres, remind yourself (and your guests) that you're honing your digital hub skills.

When your skills and tools are at the ready, you can then, oddly enough, proceed to forget about them. After all, what most people want to do isn't to play with these wonderful hardware and software tools, but to create presentations, scrapbooks of memories, courses, advertising, and a myriad of useful, interesting things that have nothing whatsoever to do with technology.

Summary

This chapter has looked at exhibits and archives—two types of projects than complement those discussed previously in this part of the book.

You can use the digital hub tools to support exhibits in museums, schools, community centers, and commercial spaces. All the supporting materials, ranging from catalogues, posters, and labels to invitations, can easily be created on your Mac. In addition, tools such as iPhoto and iMovie can help document both the exhibit itself and the materials shown. In addition, you saw how to use a Macintosh with Mac OS X as a free-standing public kiosk.

Archiving your work involves saving it for a relatively long time. The issues involved in preservation involve what to preserve, who to preserve it for, and how long to plan for its preservation. Once you make those decisions, you can move on to the choice of media, the need to preserve relevant applications as well as operating systems, and, finally, the legal issues related to intellectual property that might need to be stored for decades or longer.

In the final section of this chapter, some comments on making the digital hub disappear should make you consider further how to integrate all these tools into your daily routines. As noted in the Introduction, the digital hub quickly turns into a social hub: all these tools are communication tools.

You have the tools, you've seen how to use them, and you have some suggestions for specific types of projects you can do. It's up to you now.

Index

INTERNATIONAL CONTACT INFORMATION

AUSTRALIA
McGraw-Hill Book Company Australia Pty. Ltd.
TEL +61-2-9415-9899
FAX +61-2-9415-5687
http://www.mcgraw-hill.com.au
books-it_sydney@mcgraw-hill.com

CANADA
McGraw-Hill Ryerson Ltd.
TEL +905-430-5000
FAX +905-430-5020
http://www.mcgrawhill.ca

**GREECE, MIDDLE EAST,
NORTHERN AFRICA**
McGraw-Hill Hellas
TEL +30-1-656-0990-3-4
FAX +30-1-654-5525

MEXICO (Also serving Latin America)
McGraw-Hill Interamericana Editores S.A. de C.V.
TEL +525-117-1583
FAX +525-117-1589
http://www.mcgraw-hill.com.mx
fernando_castellanos@mcgraw-hill.com

SINGAPORE (Serving Asia)
McGraw-Hill Book Company
TEL +65-863-1580
FAX +65-862-3354
http://www.mcgraw-hill.com.sg
mghasia@mcgraw-hill.com

SOUTH AFRICA
McGraw-Hill South Africa
TEL +27-11-622-7512
FAX +27-11-622-9045
robyn_swanepoel@mcgraw-hill.com

**UNITED KINGDOM & EUROPE
(Excluding Southern Europe)**
McGraw-Hill Education Europe
TEL +44-1-628-502500
FAX +44-1-628-770224
http://www.mcgraw-hill.co.uk
computing_neurope@mcgraw-hill.com

ALL OTHER INQUIRIES Contact:
Osborne/McGraw-Hill
TEL +1-510-549-6600
FAX +1-510-883-7600
http://www.osborne.com
omg_international@mcgraw-hill.com